POMPEII

On 24 August AD 79, a massive eruption of Mount Vesuvius destroyed the unremarkable Roman town of Pompeii and its population of 12,000. Today, up to five hundred times that number visit Pompeii each year, attracted by the unique insight it gives into everyday life in Roman times, as well as by the awesome power of the still-active volcano.

What is less obvious to the visitor is the quality and range of written records which survive. This book presents translations of a wide selection of these sources, giving a vivid impression of what life was like in the town. The individual chapters explore the early history of Pompeii, its destruction, leisure pursuits, politics, commerce and religion, plus early reports of its excavation. While information about the city from authors based in Rome is included, the great majority of sources come from the city itself, written by its ordinary inhabitants – men and women, citizens and slaves. They range from the labels on wine jars to scribbled insults, from advertisements for gladiatorial contests to love poetry.

With helpful introductions, notes and illustrations, this sourcebook will appeal to anyone with an interest in Pompeii and in daily life in Roman times. It is also designed to be directly relevant to those studying the Romans in translation, at school or university level.

Alison E. Cooley is a lecturer in the Department of Classics, University of Warwick. Her previous publications include *Becoming Roman, Writing Latin?* (2002) and *Pompeii* (2003).

M. G. L. Cooley teaches Classics at King Henry VIII School, Coventry. He has recently produced a sourcebook, *The Age of Augustus* (2003).

POMPEII

A sourcebook

Alison E. Cooley and
M. G. L. Cooley

Routledge
Taylor & Francis Group

LONDON AND NEW YORK

First published 2004
by Routledge
2 Park Square, Milton Park, Abingdon, Oxon, OX14 4RN

Simultaneously published in the USA and Canada
by Routledge
270 Madison Ave, New York, NY 10016

Reprinted 2005 (twice), 2006 (twice), 2007 (twice)

Routledge is an imprint of the Taylor & Francis Group, an informa business

Typeset in Garamond by
Florence Production Ltd, Stoodleigh, Devon
Printed and bound in Great Britain by
TJ International Ltd, Padstow, Cornwall

British Library Cataloguing-in-Publication Data
A catalogue record for this book is available from the British Library

Library of Congress Cataloging in Publication Data
Cooley, Alison.
Pompeii: a sourcebook / Alison E. Cooley and M.G.L. Cooley.
p. cm.
Includes bibliographical references and indexes.
ISBN 0–415–26211–9 (hardback : alk. paper) –
ISBN 0–415–26212–7 (pbk. : alk. paper)
1. Pompeii (Extinct city) I. Cooley, M. G. L., (Melvin George Lowe),
1973– II. Title.
DG70.P7C628 2004
937'7–dc22

ISBN 10: 0–415–26211–9 (hbk)
ISBN 10: 0–415–26212–7 (pbk)

ISBN 13: 978–0–415–26211–8 (hbk)
ISBN 13: 978–0–415–26212–5 (pbk)

FOR EMMA

CONTENTS

ILLUSTRATIONS

Figures

Plates

ACKNOWLEDGEMENTS

We are grateful to Richard Stoneman for suggesting this project to us, and for his patience in awaiting its completion, delayed by the arrival of our daughter, who has nevertheless been extremely tolerant of our Pompeian preoccupations, as have her Cooley grandparents. The Davies family, as ever, gave encouragement and practical help in reading the typescript and assisting with illustrations. Jane Gardner gave invaluable advice on the Iucundus tablets. At various stages in the preparation of the book, we have become indebted to Prof. S. De Caro and Prof. P. Guzzo of Naples Archaeological Museum and Pompeii Excavations respectively for allowing us access to material, and to the Secretary of the British School at Rome, Maria Pia Malvezzi, for smoothing our path.

Illustrations

Plates 1.1, 3.2, 4.4, 5.1, 5.2, 5.3, 5.4, 5.5, 5.8, 6.1, 7.1, 7.2, 8.1, 8.2, 8.3, 8.5: A.E. Cooley; Figures 1.1, 1.3, 1.4, 4.1, 4.7, 4.8, 4.12, 5.1, 5.2, 6.1, 8.1; Plates 1.2, 5.6, 8.4, 9.1, 9.2: M.G.L. Cooley; Figure 1.2; Plates 3.3, 4.1, 4.3, 7.3, 7.4: L.H. Davies; Plates 3.1, 5.7: J. Thomas; Plate 2.1: *NSc* (1927) p. 20, fig. 5 (photo: Ashmolean Museum); Figures 4.2, 4.3, 4.4 from *CIL* IV⁴ (IV 10237, 10238a, 10236), by courtesy of *Corpus Inscriptionum Latinarum*; Figure 4.9 from *CIL* IV² (IV 4755); Figures 4.5, 4.10, 4.11 from R. Garrucci (1856), *Graffiti de Pompéi* (Paris) (Plate XI 1 + 3; Plate VI 1; Plate XVI 9); Plate 4.2: F. Mazois (1824–1838) *Les Ruines de Pompéi: Dessinées et mesurées* I (Paris), Plate 32 (by kind permission of the Bodleian Library, Oxford: shelfmark 20501 a.5, vol.1); Figure 4.6 from M. della Corte (1924) *Iuventus* 36, fig. 3 (Giovanni Fraioli, Arpino). Plates 1.1, 1.2, 4.3, 5.4, 5.5, 6.1, 8.5 by kind permission of Prof. S. De Caro, Director of the Naples Archaeological Museum; Plates 7.2, 8.1, 8.3 by kind permission of Prof. P. Guzzo, Director of Pompeii Excavations.

Warwick, August 2003

ABBREVIATIONS

AE	*Année Epigraphique*
BMC	H. Mattingly (1923) *Coins of the Roman Empire in the British Museum* I. *Augustus to Vitellius*, London
CIJ	*Corpus Inscriptionum Judaicarum*
CIL	*Corpus Inscriptionum Latinarum*
EE	*Ephemeris Epigraphica*
GC	Giordano and Casale (1991)
ILLRP	*Inscriptiones Latinae Liberae Rei Publicae*
ILS	*Inscriptiones Latinae Selectae*
NM inv.	Inventory number, National Archaeological Museum of Naples
NSc	*Notizie degli scavi di antichità*
PAH	*Pompeianarum Antiquitatum Historia*, ed. G. Fiorelli (3 vols, Naples 1860–1864)

We have used the names of gates, streets and houses commonly used in modern guidebooks, but few of these names are likely to have been used in Roman times. Otherwise, we have adopted the usual convention in referring to the location of a house or shop in Pompeii by three numbers (such as I.x.4) whereby the first number (I) represents the region (or *regio*), the second (x) the town block (or *insula*) and the third (4) the doorway. Figure 1.1 shows the regions and town blocks.

INTRODUCTION

Pompeii

Pompeii was not a particularly significant Roman town. Even within its region of Campania, it was not as large or important as Naples or Puteoli; not as fashionable as Baiae or Stabiae; not as strategically important as Misenum nor as celebrated in literature as Cumae. No Pompeian made his mark on Roman literature or politics. No crucial moments in Rome's history hinge on Pompeii.

Yet today, because of the accident of its fate, Pompeii is a Unesco world heritage site, attracting up to five hundred times as many visitors each year as actually used to live in the town. The reason for this lies partly in the very ordinariness of the town and partly in the idea that its destruction by Mount Vesuvius preserved it in a time-capsule. Images of loaves of bread found in ovens, or of meals abandoned on dinner-tables, perpetuate this impression, but it is important in using this sourcebook to appreciate that this is not entirely accurate. It is not the case that, if only the right archaeological techniques were used, we could gain a full picture of daily life in Roman times, in a town frozen at the hour of its destruction. The violence of the eruption itself, with its earth tremors and pyroclastic activity, has thrown some aspects of the archaeological record into chaos: buildings and objects were not cocooned in gently descending pumice, but were subjected to extremes of heat and, if in the path of the pyroclastic flows, violently hurled away. If they had reacted at the start of the eruption, Pompeii's inhabitants would have had time to gather together their prized possessions and flee from the town into the countryside, although they might not in the end have escaped their doom. Nor was the town perfectly sealed from the time of its burial in AD 79 until its official rediscovery in 1748; salvaging of materials from the site had been a common occurrence in the intervening period.

Nevertheless, it is easy to justify producing a sourcebook on Pompeii. Some of the written sources in this book – the inscriptions carved in stone on public and private monuments – were intended to perpetuate the memory of the individuals concerned, and, even if Vesuvius had not exploded, a few would probably have survived into modern times like the thousands of stone inscriptions from other parts of the Roman empire. But the great majority of the documents in this sourcebook were not 'written in stone' literally or metaphorically. They include notices to advertise gladiatorial games and endorsements of candidates in the local elections, written in paint upon walls, business records on wax tablets, graffiti scratched upon walls for a purpose, and casual scribblings. These are the documents which Pompeii preserves on a unique scale, and which provide a vivid picture of life in an ordinary town.

Oddly, these documents are considerably less accessible to most people than the site of Pompeii itself. They are published in mighty tomes available in university libraries, without translation, often without transcription, and with commentary in Latin. The aim of our sourcebook is to make accessible a representative sample of this material to pupils studying GCSE Classical Civilization and their teachers, to university students, and to the visitor to the site who perhaps notices some of the Latin writing around the site and is intrigued to find out what it means, or who simply wants to learn more about the life of the people in Pompeii.

Notes on literary authors

Appian wrote a history of Rome's civil wars in Greek during the second century AD.

Cicero 106–43 BC; statesman and orator, who wrote prolifically. His letters to his close friend Atticus, not originally written for publication, often give an intimate picture of his hopes and fears during the political turmoil of the late Republic.

Dio Cassius AD *c*.155–*c*.235; senator who wrote an extensive history, some of which survives only in summary form.

Diodorus of Sicily (Siculus) wrote a world history in *c*.60–30 BC, taking events from earliest times to Caesar's campaigns in Gaul, reproducing traditions of earlier historians and geographers.

Eusebius AD *c*.265–*c*.339; bishop and writer on church history. His *Chronicle* is a world chronological table from Abraham.

Florus first or second century AD; wrote an abridgement (or epitome) of Roman history with special reference to wars waged up to the time of Augustus.

Frontinus AD *c*.30–103; best known for his work *On Aqueducts*, he also composed a guide to military strategy.

Josephus AD 37/8–after 103; Jewish historian brought to Rome from the sacked Jerusalem by Vespasian. Wrote two extensive historical works, *Jewish War* and *Jewish Antiquities*.

Livy 59 BC–AD 17; during the Augustan era, he wrote *Ab Urbe Condita*, a large-scale history of Rome from its foundation to 9 BC.

Macrobius one of the topics covered in Macrobius' *Saturnalia*, a wide-ranging dialogue, set over the period of the Saturnalia festival of AD 383?, is witty sayings of and about famous people, taken from earlier authors.

Martial AD *c.*40–102; *Epigrams* published in AD 88.

Pliny the Elder AD 23–79; wrote an encyclopaedic work on Natural History (which survives) and a history (which does not); commander of the Roman fleet at Misenum; died at Stabiae during the eruption of Vesuvius.

Pliny the Younger *c.* AD 61–*c.*112; nephew and adopted son of Pliny the Elder. Witness of Vesuvius' eruption. He published ten books of *Letters* in the reign of Trajan.

Plutarch AD *c.*45–125; his *Parallel Lives* presented biographies of pairs of Greek and Romans. His *Moralia* deals with a huge range of topics.

Seneca the Younger 4 BC–AD 65; Stoic philosopher and tutor to the young emperor Nero, forced to commit suicide after falling from favour. His *Natural Questions* investigates natural phenomena.

Sibylline Oracles a collection of oracles in Greek hexameter verse, compiled in the fifth century AD. They are of varying date and anonymous authorship, imitating the pagan prophecies uttered by the Sibyls.

Statius AD *c.*45/50–96; court poet of Domitian, born in Naples, whose selection of poems known as the *Silvae* (AD *c.*93–95) often comments upon his native region.

Strabo geographer and historian, born in the Black Sea region, wrote in Greek at the time of Augustus and Tiberius (late first century BC to early first century AD).

Suetonius AD *c.*70–*c.*140; best known for his biographies of emperors, he had earlier (under Trajan) composed a work *The Lives of Illustrious Men*, taking grammarians, orators, poets and historians as his subjects. The biographical sketch of Pliny the Elder (included in his capacity as a distinguished historian) survives only partially.

Tacitus AD *c.*54–*c.*120; orator and senator who wrote two major historical works, the *Annals*, covering the period from the death of Augustus in AD 14 to that of Nero in AD 68, and the *Histories* from the civil wars of AD 68/9 to the death of Titus in AD 81. Neither work survives in its entirety.

Velleius Paterculus *c.*17 BC–AD *c.*30; wrote a panegyrical summary Roman history in only two volumes, which dealt very briefly with Rome's Republican history and focused upon more recent events. Served in the Roman army under Julius Caesar and Tiberius.

Vitruvius mid–late first century BC; wrote his work *On Architecture* in the early Augustan era.

Notes on epigraphic sources

Pottery inscriptions

A great many inscriptions have been found on the clay vessels discovered throughout Pompeii, as through the Roman world. (In Rome, Monte Testaccio, a hill 35 metres high, has been formed from *amphorae* dumped there, and rows on rows fill Pompeii's stores.) These inscriptions, some scratched on the clay by a sharp point, and others written in carbon, were essentially labels, usually abbreviated and needing only to be meaningful to one or two people. Despite this, most can be read, and enough examples do survive to give us some interesting glimpses of trade and life at Pompeii. They are published in *Corpus Inscriptionum Latinarum* (*CIL*) IV.

Monumental and parietal inscriptions

The monumental stone inscriptions found at Pompeii before the twentieth century are mostly published in *Corpus Inscriptionum Latinarum* X (two fascicles), which is supplemented by *Ephemeris Epigraphica* (*EE*) VIII. In addition, Giordano and Casale (1991) (*GC*) published some of the inscriptions found in the period 1954–1978. Otherwise, inscriptions found since the 1950s are scattered through archaeological reports, journal articles and monographs, and can be tracked down only by going through *Année Epigraphique* (*AE*), but even this does not pick up everything that has been published.

Painted inscriptions, graffiti and wax tablets have received better coverage, since four fascicles of *Corpus Inscriptionum Latinarum* IV have been published, with the latest in 1970 (but the accuracy of Della Corte's work has been questioned by some). For those interested in looking at the original sources, in addition to giving references to *CIL*, we have given references to *Inscriptiones Latinae Selectae* (*ILS*) wherever possible, since these texts are accessible on the Internet.

Brackets

[ ] indicate part of the original text is missing.
( ) indicate that the translation is expanding words abbreviated in the Latin.
† † enclose letters omitted by error from the original text.
[[ ]] indicate that part of a text has been deliberately erased in antiquity.
{ } indicate explanatory notes.
< > indicate letters which appear enclosed within a larger letter in a painted inscription

1

PRE-ROMAN POMPEII

Ancient literary sources rarely mention Pompeii's history prior to the first century BC. In addition, the vast majority of archaeological exploration has been concerned with uncovering the town's appearance at the time of its burial by Vesuvius in AD 79, so relatively little is known of the town's early history.

The earliest writing from the site is scratched upon fragments of pottery, notably in a deposit of votive offerings in the Temple of Apollo. Some of these texts are dedications, and others record the identity of the owner of the pottery. They range in date from the first quarter of the sixth century to c.475 BC, and are written in Etruscan. Otherwise, the earliest decipherable writing from the site (second–first centuries BC) appears in Oscan, an Italic language used in parts of southern Italy. Written from right to left, it uses an alphabet different from that of Latin, although some words mirror Latin usage. Monumental inscriptions and graffiti in Oscan provide our main documentary source for life in Pompeii before it became Roman. Some inscriptions were still on public display in AD 79; others were found where they had been reused as building material.

We know even less about the deaths than about the lives of the town's pre-Roman inhabitants. Twenty-nine inhumations from the fourth to mid-second centuries BC were found beyond the Herculaneum Gate, in the area to the west of the last shops along the north side of the street and in the area of the Villa of the Mosaic Columns. These were not monumental tombs, and contained a few grave goods, including pottery, coins and a bronze mirror. For a necropolis of the Epidii family, see G1–3.

This chapter starts by presenting some evidence for the character of the earliest settlement at Pompeii, before turning to its mythological foundation by the Greek hero Hercules, Roman traditions about its early inhabitants and the earliest appearance of Pompeii in the Roman historical record (A1–7). It then shows how the preservation of Oscan inscriptions allows us to piece together a picture of the town's administration, urban development and religious life from the second century BC (A8–14). By the late second century BC, we can see the impact of Hellenistic culture from the Greek East upon the town's public and private buildings (A15–21). The monumentalization of the Sanctuary of Dionysus just outside Pompeii in the late third to early second century BC and construction of the Basilica at its heart in the late second century BC illustrate the impact of Hellenistic culture upon the town's public character. The long-established Sanctuary of Apollo adjacent to the Forum was also remodelled along Hellenistic lines in the second century BC, when a temple in stone replaced the wooden temple. The addition of a *palaestra* and portico to the Stabian Baths in the mid-second century BC also reflects the same tendency. At about the same time, the town's elite increasingly adopted Hellenistic culture in their private lives too, and the House of the Faun provides an outstanding example of this. The impact of the Greek language is evident in the names of Oscan measures inscribed (and later erased) upon the Forum's measuring table, which were derived from Greek (**H64**). Finally, a selection of sources present a picture of one particularly prominent local family, the Popidii (**A22–26**).

Pompeii's origins and early history (A1–7)

The earliest settlement (A1)

The earliest settlement was founded on a lava plateau at the mouth of the River Sarno, controlling access to the interior. The Sanctuary of Apollo and the temple in the Triangular Forum were probably its focal points. It is generally thought that it is possible to discern in the current street pattern the less regular layout of this earliest settlement, covering an area of about fourteen hectares (the so-called 'Altstadt' or 'Old Town'). By the mid-sixth century BC, the site of sixty-six hectares was enclosed within a defensive circuit, and these impressive fortifications went through many phases of strengthening and rebuilding until the first century BC.

Figure 1.1 **A1 Map of Pompeii, with 'Old Town' highlighted**

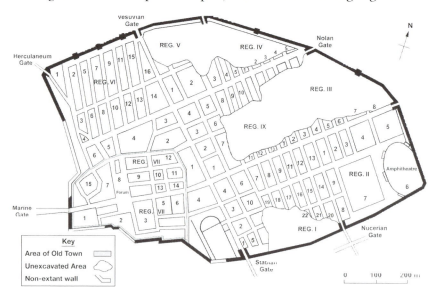

Hercules at Pompeii (A2–3)

As one of his twelve labours, Hercules was sent to the western edge of the world, to Gades (modern Cadiz, Spain). Having defeated the monster Geryon there, he drove Geryon's herd of cattle back to Greece, passing through Italy in his travels. As he did so, he was said to have bestowed upon Pompeii its name, derived from the word for procession common to Greek and Latin (*pompe/pompa*). Nearby Herculaneum was also reputedly founded by the Greek hero and named after him. The cult of Hercules may therefore have had early origins at Pompeii, but there is some dispute about the location of his cult. He is represented on a fourth-century BC terracotta antefix from the Triangular Forum, whose Doric Temple may have honoured him alongside Athene. A bronze statuette of the Hellenistic period representing Hercules was also found in the area of the Temple of Isis.

Isidore was a late antique writer (sixth–seventh centuries AD) from Spain. Servius was a scholar who wrote during the fourth–fifth centuries AD.

A2 Isidore, *Etymologies* 15.1.51

Pompeii (was founded) in Campania by Hercules, who had led a procession (*pompa*) of cattle from Spain as victor.

A3 Servius, *Commentary on Virgil's* Aeneid VII, 662

As he was coming through Campania from Spain, Hercules made a triumphal procession (*pompa*) in a Campanian town: this is how the town of Pompeii gets its name.

The geography and ethnography of Pompeii (A4–6)

Figure 1.2 A4 Map of the Bay of Naples
(*Modern place names given in italics*)

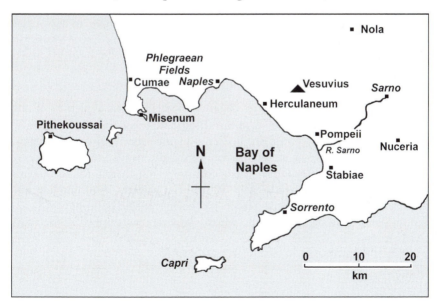

A5 Strabo, *Geography* 5.4.8

The Oscans used to occupy both Herculaneum and Pompeii next to it, past which the River Sarno flows. Then the Etruscans and the Pelasgians, and after that, the Samnites; these peoples were also thrown out of these places.

A6 Pliny the Elder, *Natural History* 3.60–2

From this point is famous productive Campania ... It was inhabited by Oscans, Greeks, Umbrians, Etruscans, and Campanians. On the coast is Naples ... Herculaneum, and Pompeii: Mount Vesuvius can be seen not far away and the Sarno river flows past.

Rome and Pompeii: an episode in the Second Samnite War, 310 BC (A7)

The region of Samnium (adjacent to Campania to the north) opposed Rome's expansion in a series of wars. The Second Samnite War lasted for some twenty years from 326 BC. Some of the Samnites' opposition to Rome was based in Campania: Rome pursued an aggressive campaign aimed at encircling the Samnites. Pompeii is here merely mentioned in passing, as the point of entry into the territory of Nuceria, upon which Pompeii was probably dependent at this time. Compare H2.

A7 Livy 9.38.2

At about the same time, a Roman fleet, under Publius Cornelius, whom the Senate had put in command of the coast, sailed to Campania. When it had put ashore at Pompeii, Italian marines set out from there to lay waste Nucerian territory.

Oscan inscriptions (A8–14)

The monumental inscriptions in Oscan provide us with a picture of the town's pre-Roman system of administration and urban development. The town was governed by two main bodies, a popular assembly and a council. Some aspects of the town's organization were quite similar to contemporary Roman practices. For example, the aediles were responsible for the town's roads, and the quaestors (*kvaísstur*) for financial matters. Building inscriptions reveal the role of magistrates in sponsoring public buildings (**A8–12**) and religious dedications illustrate which gods were worshipped in the town (**A13, A15–17**).

Road-building (A8)

This inscription, regulating road construction, appears on a travertine block found sunk into the ground just inside the Stabian Gate. The first sentence may end 'Stabian bridge' rather than 'lower Stabian road'. The identity of the Temple of Jupiter Meilichios mentioned here is disputed: traditionally identified as the small temple to the north of the theatres, it may alternatively be a small shrine in a sanctuary just outside Pompeii, in the Fondo Iozzino. Another fragmentary inscription, Vetter (1953) nos. 9–10, records a similar project.

A8 Vetter (1953) no. 8

M. Suttius, son of M., and Numerius Pontius, son of M., aediles, marked out this road as far as the lower Stabian road. The road is marked out over 100 feet. The same magistrates marked out the Pompeian road over 30 feet as far as the Temple of Jupiter Meilichios. They officially established from scratch these roads and the road of Jupiter and the (?) road by order of the Pompeian chief magistrate. The same aediles approved the work.

Testamentary donation to the town (A9)

This carefully inscribed travertine plaque was found in the Samnite Palaestra (VIII.vii.29) and probably commemorates its construction.

A9 Vetter (1953) no. 11

Vibius Atranus, son of Vibius, granted money in his will to the people of Pompeii; with this money, the Pompeian quaestor, Vibius Vinicius, son of Maras, by decree of the assembly, issued a contract for this to be built, and he himself approved it.

Sundial in the Stabian Baths (A10)

This inscription appears on the base of a small sundial, found near the main entrance to the Stabian Baths (VII.i.8) from the Street of Abundance. The use of money from fines to fund a public project was also common Roman practice. The Oscan expression for 'with the money raised from fines' ('eitiuvad multasikad') directly mirrors the equivalent archaic Latin phrase ('aere moltaticod'). Maras Atinius also appears as aedile on the altar in the Sanctuary of Dionysus (A16).

Plate 1.1 A10a Sundial in the Stabian Baths

A10b Vetter (1953) no. 12

Maras Atinius, son of Maras, quaestor, with the money raised from fines, by decree of the assembly, saw to this being set up.

Monumentalization of a well in the Triangular Forum (A11)

This text was inscribed upon the architrave of a small circular structure, or *tholos*, in the Triangular Forum, which stood above a well. Like the Popidii (A22–26), members of the Trebii are also found as public figures right down until AD 79.

A11 Vetter (1953) no. 15

Numerius Trebius, son of Trebius, chief magistrate, saw to this being built.

Refurbishing the Temple of Apollo (A12)

This inscription is highly unusual in form, surviving as a series of dots stamped upon the paving, at the threshold to the temple's inner room (*cella*). These were possibly once joined up or filled with metal. It is unclear exactly what the inscription refers to, but it may well commemorate work on the elaborate geometrically patterned paving rather than on the temple as a whole.

A12 Vetter (1953) no. 18

Ovius Camp[anius, son of ?], quaestor, by decree of the assembly, with the money of Apollo [————] issued a contract and approved it.

Altar to the goddess Flora (A13)

This small travertine altar dedicated to Flora was found in the *atrium* of the House of the Faun (VI.xii.2). A bronze female statuette, perhaps representing the goddess Flora, was also found nearby.

A13 Vetter (1953) no. 21

To Flora.

An improbable tombstone (A14)

This text is carefully cut into plaster, then coloured in red.

A14 Vetter (1953) no. 70

Audia, daughter of Numerius, aged 112.

Hellenistic culture at Pompeii (A15–21)

Sanctuary of Dionysus, 'S. Abbondio' (A15–17)

A sanctuary to Dionysus (Bacchus) was uncovered by bombardment in the Second World War, just to the south-east of Pompeii, under a kilometre beyond the Amphitheatre. An inscribed altar stands in front of the Doric temple. The temple's pediment depicts Dionysus holding a bunch of grapes and a wine cup, together with other figures commonly associated with him (such as a panther) and a female figure who has been variously interpreted as Ariadne or Aphrodite. The following inscriptions show that Pompeii's magistrates were directly involved in establishing the cult, perhaps in the second half of the third century BC. Despite the Roman Senate's decree in 186 BC banning worship of Bacchus not only at Rome but also among Rome's Italian allies, there is no evidence that the cult at Pompeii was interrupted. This may be one indication of how deeply culture and society in Pompeii were influenced by Hellenistic traditions during the second century BC. The temple was still in use in AD 79.

Figure 1.3 A15 Plan of the Sanctuary of Dionysus

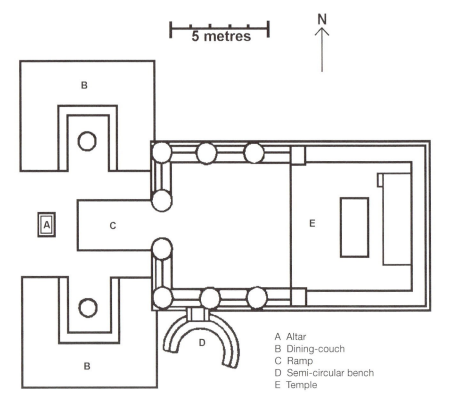

Inscribed altar (A16)

This inscription appears on both front and back of the tufa altar. Traces of the red paint high-lighting its lettering were still visible when it was found. The same individual is named as quaestor (*kvaísstur*) on the inscribed sundial in the Stabian Baths (A10b).

A16 Poccetti (1979) no. 107

Maras Atinius, son of Maras, aedile, at his own expense.

Mosaic inscription on ramp leading into temple (A17)

A17 Poccetti (1979) no. 108

Ovius Epidius, son of Ovius, and Trebius Mettius, son of Trebius, aediles.

House of the Faun (A18–21)

Figure 1.4 A18 Plan of the House of the Faun

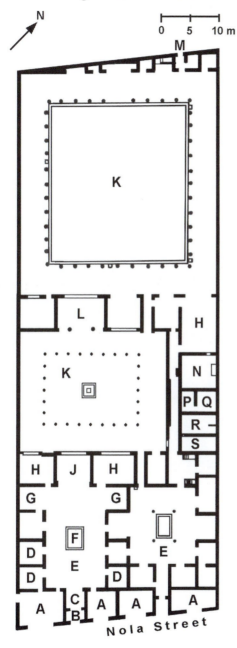

A	Shops	K	Peristyle
B	Vestibulum	L	Alexander
C	Fauces		Mosaic
D	Cubiculum	M	Back door
E	Atrium	N	Kitchen
F	Impluvium	P	Tepidarium
G	Ala	Q	Caldarium
H	Triclinium	R	Latrine
J	Tablinum	S	Stable

13

Plate 1.2 A19 The Alexander mosaic (NM inv. 10020)

The Alexander mosaic (**Plate** 1.2), consisting of over one and a half million tiny *tesserae*, or coloured cubes, is one of the artistic highlights of Pompeii. Experts agree that the use of colour, foreshortening, and the treatment of light and shade in the mosaic all show that it copied, in mosaic form, a Hellenistic (third century BC) painting. This original may have been the picture painted for King Cassander of Macedonia (ruled 316–297 BC) mentioned by Pliny the Elder in his chapters on art history (**A21**).

The mosaic depicts the turning-point in a battle between Alexander the Great and the Persian king Darius, as the latter turns to flight. Its depiction of the equipment used by the two armies is accurate. Whether the artist intended to depict an actual moment of a particular battle cannot be determined. **A20** is a Roman historian's account of the Battle of Issus in 333 BC, probably written in the mid-first century AD, based on historical accounts from Alexander's time. The mosaic and this account have some details in common, but also differences.

It was prominently situated in the house where it could be viewed from the peristyles on either side. Around it were mosaics depicting scenes of life on the River Nile, near Alexandria, one of the great cities founded by Alexander. For excavation reports relating to the House of the Faun, see **J55–58**.

Plate 1.2   A19   The Alexander mosaic

A20 Quintus Curtius Rufus, *History of Alexander*, 3.11.7–12

Alexander took the role of a soldier as much as that of a leader in actively pursuing the highest honour, that of killing the king. Darius indeed stood high in his chariot, a great incentive for his men to defend and for his enemy to attack. Therefore Darius' brother, Oxathres, on seeing Alexander pressing on the king, interposed the cavalry under his command right in front of the king's chariot. Towering above the others in weapons and his own strength, and conspicuous among the few for his bravery and loyalty, Oxathres certainly achieved renown in that battle and laid low some who pressed on recklessly and turned others to flight. But the Macedonians around their king, shouting encouragement to one another, broke into the ranks of cavalry with Alexander himself. Then men fell like a collapsed building. Darius' noblest leaders lay around his chariot, killed bravely before the eyes of their king, all lying on their faces just as they had fallen in the fight, with wounds on their fronts. Notable among them were commanders of great armies: Atizyes, Rheomithres and Sabaces, governor of Egypt; around them were heaped less famous infantry and horsemen. As for the Macedonians, not many, but some of the boldest were slain; and Alexander was slightly wounded in the right thigh by a sword.

Now the horses which were pulling Darius, struck by spears, and wild with pain, had began to throw off their yoke and shake the king from the chariot. Then he, fearing being taken alive by the enemy, leapt down and mounted a horse which followed for that very purpose, dishonourably throwing away his royal regalia so that it would not betray his flight. Then indeed the rest were scattered in terror . . .

A21 Pliny the Elder, *Natural History*, 35.110

Nicomachos, son of Aristides, had as a pupil Philoxenos of Eretria, whose picture, painted for King Cassander, *Battle of Alexander with Darius*, is second to none.

The Popidii family (A22–26)

The Popidii were a prominent family in Pompeii throughout the town's documented history. A remarkable degree of continuity in their contribution to Pompeii's urban development emerges from A22–23, two similar inscriptions, albeit one in Oscan and the other in Latin, recording building work by individuals from different generations. See also C5.

Construction of a portico (Oscan) (A22)

Since this inscription was found reused in the House of the Skeleton (VII.xiv.9), we can only guess where it might originally have been displayed. The portico has sometimes been identified as the tufa portico on the south side of the Forum, but it could equally well be some portico since demolished. The same man also oversaw the construction of the Nolan Gate (A24) and his name appears on an *amphora* (A25).

A22 Vetter (1953) no. 13

Vibius Popidius, son of Vibius, chief magistrate (*meddix tuticus*), issued a contract for the construction of this portico and officially approved it.

15

Construction of a portico, late 80s BC? (Latin) (A23)

This portico has also been interpreted as being one in the Forum, and the inscription's find-spot, near the entrance to the Basilica, makes this quite possible. Various interpretations have been offered of the magistracy abbreviated simply as 'Q': it could be *q(uaestor)*, *q(uattuorvir)* or *q(uinquennalis)*. If we follow the usual interpretation, of quaestor (a post not used in Roman colonies), the inscription may date to a period of interim administration, when the town had the status of a *municipium*.

A23 CIL X 794 = ILS 5538

Vibius Popidius son of Epidius, *q(uaestor)*, saw to the building of the porti-coes.

Construction of Nolan Gate (A24)

This inscription was found built into the inner arch of the Nolan Gate, near the keystone, together with the sculpture in tufa of a female head, probably representing the town's protective deity.

A24 Vetter (1953) no. 14

Vibius Popidius, son of Vibius, chief magistrate (*meddix tuticus*) saw to this being built and officially approved it.

Amphora inscription (A25)

These words are painted in black upon a wine *amphora*, found among ancient rubbish, which had accumulated at the foot of the town wall near the Vesuvian Gate. They illustrate how the name of the local annual magistrate (*meddix*) was used as a means of dating, here for a vintage of wine (compare **H6–7**).

A25 Vetter (1953) no. 71

Vibius Popidius, son of Vibius, magistrate.

Roof-tile stamp from the Basilica (A26)

A26 CIL X 8042.154

Numerius Popidius

2

ROMAN COLONIZATION
OF POMPEII

This chapter explores the period when Pompeii became Roman, following its colonization by Rome, c.80–40 BC. The Pompeians were among the Italian allies opposed to Rome in the Social, or Italic, War (91–87 BC) and the town was successfully besieged by the Roman general Lucius Cornelius Sulla Felix in 89 BC. The first group of sources traces Pompeii's opposition to Rome (B1–5). Some time later (c.81 BC), in punishment for Pompeii's resistance, Sulla imposed upon the town a colony of his veteran soldiers (perhaps between two and four thousand of them), led by his nephew Publius Cornelius Sulla. At this point, the town was renamed as *colonia Veneria Cornelia Pompeianorum* (see E1), a name recording its links to the goddess Venus and to the family name (Cornelius) of its new founder, Sulla, who also claimed Venus as his protectress. It adopted the constitution of a Roman colony, and Latin supplanted Oscan in all public inscriptions. Latin inscriptions from this period illustrate the impact of the colonists upon the buildings of the town (B7–12). The names of Sullan veterans dominate the inscriptions of the first couple of generations following colonization, down to the Augustan period, and it is possible that the original Pompeians were formally excluded from fully participating in local politics for a couple of decades (B15–16). Although Rome's grip upon the Italian peninsula in the mid-first century BC, following the Social War, perhaps seems secure to us, some Pompeians may have been prepared to exploit times of insecurity at Rome, notably in the wake of Spartacus' slave revolt and of the so-called Catilinarian conspiracy (B13–16).

Not only Sullan veterans, however, but other Romans – notably Cicero – also came to acquire property around Pompeii by the mid-first century BC (B17–22). Excavators in the eighteenth century identified a villa on the outskirts, just beyond the Herculaneum Gate, as belonging to Cicero. This was covered over again after excavation in 1749 and 1764, as was usual practice at that time (compare J24). In any case, he is more likely to have possessed a country estate further away from the town, but in its territory.

Pompeii's participation in the Social War (B1–6)

The start of the war, 90 BC (B1)

B1 Appian, *Civil Wars* 1.39

When the revolt broke out in Asculum, all the neighbouring peoples joined
in showing that they were ready for war: the Marsi, the Paeligni, the Vestini,
the Marrucini; in addition, the Picentines, the Frentani, the Hirpini, the
Pompeians, the Venusini, the Apulians, and the Samnites, all peoples who
had been hostile to the Romans before . . . They sent ambassadors to Rome
complaining that they had done everything to help the Romans with their
empire, but the Romans did not think that those who had helped them
deserved citizenship.

Siege of Pompeii, 89 BC (B2–6)

In dealing with certain aspects of the Italian War, Velleius (**B2**) mentions the leading generals
on either side, and pays especial attention to his own maternal ancestor, Minatius Magius of
Aeclanum. Titus Didius was killed in taking Herculaneum on 11 June. Appian's notice (**B3**)
relates to the episode when Lucius Cluentius, one of the allies' military leaders, came to help
the besieged Pompeians, but after an initial success was defeated by Sulla somewhere between
Pompeii and Nola. Nearby Stabiae was sacked on 30 April 89 BC. The testimony of the fifth-
century Christian historian, Orosius (**B4**) must be treated with caution.

At Pompeii itself, traces of Sulla's presence may be seen in a graffito (**B6**), in notices orga-
nizing the Pompeians' resistance (**B5**), and in the damage left in the town fortifications by
the bombardment of Sulla, some of whose missiles have even been found alongside the northern
stretch of the walls.

B2 Velleius Paterculus 2.16.2

In this war he {Minatius Magius} showed such loyalty to the Romans that
with a legion which he had enlisted from the Hirpini, he captured
Herculaneum with Titus Didius and attacked Pompeii with Sulla.

B3 Appian, *Civil Wars* 1.50

Lucius Cluentius contemptuously encamped 600 metres from Sulla who was
encamped near the Pompeian hills.

B4 Orosius, *Histories against the Pagans* 5.18.22

In the 661st year from the founding of the city {= 93 BC}, the Roman army
went to besiege the Pompeians. Postumius Albinus, an ex-consul, at that
time was a commander of Lucius Sulla. He had aroused the hatred of all the
soldiers towards him by his unbearable arrogance, and was stoned to death.

Organization of Pompeii's Military Resistance (B5)

A series of Oscan inscriptions painted upon the outer walls of houses near street corners came to light once their overlying plaster had peeled off after excavation. Examples have been found at VI.ii.4, VII.vii, VI.xii.23–25 (House of the Faun), VIII.v/vi (Street of Abundance), III.iv.1–2 (east end of Street of Abundance). They are thought to relate somehow to military operations, from the time when Sulla was besieging Pompeii. They are usually taken to be notices relating to individual urban districts giving the location of mustering points in case of an emergency. The Salt Gate mentioned in **B5** is the Oscan name for what is now known as the Herculaneum Gate.

B5 Vetter (1953) no. 23

Go by this route between the 12th tower and the Salt Gate, where Maras Atrius, son of Vibius, gives instructions.

Traces of Sulla at Pompeii (B6)

Sulla's name appears twice (*CIL* IV 5385, 10217a) in graffiti on the first tower to the west of the Vesuvian Gate (Tower 10). One of these texts is written on plaster next to a window in the lower part of the tower.

B6 *CIL* IV 5385

L. Sula

Colonists at Pompeii (B7–12)

The arrival of the Roman veteran soldiers as colonists heralded a major transformation of the town's fabric, typical of this period as a whole in Italy (**B7–11**). Following colonization, the town's annual magistrates were obliged by law to spend a certain amount of money either on a building project or upon games (**B11**). Individual colonists built a number of new impressive public buildings, including the Amphitheatre, Forum Baths and Covered Theatre, and modified existing ones, such as the Stabian Baths. In addition, some repairs were carried out on the town walls, which had been damaged during the siege. It is commonly thought that colonists built the large temple adjacent to the Basilica in honour of Venus in her capacity both as guardian deity of Pompeii and as Sulla's protectress, but the evidence for this is rather slight (a single fragmentary statue of the goddess). Otherwise, the colonists took over the town's existing cults, dedicating a new altar in the Temple of Apollo (**B7**). They also brought with them new funerary customs, setting up monumental tombs along the roads leading out of the town (**B12**).

Dedication of the altar in the Temple of Apollo (B7)

This inscription appears on both sides of the large altar in front of the temple. The title given to the magistrates of quattuorvirs (i.e., the Four) indicates that it dates to a little after 80 BC when this title was used for only a short time to refer collectively to the town's two duumvirs and two aediles. This is therefore one of the earliest actions performed by the colonists in the town. For Marcus Porcius, see also B9–10, B12. For other inscriptions in the Temple of Apollo, see E1–2.

B7 *CIL* X 800 = *ILS* 6354

Marcus Porcius, son of Marcus; Lucius Sextilius, son of Lucius; Gnaeus Cornelius, son of Gnaeus; Aulus Cornelius, son of Aulus, quattuorvirs, awarded the contract for its construction, in accordance with a decree of the town councillors.

Building work on the town walls (B8)

Five fragments of this inscription were found reused in the House of Mars and Venus (VII.i.8).

B8 *CIL* X 937 = *ILS* 5335

[———] Cuspius, son of Titus and Marcus Loreius, son of Marcus, duumvirs, [by decree] of the town councillors, saw to the construction of the wall and tower and also approved it.

Construction of the Covered Theatre (B9)

Two copies of this inscription were set up near the main entrances to the Covered Theatre, from the Stabian Road and from the Large Theatre. It is possible that the construction of the Covered Theatre was not a brand new project initiated by the colonists, but that they completed a design already underway. The same magistrates later built the Amphitheatre (B10). For Marcus Porcius, see also B7 and B12. For further interpretation of the Covered Theatre's significance, see commentary on D57.

B9 *CIL* X 844 = *ILS* 5636

Gaius Quinctius Valgus, son of Gaius, and Marcus Porcius, son of Marcus, duumvirs, by decree of the town councillors awarded the contract for the construction of the Covered Theatre and also approved it.

Construction of the Amphitheatre (B10)

Two copies of its dedicatory inscription originally stood over the west and east entrances to the Amphitheatre. Gaius Quinctius Valgus may be the father-in-law of the tribune Publius Servilius Rullus, who proposed the agrarian law vehemently attacked by Cicero in his speech *On the Agrarian Law*. Cicero portrays him as one of Sulla's partisans, a profiteer of the worst kind. Even if this identification is not correct, Valgus was certainly a man of wide influence, since he also appears on inscriptions at Aeclanum, Cassino, and Frigento as public magistrate and benefactor (*CIL* X 5282, IX 1140, *ILLRP* 598). The same magistrates had already supervised the construction of the Covered Theatre (**B9**). For Marcus Porcius, see also **B7** and **B12**. For the later building history of the Amphitheatre, see **D1–7**.

B10 *CIL* X 852 = *ILS* 5627

Gaius Quinctius Valgus, son of Gaius, and Marcus Porcius, son of Marcus, quinquennial duumvirs, for the honour of the colony, saw to the construction of the amphitheatre at their own expense and gave the area to the colonists in perpetuity.

Improvements to the Stabian Baths (B11)

This inscription was found in the Baths, which had originally been established perhaps as early as the late fourth century BC, and had been modified along Hellenistic lines in the mid-second century. See also **D105**. This text also provides us with valuable evidence regarding the colony's charter, otherwise lost, which evidently required local magistrates to spend a certain sum of money in their year of office on a public building or on games.

B11 *CIL* X 829 = *ILS* 5706

Gaius Uulius, son of Gaius, and Publius Aninius, son of Gaius, duumvirs with judicial power, contracted out the construction of the sweating-room (*laconicum*) and scraping-room (*destrictarium*) and the rebuilding of the porticoes and the exercise area (*palaestra*), by decree of the town councillors, with that money which by law they were obliged to spend either on games or on a monument. They saw to the building work, and also approved it.

Tomb of colonist, Marcus Porcius (B12)

This tomb, in the form of an altar, probably belongs to one of the leading colonists. It is in a prominent position, just outside the Herculaneum Gate (tomb 3 left), and its site was awarded to the deceased as a public honour. For M. Porcius, see **B7**, **B9–10**.

B12 *CIL* X 997

Of Marcus Porcius, son of Marcus, by decree of the town councillors, 25 feet wide, 25 feet deep.

Dissent at Pompeii (B13–16)

The slave revolt of Spartacus (B13–14)

The gladiator Spartacus led a slave revolt in 73–71 BC, which started at Capua in northern Campania, and spread through Italy, causing great consternation to the authorities at Rome. As they initially headed south from Capua, the slaves surprised their opponents by hiding in the crater of Mount Vesuvius and then re-emerging. Other accounts of this episode appear in Velleius Paterculus 2.30.5; Florus 2.8.4–5; Plutarch, *Crassus* 9; Orosius 5.24.1.

Spartacus in Vesuvius' crater, 73 BC (B13)

B13 Frontinus *Strategems* 1.5.21

When besieged on Vesuvius, Spartacus constructed ropes out of wild vine in that part of the mountain which was most precipitous and for that reason unguarded. Let down by these, not only did he break out, but he even terrified Clodius so much on his blind side, that a number of cohorts gave way to seventy-four gladiators.

A painting of Spartacus in battle? (B14a–b)

A sketchy picture of four fighters was found painted on a lower layer of plaster, inside the entrance way of a house (I.vii.7). Two figures on horseback, armed with spears and shields, are flanked by a figure, to their right, standing with raised trumpet, and by two other fighters on foot, to their left. All four fighters were originally labelled, but only the name of one of the horsemen can now be deciphered. This name written in Oscan – Spartacus – probably alludes to the leader of the infamous slave revolt.

B14a A painting of Spartacus in battle?

See **Plate** 2.1.

B14b Vetter (1953) no. 35

Spartacus

Unrest at Pompeii following colonization, before 62 BC (B15)

Early in January 62 BC, the turbulent political career and life of Lucius Sergius Catilina (Catiline) ended on the battlefield of Pistoria in Northern Italy. The previous year, Cicero, as consul, had had Catiline declared a public enemy. Later in 62 BC, however, Cicero defended Publius Sulla (the dictator's nephew, who had been in charge of establishing the colony at Pompeii) against a charge of involvement in political violence, as a supporter of Catiline in 66 and 63 BC, though several specious arguments in Cicero's speech suggest that the defence case may have been rather weak. Cicero indicates that there was some sort of tension between local Pompeians and colonists, perhaps relating to political rights, though the reasons for the dispute remain uncertain, since the precise meaning of a crucial Latin word (*ambulatio*) is unclear. He also says the dispute began during the early years of the colony. Nevertheless, the possibility remains that Sulla had intended to exploit existing tensions in order to gain support for Catiline.

B15 Cicero, *Pro Sulla* 60–62

[60] Now, as for the accusation that has been made, that the Pompeians were driven by Sulla into joining that conspiracy and this disgraceful crime, I cannot understand how this can be. Do you think the Pompeians conspired? Who has ever said so? Is there even the slightest trace of this? The prosecution

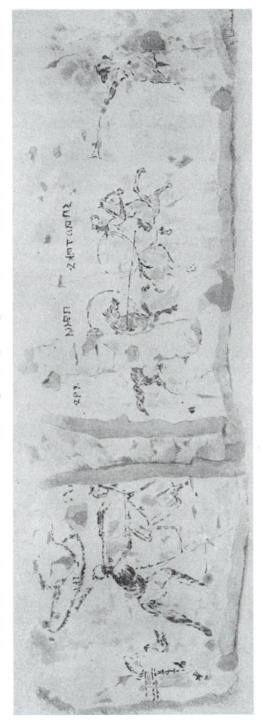

Plate 2.1 B14a A painting of Spartacus in battle?

said that Sulla divided the Pompeians from the colonists so that when this dispute and disagreement had been brought about, he would be able to have the town in his control through the Pompeians. First, the whole disagreement between Pompeians and colonists was brought before the town's patrons, when it was already long-established and had caused many years of trouble. Second, the result of the enquiry was that Sulla in no respect differed from the findings of the other patrons. Finally the colonists themselves realize that Sulla looked after their interests as much as those of the Pompeians. [61] You can appreciate this, gentlemen of the jury, from this large group of dignitaries from the colonists. Although they have not been able to keep him secure in high position and office, now that he lies crushed by this fall, they are here, working hard and earnestly hoping for you to help and preserve their patron and protector, the defender of their colony. The Pompeians are here with equal enthusiasm, who are still being accused by the colonists: though in disagreement with the colonists over a promenade (*ambulatio*) and their voting rights, they agree about their common interest. [62] Furthermore, I do not think I should fail to mention this virtue of Publius Sulla, that although the colony was founded by him, and although the privileged position of the colonists was at the expense of the Pompeians, he is so dear to both and so charming that he seems not to have dispossessed one group but to have established both.

Catilinarian omens at Pompeii (B16)

This passage perhaps preserves a hint of Pompeii's involvement in Catiline's uprising, and suggests that the Pompeians' leanings to Catiline were not entirely the invention of the prosecutors of Publius Sulla. Herennius is an old Pompeian family name, suggesting that such families were not all excluded from participating in local politics by 63 BC, even if they had been in the immediate aftermath of colonization.

B16 Pliny the Elder, *Natural History* 2.137

Among the Catilinarian omens, a town councillor from the town of Pompeii, Marcus Herennius, was struck by lightning on a clear day.

Cicero's Pompeian property (B17–22)

Cicero owned eight properties in the country, in addition to his prestigious town house on the Palatine Hill in Rome. One of these was in the territory of Arpinum (modern Arpino), a hill town in the Liris valley, where he was born. In addition to farms at Neapolis (Naples) and Pompeii, Cicero also owned property at Formiae on the Appian Way (modern Formia) and at the fashionable Tusculum, fifteen miles to the south-east of Rome (near modern Frascati). His Pompeian villa served at times both as a retreat from the politically oppressive atmosphere of Rome and as a potentially good location for a hasty escape by sea.

Cicero's purchase of a property at Pompeii (B17–18)

In this letter to his intimate friend, Atticus, Cicero implies that he has only just bought his two estates at Tusculum and Pompeii at great expense. He puns on different meanings of the Latin word *aes* (copper or bronze). 'Borrowed copper' (*aes alienum*) is 'debt': Cicero is alluding here to his opposition to Catiline's campaign to cancel debt. 'Corinthian copper' is a special type of bronze produced at Corinth, and used to make highly valued *objets d'art*. 'Copper of the forum' is another way of saying 'debt', the forum being the place where business deals were transacted.

B17 Cicero, *Letters to Atticus* 2.1.11, *c.*3 June 60 BC

My properties at Tusculum and Pompeii please me very much, except that they have overwhelmed me (that well-known champion of borrowed copper) with copper not of the Corinthian type but of the forum.

B18 Plutarch, *Life of Cicero* 8

He possessed a fine property at Arpinum, a farm near Neapolis and another near Pompeii, neither of which was large.

Sale of a farm (B19)

This letter illustrates other property interests in the area.

B19 Cicero, *Letters to Atticus* 13.8, 9 June 45 BC, Tusculum

Please give someone the task of finding out whether a farm of Quintus Staberius is for sale in the area of Pompeii or Nola.

Troubled times (B20–21)

In 49 BC, Julius Caesar crossed the River Rubicon, thus invading Italy and prompting the outbreak of civil war. Cicero fled from Rome in January, and remained in Campania for some months, torn between his desire to broker peace between Caesar and Pompey and his instinct to flee abroad to join Pompey and the consuls. Caesar met him in March to try to win his support. By May, Cicero had decided to leave Italy, and used a trip to his Pompeian property to disguise his plans to do so (B20–21). Despite his best endeavours, however, he had to take swift action in order to avoid becoming involved in tricky negotiations with some centurions based at Pompeii, who wished to oppose Caesar (B21). Cicero's response to news that they wanted to meet him was to leave his villa before daybreak the next day in order to avoid them. Cicero had no desire to lead armed resistance against Julius Caesar and was well aware that the forces of a mere three cohorts would not be able to resist him. Lucius Ninnius Quadratus had been an opponent of Publius Clodius, Cicero's arch enemy.

B20 Cicero, *Letters to Atticus* 10.15.4, 10/12 May 49 BC, Cumae

I am making an excursion to my Pompeian property while bread and other things are being prepared for the ship.

B21 Cicero, *Letters to Atticus* 10.16.4, 14 May 49 BC, Cumae

In order to lessen suspicion of my departure or of my intention to depart, I set out for my Pompeian property on the 13th, so that I might be there while what was necessary for the voyage might be prepared. When I arrived at the villa, a message came to me that the centurions of three cohorts, which were at Pompeii, wanted to meet me on the following day – our friend Ninnius discussed this with me – and that they wanted to hand over themselves and the town to me.

Aftermath of Caesar's assassination (B22)

In the aftermath of the assassination of Julius Caesar, Cicero again used his property at Pompeii as a refuge from the turbulent political situation in Rome, despite apparent appeals from Octavian (later Augustus) for him to return. Cicero's suppression of the Catilinarians in 63 BC (see note on B15) was when he had 'saved the state'.

B22 Cicero, *Letters to Atticus* 16.11.6, 5 November 44 BC, Puteoli

I have not hidden myself away at my Pompeian property, as I wrote I would, first because of the vile weather, and second because letters every day from Octavian urge me to take up public affairs, come to Capua, save the state for a second time, and immediately get to Rome, somehow.

3

DESTRUCTION OF POMPEII

In the years leading up to the eruption, Pompeii was rocked by earthquakes, one of which, in AD 62, even impressed writers at Rome (**C1–2**). Two relief panels from Pompeii depict an earthquake, possibly, but not necessarily, that of AD 62 (**C3**). Otherwise, it is possible to see signs of earthquake damage and of structural repairs all around the site today, but these are the consequence not only of the famous tremor of AD 62 (**C4**). In one case – the Temple of Isis – an inscription records restoration work after extensive damage in an earthquake (**C5**).

Comments about Vesuvius by writers of the Augustan era reveal that at least some people were aware of the character of the dormant volcano before it erupted in AD 79 (**C6–8**). The Younger Pliny's two letters describing the eruption have long been famous, but only recently have modern studies analysing the letters in the light of scientific data shown that they provide a surprisingly accurate picture of the eruption (**C9, C12**). Although these are the best known and most useful sources, other authors also provide accounts of the eruption, both brief and elaborate (**C11, C13–15**).

The eruption had a devastating impact upon the economy, society and geography of the Bay of Naples, destroying towns, villages, villas and farms as far as Stabiae and Herculaneum, and changing the landscape (including the coastline and course of the River Sarno) (**C24-C25**), but we hear surprisingly little of its human victims (**C16**). It was one of several natural disasters to occur during the brief reign of the emperor Titus (AD 79–81), whose attempt to help the stricken area was diverted almost immediately by the outbreak of a serious fire at Rome (**C17–18**). Several contemporary authors recorded their reactions to the region's fate, notably the poet Statius, whose home town was Naples (**C20–23**). Other contemporary poets were inspired to allude to the eruption in vivid metaphors or similes (**C26–27**). Finally, the apocalyptic nature of the eruption provoked discussion of the role of the gods among Jewish, Greek and Christian writers alike (**C28–30**).

Earthquake of AD 62 (C1–5)

This disaster inspired the Younger Seneca to discuss earthquakes at length in his *Natural Questions* (**C1**). The disaster was highly topical as Seneca's work was written between AD 62 and his death in AD 65. Another reason for Seneca's focus upon Pompeii in his account may be the local connections of the dedicatee of this work, Lucilius, alluded to in *Letters* 5.49.1 and 8.70.1. His dating of it by the consuls of AD 63, however, is at odds with Tacitus' inclusion of it in his *Annals* under AD 62 (**C2**).

A contemporary account of the earthquake (C1)

C1 Seneca the Younger, *Natural Questions* 6.1.1–3, 6.1.10, 6.27.1, 6.31

We have heard, my dear Lucilius, that Pompeii, a busy town in Campania, has subsided under an earthquake. It is situated where the shore of Sorrento and Stabiae from the one side and from the other the shore of Herculaneum come together and encircle with a beautiful bay the sea where it has been brought in from open waters. All the surrounding areas have also been affected. What is more, this happened during winter, a time our ancestors used to promise us was free from danger of this kind. This tremor was on 5 February in the consulship of Regulus and Verginius, and it inflicted great devastation on Campania, a region never safe from this evil, yet which has remained undamaged and has so often got off with a fright. For part of the town of Herculaneum too fell down and even the structures that remain are unstable, and the colony of Nuceria, though it escaped disaster, nevertheless is not without complaint. Naples too lost many private buildings, but no public ones, being stricken only lightly by the great disaster; even villas have collapsed, everywhere things shook without damage. In addition, the following events occurred: a flock of 600 sheep died and statues split, some people have lost their minds and wander about in their madness. Both the plan of my proposed work and the coincidence of the misfortune at this time demand that we explain the reasons for these things.

[10] Therefore let us adopt great courage in the face of that disaster, which can neither be avoided nor predicted and let us stop listening to those who have renounced Campania, who have emigrated after this misfortune and say that they will never go there again. For who can promise them that this or that piece of ground stands on better foundations? [12] We are mistaken if we believe any part of the world is exempt and immune from the danger of an earthquake.

[27] In this Campanian earthquake some peculiar things are said to have occurred, of which an account ought to be given. We have said that a herd of 600 sheep died in the area of Pompeii.

[31] Yet why did the earthquake last several days? For Campania shook continuously and did not stop though it became less violent. Nonetheless there was great damage, because it was shaking things that had already been shaken, and things that are hardly standing do not need to be overturned, but merely pushed, to fall down.

Bad omens for Nero's reign (C2)

The earthquake appears here in the *Annals* in a section reviewing the minor events of AD 62.

C2 Tacitus, *Annals* 15.22

Under the same consuls a gymnasium burned down as a result of being struck by lightning, and a statue of Nero in it was melted into shapeless bronze. And the busy town of Pompeii in Campania largely collapsed because of an earthquake; and the Vestal Virgin Laelia died: her place was taken by Cornelia from the family of the Cossi.

Relief panels depicting an earthquake, House of Caecilius Iucundus (V.i.26) (C3)

Two relief panels depict scenes during an earthquake, representing identifiable areas of Pompeii, namely the Forum (C3) and area outside the Vesuvian Gate. At least one of these reliefs (C3) belonged to the household shrine (*lararium*) of Caecilius Iucundus, and the other is probably a companion piece. For other finds from the House of Caecilius Iucundus, see D77, E55, F17 and H69–82.

The first panel (C3) depicts the northern side of the Forum, with the Temple of Jupiter, flanked by two equestrian statues and a monumental arch, and an altar flanked by sacrificial implements and a bull sacrifice. Gradel (1992) has argued that the altar is that of the Temple of the *Genius* of the Colony (otherwise generally known as the Temple of Vespasian or Temple of the *Genius* of Augustus).

The other panel shows the area at the Vesuvius Gate, with the water-distribution tower (*castellum*), the gate itself, part of the town walls, and an altar next to a tree. This gate is only a short distance to the north of Caecilius Iucundus' house. The reliefs were perhaps set up as a thank-offering to the household gods for protecting life and/or property during an earthquake.

Plate 3.1 C3 Relief panel on the *lararium* of Caecilius,
depicting an earthquake in the Forum

Plate 3.2 C4 Repairs in brick to the north enclosure wall
of the Temple of Apollo

Rebuilding the Temple of Isis following an earthquake (C5)

This building inscription was set over the main entrance to the sanctuary. The Popidii were an old, established family at Pompeii (see A22–26), but Celsinus was almost certainly the son of one of that family's freedmen (Popidius Ampliatus) rather than descended from the distinguished family itself. As an ex-slave himself, his father was barred from becoming a member of the local council, but by rebuilding the temple in the name of his young son, Ampliatus ensured promotion up the social hierarchy for the next generation. For premature promotion of children in another family, see G21 and G24. For other finds in the Temple of Isis, see E3–5. Rebuilding after earthquake damage is also known from inscriptions at Herculaneum, where two major projects were sponsored by the emperor Vespasian: *CIL* X 1406 and *AE* (1979) 170.

C5 *CIL* X 846 = *ILS* 6367

Numerius Popidius Celsinus, son of Numerius, rebuilt at his own expense from its foundations the Temple of Isis, which had collapsed in an earthquake; because of his generosity, although he was only 6 years old, the town councillors nominated him into their number free of charge.

Eruption of Vesuvius, AD 79 (C6–15)

The sleeping volcano (C6–8)

The following references to Vesuvius show how ancient authors appreciated the ongoing effects of past volcanic activity, which had made the area particularly fertile (see also H1) and had also produced pumice. The plain to the north of Naples was (and still is) known as 'Phlegraean' or 'Fiery'. In C6, Diodorus is describing Hercules' journey through Italy (A2–3), when he defeated giants in Campania.

C6 Diodorus of Sicily 4.21.5 (written before 30 BC)

This plain is called Phlegraean from the mountain which formerly poured forth monstrous fire like Etna in Sicily: but now the mountain is called Vesuvius and shows many signs of having burnt in ancient times.

C7 Vitruvius, *On Architecture* 2.6.2 (written before 27 BC)

Also worth mentioning are the conflagrations that arose long ago and have been plentiful beneath Mount Vesuvius, and from there spewed forth fire over the fields. For this reason then what is called sponge or Pompeian pumice seems to have been melted down from another type of stone and converted into this characteristic type.

C8 Strabo, *Geography* 5.4.8 (written before AD 25)

Mount Vesuvius is situated above these places and people live all around on very beautiful farms, except at the summit. This is flat for the main part, but completely unfruitful, like ashes to look at, and it displays porous hollows of rocks blackened on the surface, as if devoured by fire. As a result, one would deduce that this area was previously on fire and held craters of fire, and that it was extinguished when the fuel failed. Perhaps this is also the reason for the fruitfulness of the surrounding area, just as at Catana they say that the part covered by ash carried up by the fire of Etna made the country suited to vine-growing.

The death of the Elder Pliny in the eruption (C9–11)

At the time of the eruption, the Elder Pliny was commanding the Roman fleet stationed at Misenum, a promontory on the northern side of the Bay of Naples. On first noticing the eruptive cloud, his spirit of scientific curiosity roused him to investigate further (he had just completed writing an extensive *Natural History*). His plan took on a humanitarian aspect on receiving a message begging for help from a friend. His nephew, the Younger Pliny, chose not to accompany him on his voyage, preferring to finish his homework, but observed the eruption from Misenum. Many years later, the historian Tacitus asked the Younger Pliny to provide him with an account of his uncle's death in the eruption, since he wanted to narrate the end of this distinguished Roman in his *Histories*. The part of this work dealing with this episode has not survived, but we do have Pliny's letters (written AD *c.*106–7), intended to provide vivid material for a dramatic history. For a much later eye-witness account of an eruption, see J53–54.

C9 Pliny the Younger, *Letters* 6.16

Pliny greets his friend Tacitus:

Thank you for asking me to write to you about my uncle's death, so that you can pass on a more accurate account to future generations. I realize that his death will be granted undying fame if it is celebrated by you. [2] For although he died a memorable death that will make him survive for ever, in a disaster affecting the most beautiful areas, involving people and cities, and although he himself has written many works of lasting value, nonetheless your immortal writing will do much to perpetuate his name. [3] In my opinion, lucky are those with the God-given gift either of doing something worth writing about or writing something worth reading, but luckiest of all are those who have done both. My uncle will count as one of these, through his own books and yours. Therefore I am more willing, indeed insist on undertaking what you ask.

[4] He was at Misenum, commanding the fleet in person. On 24 August in the early afternoon, my mother pointed out to him that a cloud of unusual size and form was appearing. [5] He had been enjoying the sun, had taken a cold bath, had eaten a light lunch while lying down, and was working.

He called for his sandals and climbed to the place from which he would have the best view of the phenomenon. A cloud was rising from a mountain (those seeing it from far away could not tell which, but it was later known to be Vesuvius). Its appearance can best be expressed by comparing it to an umbrella pine, [6] for carried up to a very great height as if on a tree-trunk, it began to spread out into various branches. This was, I believe, because it was lifted up by the fresh blast, then as that died down, defeated by its own weight, it began to disperse far and wide. Sometimes it was white, sometimes dirty and speckled, according to how much soil and ash it carried. [7] To a man of my uncle's great intellect, it seemed important and worth learning about from closer at hand. He ordered a fast warship to be fitted out; he gave me the opportunity, should I wish, of coming with him. I replied that I should prefer to work, and as it happened he had given me some writing.

[8] As he was leaving the house he received a note from Rectina, the wife of Tascius, who was terrified by the imminent danger (for her villa lay at the bottom of the mountain and there was no escape except by boat) and who begged him to rescue her from so great a danger. [9] He changed his plan and what he had begun in a spirit of enquiry he ended as a hero. He ordered warships to be launched and embarked, aiming to bring help to many others besides Rectina (for the beautiful coastline was thickly populated). [10] He hurried to the place from which others were fleeing and steered his course straight for the danger. So fearless was he that he dictated notes on each movement and change in shape of the disaster as he observed them.

[11] By now ash was falling on the ships: the closer they came, the hotter and denser the ash. Then pumice and blackened stones, burnt and shattered by the fire. Next sudden shallow water and the shore blocked by debris from the mountain. He delayed a little, wondering whether to turn back, but then said to the helmsman when he warned him to do so, 'Fortune favours the brave: head for Pomponianus.' [12] Pomponianus was at Stabiae, cut off by being in the middle of the bay (for as the shore gradually curves round, the sea pours into it). There, although it was not yet imminent, the danger was clear, and since it was growing very close, he had carried luggage into ships, determined to flee if the adverse wind died down. My uncle, then, sailed in on a strong following wind; he embraced, consoled and encouraged the fearful Pomponianus, and in order to lessen his friend's fear by his own assurance, he ordered that he be taken to the baths. Having washed, he reclined to dinner, either cheerful or (equally impressively) pretending to be cheerful.

[13] Meanwhile from many points on Mount Vesuvius, wide sheets of flame and soaring fires were blazing, their brightness and visibility increased by the darkness of night. My uncle, to soothe their fears, kept saying that these were fires abandoned by country folk in their panic and villas that were

burning through being left uninhabited. Then he went to bed and actually fell asleep; for his breathing, which because of his large build was rather heavy and loud, was heard by those who were keeping watch by his door. [14] But the level of the courtyard from which his rooms were approached had so risen, by being filled with ashes mixed with pumice, that any further delay in the bedroom would have prevented escape. On being woken, he went out and returned to Pomponianus and the others who had remained awake. [15] They consulted together whether to stay indoors or wander in the open. For the buildings were shaking with frequent and severe tremors and seemed to be swaying to and fro as if removed from their own foundations. [16] Then again, in the open there was the fear of falling pumice stones, even though these were light and porous. On comparing the dangers, they chose the latter (in my uncle's case, reason won out; but fear in the case of the others). They put cushions on their heads, tied with cloth, as protection against falling objects. [17] Now it was day elsewhere; there it was night, blacker and denser than any night, though many torches and various lights broke it up. He decided to go down to the shore and see from close up if the sea allowed any escape, but it remained high and hostile. [18] There, lying on a cloth spread out for him, he twice demanded and drank cold water. Then the flames and the smell of sulphur which heralded the flames, made the others turn to flee, and made him get up. [19] Leaning on two young slaves he stood up and immediately collapsed, because, I gather, his breathing was obstructed by the thicker smoke, and his windpipe, which was naturally weak, narrow and often inflamed, was blocked. [20] When day returned (two days after the last he had seen), his body was found, intact, uninjured, covered and just as he had been dressed: the appearance of the body was more like someone asleep than dead.

[21] Meanwhile at Misenum, my mother and I – but this is nothing to do with your history, nor did you want me to write about anything other than his death. So I stop. One thing I shall add, that I followed up everything I witnessed or heard immediately after, when things are most accurately remembered. You will select the most important things: for it is one thing to write a letter, another to write history; one thing to write to a friend, another to write to everyone.

Farewell.

Plate 3.3 C10 An umbrella pine, with Vesuvius
in the background

C11 Suetonius, *On Distinguished Men*

Pliny the Elder died in a disaster in Campania; for when he was in command
of the fleet at Misenum, during the eruption of Vesuvius he claimed that
the reasons ought to be investigated at closer hand in a warship, and was
unable to return in the face of adverse winds. He was overcome by the force
of dust and ashes, or, as some think, he was killed by his slave, whom he
had asked to hasten his death when he was being overcome by the heat.

A narrow escape (C12)

For Pliny's first letter about the eruption, see C9.

C12 Pliny the Younger, *Letters* 6.20

Pliny greets his friend Tacitus:
   You say that you are encouraged by the letter in which I wrote, at your
request, about the death of my uncle, to wish to learn what fears and actual
dangers I endured, left at Misenum (for I began but broke off my account).
'Although the mind shrinks from remembering ... I shall begin.' {Pliny

here quotes Virgil, *Aeneid* 2.12–13, Aeneas reluctantly beginning to tell Dido the story of the sack of Troy.}

[2] After my uncle set out, I spent the rest of my time on work, since this was the reason I had stayed behind; then I had a bath, dinner, and a short, disturbed sleep. [3] For many days previously there had been earth tremors, less alarming because frequent in Campania; but that night they grew so strong that it seemed everything was not so much being moved, but being overturned. [4] My mother burst into my bedroom: I was getting up anyway but would have been woken had I been asleep. We sat in the courtyard of the house, which formed a small area separating the sea from the living quarters. [5] I am not sure whether I should call it brave or foolish (I was seventeen at the time) but I called for a book of Livy and as if reading for pleasure I continued to make the summaries I had begun. Then a friend of my uncle, who had recently come to visit him from Spain, saw my mother and me sitting down, and me actually reading, and attacked her over-indulgence and my complacency. I remained as eagerly engrossed in my book.

[6] Now it was the first hour of daylight, but the light was still weak and uncertain. Now the surrounding buildings were shaking and although we were in the open, being in a confined space, we were in great and real danger from the house collapsing. [7] Then finally we decided to leave the town: a dazed mob followed us, preferring someone else's plan to their own – the nearest they could get to prudence in their panic. They hurried us on our way, pressing in a thick crowd behind us. [8] Once out of the built-up area we stopped. There we experienced many remarkable and terrifying phenomena. The carriages which we had ordered to be brought began to move in different directions although the ground was quite level and they did not even stay still when secured by stones placed in their tracks. [9] In addition we watched the sea apparently sucked out and driven back by the earthquake. Certainly the shoreline had advanced and stranded many sea creatures on dry sand. On the other side, a terrifying black cloud, split by twisted blasts of fire shooting in different directions, gaped to reveal long fiery shapes, similar to flashes of lightning only bigger. [10] Then that same friend from Spain spoke more pointedly and urgently. 'If your brother and your uncle lives, he would wish you to be safe; if he has died he would have wished you to survive. So why do you abandon your escape?' We replied that we could not undertake to think about our own safety while uncertain about his. [11] Delaying no longer, he rushed off away from the danger at great speed. Soon after, that cloud sank down over the land and covered the sea. It had already shrouded and concealed Capri and hidden the part of Misenum that juts out. [12] Then my mother begged, encouraged and ordered me to escape by whatever means I could, being a young man; she, being old and stout, would die content as long as she had not brought about my death. I however said I would not escape unless we did so together; then grasping her hand, I forced

her to quicken her pace. She reluctantly complied and accused herself of delaying me.

[13] Now ash was falling, though still lightly. I looked back: behind our backs loomed thick blackness, which like a torrent pursued us, spreading over the earth. 'Let us turn aside,' I said, 'while we can see, to avoid being knocked down and trampled on in the darkness by the crowd around us.' [14] We had only just sat down when darkness fell, not like a moonless or cloudy night, but like when a light is extinguished in a closed room. You could hear women screaming, babies wailing, men shouting: some were calling out for their parents, others for their children, others for their spouses, and trying to recognize their voices; some lamented their own misfortune, others that of their relatives; there were some who in their fear of dying prayed for death; [15] many raised their hands to the gods; more still concluded that there were no gods and that this was the world's final and everlasting night. And there were people who exaggerated the real dangers by inventing fictitious terrors. Some were there with the news that one part of Misenum had collapsed and another part was on fire: though false, people believed it. [16] A little light returned, which seemed not to bring daylight to us, but to indicate that the fire was approaching. The fire actually halted some way off, but darkness returned, and ash in heavy falls. We repeatedly got up to shake this off, otherwise we would have been covered and even crushed by the weight. [17] I could have boasted that no groan or feeble cry escaped me in these dangers had I not believed, as a considerable consolation for my death that I was dying along with everyone and everything was dying with me.

[18] At last the darkness thinned and dissipated as into smoke or cloud; soon there was proper daylight; the sun even shone, though pale as in an eclipse. A completely changed landscape met our frightened eyes – one covered deep in ash as if by snow. [19] Returning to Misenum we saw to our physical needs and spent an anxious night wavering between hope and fear. Fear was stronger since the earthquakes continued and many people hysterically made their own sufferings and those of others seem ludicrous by their terrifying predictions. [20] As for us, not even then did we think of leaving, although we had been through dangers and expected more to come, until there was news of my uncle.

All this is not worthy of serious history and you will read it without any intention of writing it up. But you will have only yourself to blame for asking for the account if it does not even seem worth including in a letter. Farewell. *play down fear, heroisize Uncle?*

Disasters in Italy (C13)

This brief allusion to the eruption in the swift-moving programmatic prologue to the *Histories* is all that survives of Tacitus' treatment of the disaster.

C13 Tacitus, *Histories* 1.2

In that period, Italy was afflicted by disasters which were either unprecedented or had not been experienced for many centuries. Cities were burnt or buried on the very fertile shore of Campania; Rome itself was devastated by fires, which gutted its most venerable shrines, and the Capitol itself was burnt by the hands of citizens.

A later dramatic account of the eruption (C14)

Even though Dio himself was alive at the time of the later eruption of AD 202, the details of this passage are far from accurate, since the author's aim here is dramatic description rather than historical veracity. In addition, this description is only preserved though a summary by Xiphilinos.

C14 Dio Cassius 66.21–23 (continued in C18)

[21] In Campania some amazing and terrifying events took place: for during the autumn, a great fire was suddenly kindled. For Mount Vesuvius stands opposite Naples by the sea and has unquenchable fountains of fire. It was once an equal height all around and fire sprang from its centre. Only this part of the mountain is burnt, while the outside is unburnt and remains so even now. Therefore as these parts are always unburnt, while the middle is parched and burnt to ashes, the peaks around the centre preserve their original height to this day, while the whole fiery section has been consumed over time and has subsided into a hollow shape, so that the whole mountain, if I can compare great things to small, resembles an amphitheatre.

The heights of Vesuvius support trees and many vines, but the crater is given over to the fire, and gives smoke by day and flame by night, so that it seems that great quantities of all kinds of incense are being burnt in it. This happens continually to a greater or lesser extent. Often it throws up ashes whenever there is a general subsidence, and sends up stones whenever there are violent winds. It roars and bellows since its vents are not compacted but are narrow and hidden.

[22] This is what Vesuvius is like and these phenomena generally happen each year. But all the other things that have happened there over the years, although they always seem impressive and unusual to those who see them, would, even if all put together, be thought trivial in comparison with what then took place. This was as follows.

Many huge men, greater than human size, as giants are depicted, made an appearance, now on the mountain, now in the surrounding countryside and the cities, wandering day and night on the earth and passing through the air. After this were terrible droughts and sudden violent earthquakes, so that the whole plain seethed and the summits leapt up, there were roars, some underground like thunder, some on the surface like bellowing of oxen. The sea too roared and the sky re-echoed it. Then a sudden portentous crash was heard as if the mountains were collapsing, and first enormous stones were thrown up to reach the height of the mountain-tops themselves, then great quantity of fire and endless smoke so that the whole sky was shaded, the sun completely hidden as if eclipsed. [23] So day became night, light darkness. Some thought the giants were rising in revolt (for many of their forms could be seen through the smoke, and in addition a sound of trumpets was heard). Others thought that the whole universe was being consumed by chaos or fire. Therefore they fled, some from their houses into the streets, some from outside indoors; from the sea inland and from there to the sea, since in their confusion they thought that wherever they were not was safer than where they were. At the same time, an unbelievable quantity of ash was blown out, covering land, sea and all the sky. Not surprisingly it did a great deal of damage to men, farms and cattle. It destroyed all fish and birds and, in addition, it buried two whole cities, Herculaneum and Pompeii, while its population was sitting in the theatre. The whole cloud of dust was so great that some of it reached Africa, Syria and Egypt; it also reached Rome, filling the sky above it and darkening the sun. It occasioned no little fear for several days since people did not know and could not imagine what had happened, but thought that everything was being turned upside down and that the sun was vanishing into the earth and the earth being lifted into the heavens. However this ash did them no great damage, but later brought a terrible plague on them.

C15 Eusebius, *Chronicle* AD 79

Mount Vesuvius burst open at its summit, and so much fire spurted forth that it consumed the surrounding countryside together with the towns.

The aftermath of the eruption (C16–30)

Victims of the eruption (C16)

Individual victims of Vesuvius are rarely mentioned. One exception, mentioned by Josephus, is Agrippa, the son of Antonius Felix and Drusilla. Felix was an imperial freedman, and extraordinarily the emperor Claudius' procurator (governor) of Palestine (AD *c.*52–60). He made three exceptional marriages, all to royalty. Drusilla was a Jewish princess, daughter of Agrippa I. Josephus does not fulfil his promise to describe Agrippa's death. For possibly a less direct allusion to death caused by the eruption, see C22.

C16 Josephus, *Jewish Antiquities* 20.7.2

How that young man was killed with his wife in the eruption of Mount Vesuvius in the times of Titus Caesar, I shall reveal after this.

Relief work by the emperor Titus (C17–18)

Titus had succeeded his father Vespasian as emperor only two months before the eruption occurred. The significance of Titus' action in allocating the property of those who died without heirs to relief work lies in the fact that such property would otherwise have entered the imperial coffers. A series of coins minted in the following year (H. Mattingly (1923) *Coins of the Roman Empire in the British Museum* I. *Augustus to Vitellius* (*BMC*) *Titus* 49–82) commemorates attempts to assuage the gods' wrath, which had been revealed by these natural disasters (compare C28). Inscriptions at Naples, Salerno and Sorrento show how Titus contributed to the rebuilding of towns damaged, though not destroyed, during the eruption, and one at Nuceria shows the emperor Domitian rebuilding the theatre there.

C17 Suetonius, *Titus* 8.3

In his reign, several dreadful disasters occurred – an eruption of Mount Vesuvius in Campania, a fire at Rome which burned for three days and nights, and one of the worst ever outbreaks of the plague. In the face of all these disasters, he displayed not merely the concern of an emperor but also the deep love of a father, whether by offering messages of sympathy or by giving all the financial help he could. He selected by lot some senators of consular rank to regenerate Campania, and allocated the property of those who had died in the eruption and who had no surviving heirs to the renewal of the afflicted towns.

C18 Dio Cassius 66.24.1, 3–4 (continuation from C14)

In the following year, a fire on the ground spread over a very large part of Rome while Titus was away following the disaster in Campania . . . Titus therefore sent two ex-consuls to Campania to refound the settlements and gave money and the possessions of those who had died without heirs. Titus himself took no money from individuals or cities or kings although many kept giving and promising him large sums, but restored all the damage from his resources.

Salvaging on site (C19)

The extent of salvaging in the immediate aftermath of the eruption is much debated, but the following text (Latin, but written in Greek letters) was clearly scratched upon the right wall of the entrance way. It appears to be a statement that the house has been explored and salvaged. This is supported by holes in the walls and by the fact that hardly anything was found in the house, except for a bronze statue, which had been stored in a more out-of-the-way place. This suggests that the salvaging was the act not of the house's owner, nor of someone acquainted with the house, but perhaps took place some time after the eruption. Compare J32 for other possible indications of salvaging in antiquity.

C19 *CIL* IV 2311, House of N. Popidius Priscus (VII.ii.20)

House tunnelled through.

The eruption's impact, according to a local poet (C20–23)

Statius was particularly moved by the fate of his region of birth, not least since he knew individuals who were affected by the eruption. In **C20**, the poet may be alluding to towns other than Pompeii, Herculaneum and Stabiae, such as Naples and Sorrento, which must have suffered in the eruption from fallout and earth tremors, but which soon recovered. Julius Menecrates (eulogized in **C22**), also from Naples, was the son-in-law of Pollio Felix, whose villa on the Sorrentine promontory is eulogized by Statius in another poem. Statius even reveals (**C23**) his father's unfulfilled plans to write a poem about the eruption. Book 3 was published AD 93–4, Book 4 in AD 95, Book 5 posthumously, in AD ?96.

C20 Statius, *Silvae* 3.5.72–5

Vesuvius' peak and the dread mountain's fiery storm have not depleted the terrified cities of their citizens so much: they stand and their populations thrive.

C21 Statius, *Silvae* 4.4.78–85

These things I am singing to you, Marcellus, on the Cumaean shores, where Vesuvius revived its curbed anger, billowing forth fires to rival Etna's flames. Amazing truth! Will future generations believe, when crops and these now deserted places once more thrive again, that cities and peoples are buried below and that ancestral lands have disappeared, having shared in the same fate? Not yet does the mountain-top cease to threaten death.

C22 Statius, *Silvae* 4.8.3–5

Behold, now a third child increases the family of illustrious Menecrates. A noble crowd of princes grows for you and consoles you for the losses caused by mad Vesuvius.

C23 Statius, *Silvae* 5.3.205–8

It was your intention to lament the fires of Vesuvius in a poetic tribute and to spend your efforts lamenting the ruin of your country, when the Father uprooted the mountain from the earth, lifted it to heaven, and cast it down onto the pitiable cities all around.

The eruption's impact on the landscape (C24–25)

C24 Martial, *Epigram* 4.44 (published December AD 88)

Here is Vesuvius, just now covered with green shady vines; here the noble grape had squeezed out drenching pools; these the ridges, which Bacchus loved more than the hills of Nysa; on this mountain the Satyrs recently performed their dances; this was the home of Venus, more pleasing to her than Lacedaemon; this place was famous for Hercules' divine presence. Everything lies submerged in flames and sad ash: and the gods above would not wish they had such power.

C25 Tacitus, *Annals* 4.67

Capri used to look out over a very beautiful bay, before the eruption of Mount Vesuvius changed the region's appearance.

The eruption as source of poetical inspiration (C26–27)

Both Valerius Flaccus and Silius Italicus were engaged in writing melodramatic epic poems around the time of Vesuvius' eruption, which clearly made an impact upon their imagination. C26 is one of two striking similes in *The Argonauts* (written AD 70–80) in which the poet compares moments during battles with the erupting volcano (compare 3.208–10).

In his epic poem on the struggles between Rome and Carthage in the Punic Wars, Silius Italicus (AD *c.* 25–101) presents an eruption of Vesuvius as the culmination of a whole sequence of bad omens that predicted disaster for the Romans on the battlefield at Cannae (C27). This does not record a historical eruption of 216 BC, but reflects the impact of the eruption of AD 79 upon the imagination of contemporary onlookers.

C26 Valerius Flaccus, *The Argonauts* 4.507–9

As when perhaps the fatal peak of Hesperian Vesuvius thundered as it burst apart, only just has the fiery storm twisted the mountain, but already the ash has clothed eastern cities.

C27 Silius Italicus, *Punic Wars* 8.653–5

Vesuvius thundered as well, whirling Etna's fires from its rocks, and the Phlegraean peak reached the trembling stars with the boulders hurled into the clouds.

The role of the gods in the eruption (C28–30)

A Jewish prediction of doom (C28)

The fourth Sibylline Oracle is a composite oracle, containing a Hellenistic political oracle and a later Jewish insertion of the AD 80s. The Sibyl predicts the rise and fall of a succession of kingdoms, culminating in the fall of the Roman Empire. This passage follows an account of the sack of Jerusalem (by Vespasian and Titus in AD 70).

C28 Sibylline Oracle 4.130–6

But when, some day, fire escapes from an underground fissure in the land of Italy and reaches the expanse of the heavens, it will destroy many towns and men with its flames, and much dense ash will fill the great sky, and drops will fall from heaven like red ochre, then know the wrath of the heavenly God, on those who destroyed the blameless race of the pious.

A Greek defence of prophecy (C29)

This passage is part of a defence of the accuracy of the Pythian Sibyl at Delphi, and claims to illustrate how her divinely inspired prophecy predicted Vesuvius' eruption. Later on, at *Moralia* 566E (*The Divine Vengeance*), Plutarch represents his visionary as actually hearing the Sibyl make this prophecy. Dikaiarcheia is the Greek name for Puteoli (modern Pozzuoli). For the Sibylline prophecy, see C28.

C29 Plutarch, *Moralia* 398E, The Oracles at Delphi

Time has delivered the recent and new misfortunes around Cumae and Dikaiarcheia not long ago commemorated and chanted through the Sibylline books, just as it ought, with the bursting out of the mountain's fire and the sea's seething, with burning rocks thrown up by the wind, and the destruction of so many great towns, so that their location is imperceptible and uncertain to anyone going there in broad daylight, now that the land has been turned topsy-turvy.

A Christian defence against pagans (C30)

Finally, in AD *c.*197, Tertullian, writing in defence of Christianity, argues that the wrath of the pagan gods against Christians neglecting their worship cannot be sufficient explanation for natural disasters, given that no Christians lived at Pompeii when Vesuvius erupted. He uses the same pair of examples at *Ad nationes* 1.9.7.

C30 Tertullian, *Apology* 40.8

But neither Etruria nor Campania had yet complained about Christians at that time, when fire flooded Vulsinii from the sky, and Pompeii from its own mountain.

4

LEISURE

Pompeii's Amphitheatre is the oldest surviving building of its kind in the Roman world. Its dedicatory inscription shows that it was built *c*.70 BC (**B10**), and other inscriptions reveal later phases in its building history (**D1–5**). It was repaired and reinforced following earthquake damage during the last years of the town's existence, perhaps under the supervision of the Cuspii Pansae (**D6–7**). Despite the Amphitheatre being the venue *par excellence* for various sorts of shows, some were still being performed in the Forum in the Augustan era, several decades after the Amphitheatre had been built (**D8**). See also J47–52.

Some of the most distinctive sights at Pompeii today are the inscriptions painted in black and red upon the whitewashed plaster façades of shops, houses, public buildings and tombs. These inscriptions, or *dipinti*, announcing forthcoming games provide a unique insight into the presentation of shows by members of the local elite and illustrate aspects of their organization. Over seventy such inscriptions have been found in the town, from which we can discover who presented games at Pompeii, when they were staged, and information about the types of show (**D9–24**). Some of the most impressive and unusual notices are those advertising games sponsored by Gnaeus Alleius Nigidius Maius (**D19–24**). Others even advertise games in other towns in the region (**D25, 29–30**).

Gladiatorial shows were highly popular: in addition to the notices announcing future games, past games were commemorated in a variety of media, including stucco, painting and graffiti (**D26–28, D31–33, F88, G8**). Some of these pictures were commissioned by those who had provided the games, in order to provide a lasting record of their generosity. Some of the elite had depicted on their tombs the games that they had presented to the populace (**D31, F88, G8**). Graffiti drawings of gladiators and the fight results can be found in many parts of the town (**D33**). On one notorious occasion, the spectators' rivalry spilled over into a riot, giving a foretaste of football hooliganism two thousand years later (**D34–38**)! Two training grounds for gladiators have also been discovered. In the mid-first century AD, the large portico behind the Large Theatre was converted into a

Gladiatorial Barracks (**D44**; see also **J11–20**). Previously, gladiators had been trained in the 'House of the Gladiators', where many graffiti relating to gladiators have been found (**D45–49**).

We have a less vivid picture of other types of spectacles at Pompeii, but theatrical shows were also well established by Roman times. The Large Theatre at Pompeii was initially built during the second century BC, and was extensively modified during the Augustan era, probably *c.* 2 BC (**D51–56**). The presiding magistrates at the shows would have been seated upon wide honorific chairs of metal with ivory ornamentation, traces of which were found in the eighteenth century (**J22–23**). As at the Amphitheatre, spectators in the Theatre were protected by an awning, as can be seen from the brackets that remain, which supported the masts.

Adjacent to the Large Theatre, which seated around 5,000, is the Covered Theatre or Odeion. This had a much smaller seating capacity of around 2,000 (still very large by modern standards: the Royal Shakespeare Theatre at Stratford seats 1,412). Some clues remain as to the character of performances in these venues, the highbrow and lowbrow alike. What appear to be theatre tokens imply that Greek drama was staged at Pompeii (**D58–61**), while it is highly likely that the 'Atellan' slapstick farces, a traditional part of this region's culture, were also performed. Although gladiators seem to have dominated popular enthusiasms, actors could also attract fans (**D63–70**). Finds of fragmentary instruments help to create some impression of the musical accompaniments to performances (**J21**). Finally, basins for water beneath the *orchestra* of the Large Theatre may have powered a water organ, or have been used for aquatic spectacles, while a cistern above the Theatre may have provided water for sprinkling the audience – an amenity occasionally advertised on notices of games in the Amphitheatre (e.g. **D22**).

Literary pursuits spilled over into other areas of the town as well. Excerpts from all the well-known Latin poets of the time, except Horace, appear in graffiti (Appendix 2). In most cases, quotations are reproduced verbatim, but there is also a sophisticated parody upon the opening lines of Virgil's *Aeneid* (**D71**). There is even an otherwise unknown local poet, Tiburtinus, who scratched a few verses upon the walls of the Odeion (**D72**), and many other short love poems can be found (**D73–79**). In addition, word plays (including 'magic' squares – **D84–85**) and amusing sketches combining words and pictures (**D81–83**) suggest that some inhabitants spent a considerable amount of their leisure time scribbling up graffiti! Obscenities and insults are also common, and brief accounts of sexual encounters occur famously in the brothel, but are by no means confined to its walls (**D100–102**).

Three main sets of public baths existed at Pompeii – the Stabian, Forum and Central Baths, the last of which were still unfinished in AD 79 (**D105–108**). Although Pompeii was destroyed before the heyday of Roman bath buildings, the Stabian Baths at Pompeii are the oldest preserved public baths (**D105**). Other early public baths, the Republican Baths (VII.v.36) of *c.*100–80 BC, fell out of use by the Augustan period. In addition, several sets of privately owned baths tried to attract customers by advertising their amenities. Their owners aimed to make a profit by providing exclusive bathing for the discerning customer. Baths of Crassus Frugi are known only from an inscription (**D109**), but the Baths of Julia Felix (**H44**), the Sarno Baths (VIII.ii.17), Palaestra Baths (VIII.ii.23) (see also **H38**) and Suburban Baths have all been excavated. A few of the most luxurious houses boasted their own small bath suites (e.g. House of the Faun, House of the Menander, House of the Silver Wedding).

The Amphitheatre (D1–7)

Built in *c.*70 BC (**B10**), the Amphitheatre abuts on the town's defensive walls in the south-eastern district of the town. The large quantities of soil removed to create the sunken arena were piled up to support the spectators' seating. It may have had a seating capacity of *c.*24,000 – more than enough seats to cater for the whole of Pompeii's population and for an almost equally large number of visitors too. Spectators were divided up and allocated seats in different parts of the auditorium according to their social status. Intermingling of the common crowd with the elite was avoided: a system of separate entrances and tunnels gave access to the lower tiers of seating, while external staircases led directly to the upper tiers for the masses. It seems likely that women were confined to the uppermost seats, where they may have been allocated seats in 'boxes', each with a capacity of up to fourteen people. Magistrates and others funding the games would have occupied double-width honorific seats (*bisellia*) in special boxes near to the arena. A canvas awning (*vela*) stretching out over the seating, supported by tall wooden masts, protected spectators from light rain and sun alike.

Construction of stone seating in the Amphitheatre (D1–5)

In a series of inscriptions on the upper part of the wall dividing the arena from the spectators' seating appear the names of benefactors, who paid for the construction of the stone seating during the Augustan period. This replaced the earliest seating, which was probably wooden.

Each inscription relates to a particular section, or wedge, of seating (*cuneus*). The phrase 'instead of games' implies that the 'benefactors' concerned were actually thus fulfilling their legal obligation to spend a certain amount of money in their year of office either on games or on a monument (**B11** and **D57**). The references to lights allude to performances held at night under artificial illumination. The identity of the Fortunate Augustan Suburban Country District (*pagus augustus felix suburbanus*) is not known. The word *pagus* usually implies a rural location but the district was closely integrated into the life of the colony and had existed before the Augustan period as the Fortunate Suburban district.

D1 *CIL* X 853 = *ILS* 5653e

The presidents of the Fortunate Augustan Suburban Country District (built this) instead of games, by decree of the town councillors.

D2 *CIL* X 854

Titus Atullius Celer, son of Gaius, duumvir, instead of games and lights, saw to the construction of a seating sector, by decree of the town councillors.

D3 *CIL* X 855 = *ILS* 5653c

Lucius Saginius, duumvir with judicial power, instead of games and lights, by decree of the town councillors (built this) seating sector.

D4 *CIL* X 857a = *ILS* 5653b

Numerius Istacidius Cilix, son of Numerius, duumvir, instead of games and lights.

D5 *CIL* X 857d = *ILS* 5653a

Marcus Cantrius Marcellus, son of Marcus, duumvir, instead of games and lights, saw to the construction of three seating sectors, by decree of the town councillors.

The Amphitheatre restored after earthquake damage (D6–7)

The following inscriptions appear below two large niches opposite each other, which flank the passageway leading down into the arena on the north side of the Amphitheatre. This would presumably have been the entrance used by processions entering the building. Although it is generally assumed that the niches above held honorific portrait statues of the father and son named on the inscriptions, there are signs of a metal grille barring off the niches. This suggests that something of great value stood there, perhaps precious-metal statues of deities. The fact that the inscriptions are in the nominative (instead of the dative) case also implies that they are not honorific in character, but record something which the two men have done. They might, therefore, have donated such statues. Another suggestion is that Cuspius Pansa, father, was appointed as a prefect following the earthquake of AD 62, with special responsibility for helping to sort out the town. One of his tasks, then, may have been seeing to the restoration and reinforcement of the Amphitheatre. This certainly happened, as can be seen from the addition of brick buttresses to shore up existing structures. The same pair were honoured with statues in the Forum, which stood on bases decorated with gladiatorial motifs (F94–95).

D6 *CIL* X 858 = *ILS* 6359

Gaius Cuspius Pansa, son of Gaius, the father, duumvir with judicial power four times, quinquennial, prefect with judicial power by decree of the town councillors in accordance with the Petronian Law.

D7 *CIL* X 859 = *ILS* 6359a

Gaius Cuspius Pansa, son of Gaius, the son, priest, duumvir with judicial power.

Games in the Forum and Amphitheatre (D8)

This inscription (now lost) appeared on the family tomb of the Clodii, and commemorated the career of Aulus Clodius Flaccus, whose name also appears on the measuring table in the Forum (H64). It places especial emphasis on the games that he gave at the festival in honour of Apollo, each time he held the duumvirate. He was duumvir for the third time in 2/1 BC, with Holconius Rufus as his colleague. Such is the level of detail in describing exactly what performances were put on, that several words in the inscription, for different types of bull-fighters and boxers, are not found elsewhere. Pylades was a famous actor at Rome in the Augustan era, and this may explain why his name is included here. The games described include a whole variety of performers and took place not just in the Amphitheatre, but also in the Forum. This may be partly because of the proximity of the Temple of Apollo to the Forum, but may also reflect the continuation of practices predating the construction of the Amphitheatre. Vitruvius (*On Architecture* 5.1.1–2) notes that it was usual for gladiatorial fights to be displayed in the fora of Italian towns.

D8 *CIL* X 1074d = *ILS* 5053.4, early first century AD

Aulus Clodius Flaccus, son of Aulus, of the Menenian voting tribe, duumvir with judicial power three times, quinquennial, military tribune by popular demand.

In his first duumvirate, at the games of Apollo in the Forum, (he presented) a procession, bulls, bull-fighters, and their fleet-footed helpers, 3 pairs of stage-fighters, boxers fighting in bands, and Greek-style pugilists; also (he presented) games with every musical entertainment, pantomime, and Pylades; and he gave 10,000 sesterces to the public coffers.

In return for his second duumvirate, which was also his quinquennial duumvirate, at the games of Apollo (he presented) in the Forum a procession, bulls, bull-fighters, and their fleet-footed helpers, and boxers fighting in bands; on the next day in the Amphitheatre (he presented) by himself 30 pairs of athletes and 5 pairs of gladiators, and with his colleague (he presented) 35 pairs of gladiators and a hunt with bulls, bull-fighters, boars, bears and the other hunt-variations.

In his third duumvirate (he presented) with his colleague games by a foremost troupe, with extra musical entertainment.

Organization of games at Pompeii: announcements of shows (D9–24)

Most of our evidence for the organization of the games comes from painted notices advertising forthcoming shows. Games were apparently given all year round (only the month of September is missing from the surviving notices), and celebrated different occasions. Typically, the notice advertises the date, giver of the games, type of show to be exhibited, and additional attractions for the audience, such as the provision of an awning or sprinkling of water to refresh spectators in the heat. Some of the inscriptions advertise games to be given in other towns, even as far away as Puteoli (modern Pozzuoli, 25 miles from Pompeii) (D25, 29–30). The notices were painted by specialist sign-writers, who sometimes added their names. In addition to gladiatorial combat, wild beast fights and athletic shows were also exhibited.

Lavish games presented by Pompeians were calculated to win popularity and prestige, to help in climbing the greasy pole of local political advancement. Lucretius Satrius Valens, for example, appears to have arranged for gladiatorial shows in his son's name as well as his own, perhaps when his son was still a child (D11–15, commentary on G20–26). Magistrates and priests of the emperor (*Augustales*) were, however, obliged to spend a certain amount of money during their year in office, and some of the notices probably record such games, although they still give the impression that they are gifts to the town rather than obligatory payments (B11).

Plate 4.1 D9 Painted notices for games at Pompeii

Plate 4.1 shows a section of painted notices preserved along the Street of Abundance, including the end of a notice by Lucretius Satrius Valens and his son (left) (D12) and a notice of Alleius Nigidius Maius (right) (D21). In between is a political poster, calling for the election of a Satrius as quinquennial (F2). This may well be the Satrius Valens whose games are prominently advertised nearby, suggesting how electoral campaigning and the giving of games could be closely interlinked.

Plate 4.1   D9 Painted notices for games at Pompeii

D10 Bar chart showing half-monthly distribution of games in Pompeii and other towns in the region

See **Figure** 4.1. Appendix 1 provides the data upon which this bar chart is based.

Games given by father and son: the Lucretii Valentes (D11–15)

For this family, see **G20–26**. Lucretius Valens' name also appears on the painting of the riot (**D37**). The post of priest of Nero as Caesar must have been created once Nero was adopted by Claudius (here referred to simply as 'Augustus') in AD 50. In **D12** and **D14**, the name 'Nero' was plastered over, perhaps after he committed suicide in AD 68. This would imply that the notice was originally painted during Nero's reign. The writer of **D11** signs his notice twice; once within the large 'C' of 'Lucreti', and also to the right-hand side of the notice. In **D12**, the writer's name, Poly(bius?) is enclosed within the initial D of D(ecimus). See **F74–81** for more on sign-writers. The giving of games over a five-day period is unusual (**D11**), so it is not surprising that Lucretius Satrius Valens had good wishes heaped upon him (**D15** and **D37b**). The acclamation **D15** was painted on the opposite side of the doorway to **D14**, again suggesting some attention was paid to the location of these notices.

D11 *CIL* IV 3884 = *ILS* 5145, west side of IX 8, after AD 50

20 pairs of gladiators of Decimus Lucretius †Celer wrote this† Satrius Valens, perpetual priest of Nero and 10 pairs of gladiators of Decimus Lucretius Valens, his son, will fight at Pompeii on 8, 9, 10, 11, 12 April. There will be a regular hunt and awnings. Aemilius Celer wrote this on his own by the light of the moon.

D12 *CIL* IV 7992, in black and red, House of Trebius Valens (III.ii.1), AD 50–68

20 pairs of gladiators of Decimus †Poly(bius?)† Lucretius Satrius Valens, perpetual priest of [[Nero]] Caesar, son of Augustus, and 10 pairs of gladiators of Decimus Lucretius Valens will fight at Pompeii on 4 (?) April. There will be a hunt and awnings.

D13 *CIL* IV 1185, outside the Gladiatorial Barracks, on the external wall of the Large Theatre, AD 50–68

[. . . pairs of gladiators] of [Lucretius] Valens, perpetual priest of Nero, son of Augustus. [. . . pairs of gladiators] of Decimus Lucretius Valens, his son [will fight at Pompeii] on 28 March. There will be a hunt and awnings.

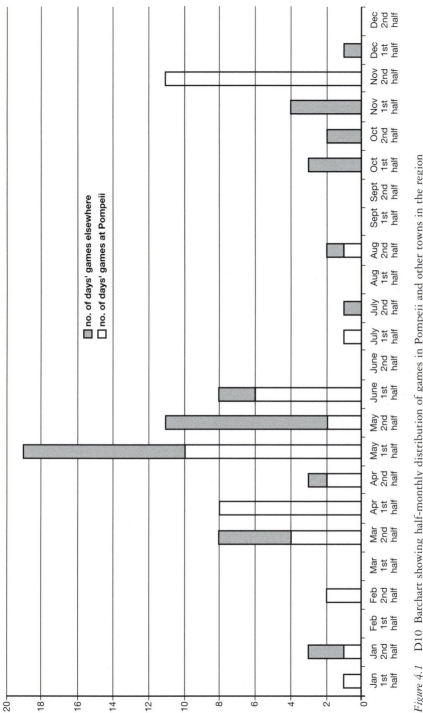

Figure 4.1 D10 Barchart showing half-monthly distribution of games in Pompeii and other towns in the region

D14 *CIL* IV 7995, in black and red, III.vi.2, AD 50–68

20 pairs of gladiators of Decimus Lucretius Satrius Valens, perpetual priest of [[Nero]] Caesar, son of Augustus, and 10 pairs of [gladiators] of Decimus Lucretius Valens, his son, on 28 March. There will be a hunt and awnings.

D15 *CIL* IV 7996, III.vii.1

[Good fortune] to the priest of Nero Caesar.

Games presented by an aedile, Suettius Certus (D16–17)

Both of these notices seem to advertise the same games, provided by Suettius Certus as aedile, who appears to have owned a troupe of gladiators.

D16 *CIL* IV 1189, in red, on the exterior wall of the Building of Eumachia, at the west end of the Street of Abundance near the Forum, AD 54–68

The gladiatorial troupe of Aulus Suettius Certus, aedile, will fight at Pompeii on 31 May. There will be a hunt and awnings.

D17 *CIL* IV 1190, Street of the Brothel, AD 54–68

The gladiatorial troupe of Aulus Suettius Certus will fight at Pompeii on the 31 May. There will be a hunt and awnings. Good fortune to all Neronian games.

Games presented by an imperial priest (Augustalis) (D18)

D18 *CIL* IV 9962, to the right of the entrance to I.ix.13

[. . .] pairs of gladiators of Lucius Valerius Primus, imperial priest (*Augustalis*), will fight at Pompeii on the [. . .] February: there will be a hunt in the morning [. . .].

Games presented by Gnaeus Alleius Nigidius Maius, leading games-giver (D19–24)

During the Neronian period, Gnaeus Alleius Nigidius Maius achieved unparalleled prominence in Pompeian society, being hailed as 'leader of the colony' and 'leading games-giver'. He attained the highest local political post, of quinquennial duumvir, in AD 55/56. Some at least of his games would have been given as a result of his holding this office, but he appears to have sponsored games on at least three different occasions. He also appears as a seller at auction in AD 55 on one of Caecilius Iucundus' wax tablets (H69–82), but the tablet (Tab.16) is too damaged to reveal much more than this. A rental notice advertising some of his urban property, which probably dates from the last year or so before the town's destruction, gives some idea of his sources of income (H50). It is also possible to deduce that at least some of his wealth may have been derived from the prominent public priestess Eumachia, since members of his family (including his mother, Pomponia Decharcis and one of his freedmen) were buried in her tomb enclosure (G17–18). This implies that this branch of the Alleii (into which Nigidius Maius was adopted) may have become a beneficiary of the Eumachii, once Eumachia's direct descendants had died out. Alleius Nigidius Maius was also priest of 'Caesar Augustus' (possibly Claudius, but more probably Vespasian). His daughter Alleia was a public priestess (E49), and one of his freedmen received honours from his peers (G18).

Quinquennial games? (D19–20)

Maius was quinquennial during the year 55/56. It has been argued that these two sets of games are the same, on the grounds that he is named as quinquennial in both. The notice on the House of Trebius Valens (D20) is one of several electoral notices and advertisements for games (which had been painted over) on its wide façade, on the north side of the Street of Abundance, not far from the Amphitheatre (D12 and D21).

In D19, the word 'Ellius' is damaged, but may be the name of a popular performer. Reference to 'substitutes' relates to the additional gladiators who took the place of defeated fighters in subsequent bouts.

D19 *CIL* IV 1179 = *ILS* 5143, in black paint, on the Nolan Street, AD 55/56 or later

30 pairs of Gnaeus Alleius Nigidius Maius, quinquennial, and their substitutes will fight at Pompeii on 24, 25, and 26 November. There will be a hunt ... Ellius. Good fortune to Maius, quinquennial, (from) Paris. Marti[alis wishes good fortune to M]aius.

D20 *CIL* IV 7991, in black and red, House of Trebius Valens (III.ii.1), AD 55/56 or later

20 pairs of gladiators of Gnaeus Alleius Nigidius Maius, quinquennial, and their substitutes will fight without any public expense at Pompeii.

Commemorative games (D21–23)

Games could be given to commemorate specific occasions, or to promote the welfare of the imperial family.

In D21, there is no agreement about what the *opus tabularum* might be: some have suggested an archive office (*tabularium*) in the Forum, others a painting, or a decorative stage building for the Theatre. One attractive suggestion is that Alleius Nigidius Maius paid for the striking paintings of gladiators and hunting around the arena's parapet wall in the Amphitheatre (J47–51). The names of the sign-writers, Ocella and Poly(bius?), appear inside the O of the word *dedicatione* in D21–22. The awnings were large canvasses drawn across the spectators' seating area in order to shield them from the sun. They can be seen on the painting of the riot in the Amphitheatre (D37a). D22, displayed in the courtyard of the men's Forum Baths, may also publicize the same event as D21. The absence of gladiators may point to a date after the riot in AD 59 (D34). For the sign-writer Poly(bius?), see also D12.

Although it is just possible that Nigidius Maius was priest of Claudius, it seems more likely that the emperor and his children referred to in D23 are Vespasian, Titus and Domitian. The altar in question here has been identified by some with the finely carved altar in the so-called 'Temple of Vespasian' in the Forum (E38), whose iconography links it with the imperial cult, making it a suitable donation to the town by a priest of Vespasian. Dobbins (1992), however, dates that altar to the Augustan period.

D21 *CIL* IV 7993, in red and black, House of Trebius Valens (III.ii.1), AD 59–69?

At the dedication †Ocella† of the *opus tabularum* of Gnaeus Alleius Nigidius Maius, at Pompeii on the 13 June, there will be a procession, hunt, athletics, and awnings. Greetings to Nigra [picture of a head].

D22 *CIL* IV 1177 = *ILS* 5144, in red, courtyard of Forum Baths, AD 59–69?

At the dedication †Poly(bius?)† of the games of Gnaeus Alleius Nigidius Maius . . . There will be a hunt, athletes, sprinklings, awnings. Good fortune to Maius, leader of the colony.

D23 *CIL* IV 1180, in red, outside the main entrance of the Gladiatorial Barracks, on the external wall of the Large Theatre, AD 70–79

For the well-being of the [emperor Vespasian] Caesar Augustus and of his children, [and on account of the] dedication of the altar, [the gladiatorial troupe] of Gnaeus [All]eius Nigidius Maius, priest of Caesar Augustus, will fight at Pompeii, without delay, on the 4 July. There will be a hunt and awnings.

Acclamation of Alleius Nigidius Maius (D24)

D24 *CIL* IV 7990, in black, II.vii.7

Good fortune to Gnaeus Alleius Maius, the leading games-giver.

Shows beyond Pompeii (D25–30)

The following is a selection of advertisements for spectacles in other towns. Most of these were displayed outside the town, on tombs lining the roads leading away from Pompeii. In addition to the following, places mentioned include Capua (*AE* 1990, 177b), Herculaneum (*CIL* IV 9969), Cumae (*CIL* IV 9976, 9983) and Forum Popilii (*AE* 1990, 177c).

Nola

D25 *CIL* IV 3881, in red on tomb 3 in Fondo Pacifico (near the Amphitheatre)

20 pairs of gladiators of Quintus Monnius Rufus will fight at Nola: 1, 2, 3 May. And there will be a hunt.

Four days' games at Nola given by Marcus Cominius Heres
(D26–28)

Much of the podium of tomb 14 EN (= 19 Maiuri, 37 Della Corte) in the necropolis outside the Nucerian Gate was originally covered with graffiti pictures of gladiatorial combat. These all seem to have been created by a single hand, and probably record a particular set of games at Nola. At least four pairs of gladiators are depicted, and a more complex scene depicts a central pair of gladiators framed by trumpeters and by horn-players. 'Neronian' gladiators were those from the imperial gladiatorial training school at Capua. The names of the gladiators are revealing: 'Princeps', 'The Chief', is obviously a 'stage-name'. He and Hilarus (possibly a 'stage-name': *hilarus* means 'merry') were slaves, having only one name. Marcus Attilius' name shows that he was a freeborn citizen. Lucius Raecius Felix may have been a freedman: Felix was a common slave name and a slave on being set free would adopt his former master's first two names, while keeping his own name as a third. Other games at Nola: *CIL* IV 9978.

Figure 4.2 D26a Victory of 'The Chief'

D26b *CIL* IV 10237

Text:
Munus Nolae de
quadridu(o)
M. Comini
Heredi(s)

Pri<n>ceps
Ner(onianus), (pugnarum) XIII, (coronarum) X,
v(icit);

Hilarus Ner(onianus), (pugnarum) XIV, (coronarum)
XII, v(icit)
Creunus, (pugnarum) VII, (coronarum) V, m(issus);

Translation:
Games at Nola of Marcus Cominius Heres over 4 days.

'The Chief', Neronian, fought 13, 10 victories, victor. Hilarus, Neronian, fought 14, 12 victories, victor. Creunus, fought 7, 5 victories, reprieved.

Figure 4.3 D27a Debut of Marcus Attilius

D27b *CIL* IV 10238a

Text:
M. Attilius, t(iro), v(icit); Hilarus Ner(onianus), (pugnarum) XIV, (coronarum) XII, m(issus)

Translation:
Marcus Attilius, novice, victor; Hilarus, Neronian, fought 14, 12 victories, reprieved.

Figure 4.4 D28a Further success of Marcus Attilius

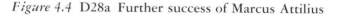

D28b *CIL* IV 10236a

Text:
M. Att(ilius)

M. Attilius, (pugnarum) I, (coronarum) I, v(icit)

L. Raecius Felix, (pugnarum) XII, (coronarum) XII, m(issus)

Translation:

Marcus Att(ilius)

Marcus Attilius, fought 1, 1 victory, victor. Lucius Raecius Felix, fought 12, won 12, reprieved.

Nuceria (D29)

D29 appears on tomb 10EN (= 12 Maiuri, 13 Della Corte), in the necropolis outside the Nucerian Gate. For other adverts for games at Nuceria, see *CIL* IV 3882, 9972.

D29 *CIL* IV 9973

20 pairs of gladiators of Lucius T[. . .]mius Felix and of [Gro]sphus, will fight on 29 and 30 October [. . .] at [Nuceria Con]stantia.

Puteoli (D30)

D30 appears in red letters on the façade of III.iv.1–2, along the lower part of the Street of Abundance. For other games at Puteoli, see *CIL* IV 9970, 9969, 9984.

D30 *CIL* IV 7994

49 pairs. The Capinian troupe will fight at the games of the Augusti at Puteoli on [12], 14, 16, and 18 May. There will be awnings. Magus (wrote this).

Commemoration of games (D31–33)

Stucco relief on 'tomb of Umbricius Scaurus/ Festius Ampliatus' (D31)

This relief in stucco from the AD 70s, belonging to a tomb outside the Herculaneum Gate (erroneously known as the 'Tomb of Scaurus' – see J29), depicts gladiatorial combat and hunting. The stucco was badly damaged by frost in 1815, and has more or less completely disappeared, apart from faint traces above the doorway to the tomb. At the top is an inscription in larger letters, which acts as a heading for the scenes (D31b). The scenes represent the final day in games given by Ampliatus, whose troupe of gladiators is advertised elsewhere in Pompeii too (*CIL* IV 1183–4). The fighters are labelled with painted inscriptions, which give their names and training school affiliations, the numbers of their fights and victories, and whether they won, were reprieved, or died in combat. The frieze provides a narrative of the day's games, from left to right, starting with a combat between two equestrian fighters, in which Bebryx (on the left) defeated Nobilior [Bebryx Iul(ianus) XV (pugnarum) v(icit) – Nobilior Iul(ianus) XIV (pugnarum)]. 'Julian' gladiators were trained in the imperial school at Capua. Then follow seven pairs of gladiators in various combinations, including Thracians, *murmillones*, heavily armed fighters and net-fighters (*retiarii*). See notes on D45–50 for types of gladiators.

Plate 4.2 D31a Stucco relief on tomb of 'Umbricius Scaurus'/Festius Ampliatus(?)

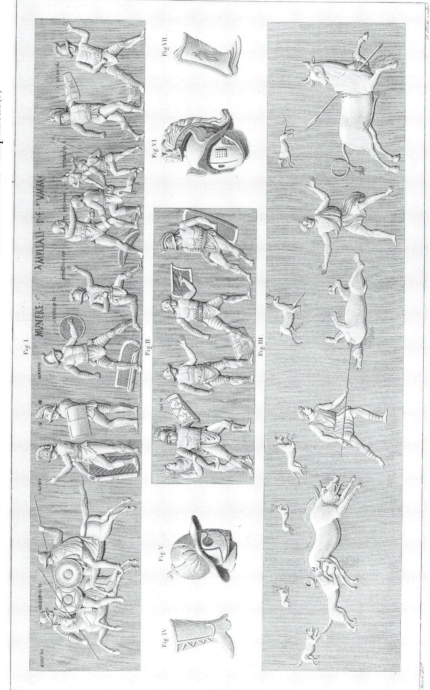

D31b *CIL* IV 1182 (extract)

At the games of [Numerius Fes]tius Ampliatus on the last day.

Review of gladiatorial games (D32)

An inscription on plaster work in Naples Museum, which is thought to have come from Pompeii, records two periods of games on several consecutive days in May. It lists the types of gladiator, names of the fighters, their affiliation, number of fights to date, and the outcome of their fights. Neronian gladiators, like Julian gladiators, were trained in the imperial gladiatorial barracks at Capua. The letters indicating the outcome of the fights (*v* – *vicit* (won), *m* – *missus* (reprieved), *p* – *periit* (killed)) were added to the list of combatants by a different hand. It is worth noting how few gladiators were actually killed. See notes on D45–50 for types of gladiator. Only the second set of games (with nine pairs of gladiators) is translated below. The text relating to the first set, with six pairs, is less well preserved.

D32 *CIL* IV 2508

Games [. . .] on the 12, 13, 14, 15 May

	Double swordsman (?) versus heavily armed fighter:
Reprieved.	[. . . .]ciens Neronian, fought 20 [. . .] 11
Won.	Nobilior, Julian, fought 2 [. . .] 14

	Thracian versus *murmillo*:
Reprieved.	Lucius Sempronius [. . .]
Won.	Platanus, Julian [. . .]

	Thracian versus *murmillo*:
Won.	Pugnax, Neronian, fought 3.
Killed.	Murranus, Neronian, fought 3.

	Heavily armed fighter versus Thracian:
Won.	Cycnus, Julian, fought 9.
Reprieved.	Atticus, Julian, fought 14.

	Thracian versus *murmillo*:
Won.	Herma, Julian, fought 4.
Reprieved.	Quintus Petillius [. . .]

	Chariot-fighters:
Reprieved.	Publius Ostorius, fought 51.
Won.	Scylax, Julian, fought 26.

	Thracian versus *murmillo*:
Won.	Nodu[. . .], Julian, fought 7.
Killed.	Lucius Petronius, fought 14.

	Thracian versus *murmillo*:
Killed.	Lucius Fabius, fought 9.
Won.	Astus, Julian, fought 14.

Graffiti drawings of gladiators (D33)

Graffiti drawings of gladiators are found in many areas of the town, and not just in areas where gladiators may have drawn them themselves. Sometimes, fighters are labelled with their names, but elsewhere there is no text alongside the drawing. The drawings demonstrate a huge diversity in artistic ability. Most common are single fighters or pairs, but occasionally quite complex scenes have been created. The overall frequency of gladiatorial themes is an index of the popularity of gladiatorial combat among spectators.

Depicted to the left in **D33a** (from the peristyle in the House of the Labyrinth, VI.xi.10) is the person presiding over the games, seated on an honorific seat upon a platform; a fighter holding a trident is descending the stairs from the platform to the right; a man in a tunic is holding out a staff (an adjudicator?); two gladiators engaged in combat; another man in a tunic holding a staff.

Figure 4.5 D33a **A complex scene at the games**

D33b *CIL* IV 1421

Faustus, slave of Ithacus, Neronian, at the Amphitheatre; Priscus, Neronian, fought 6, victor; Herennius, fought 18, killed.

Riot in the Amphitheatre, AD 59 (D34–43)

In AD 59, a notorious riot occurred in the Amphitheatre between Pompeians and Nucerians (**D34**). Nuceria was a nearby colony, where extra veteran soldiers had been settled by Nero as recently as AD 57. It is possible that the land allotments accompanying this move exacerbated feelings of local rivalry that may already have existed. As a result of the bloodshed, the Roman Senate banned gladiatorial shows for ten years from Pompeii (**D34**), and probably removed the duumvirs of the time from office (**D35–36**). Even so, some Pompeians clearly basked in the glory of their victory over their neighbours, and commemorated it in a painting and in graffiti (**D37–38**) and the Amphitheatre remained the venue for other types of spectacle (**D39**). Some scholars have argued that the emperor Nero may have lifted this ban before the end of that period (**D40–42**).

D34 Tacitus, *Annals* 14.17

At around the same time, there arose from a trifling beginning a terrible bloodbath among the inhabitants of the colonies of Nuceria and Pompeii at a gladiatorial show given by Livineius Regulus, whose expulsion from the senate I have recorded previously. Inter-town rivalry led to abuse, then stone-throwing, then the drawing of weapons. The Pompeians in whose town the show was being given came off the better. Therefore many of the Nucerians were carried to Rome having lost limbs, and many were bereaved of parents and children. The emperor instructed the senate to investigate; they passed it to the consuls. When their findings returned to the senators, the Pompeians were barred from holding any such gathering for ten years. Illegal associations in the town were dissolved; Livineius and the others who had instigated the trouble were exiled.

Penalties for the local magistrates? (D35–36)

The wax tablets of Lucius Caecilius Iucundus recording business deals (H69–82) incidentally show extraordinary repercussions of the riot and senatorial inquiry on local politics. These tablets, as usual, record the date in the standard way, giving the names of the consuls at Rome and those of the duumvirs at Pompeii. This system of dating allows us to work out that the duumvirs served their year from 1 July to 30 June (consuls at Rome served from 1 January to 31 December). D35–36 show an extraordinary situation in two respects. First, if the two Grosphi were duumvirs on 10 July AD 59 (D35), their term of office should not have ended until the end of June AD 60; but D36 shows a different pair of duumvirs in place by early May AD 60. Second, by this time there is also a prefect as well as the duumvirs, an office only used in exceptional circumstances (compare F107–108). Thus the riot seems to have led to the duumvirs being replaced before the end of their year, and an extra magistrate with legal powers being chosen.

D35 *CIL* IV 3340.143

On 10 July when Gnaeus Pompeius Grosphus and Grosphus Pompeius Gavianus were duumvirs with judicial power

{ . . . *details of the business follow* . . .}

Transacted at Pompeii when Marcus Ostorius Scapula and Titus Sextius Africanus were consuls (AD 59).

D36 *CIL* IV 3340.144

On 8 May when Numidius Sandelius Messius Balbus and Publius Vedius Siricus were duumvirs with judicial power and Sextus Pompeius Proculus was prefect with judicial power

{ . . . *details of the business follow* . . .}

Transacted at Pompeii when Nero Caesar Augustus for the 4th time and Cossus Lentulus were consuls (AD 60).

Painting of the riot, House of Actius Anicetus (1.iii.23), peristyle garden (D37)

The painting gives an aerial view of the Amphitheatre and its surroundings. The viewer can see the open space around it, with trees and perhaps temporary stalls (see also **H65**), the Large Palaestra and town walls. Painted inscriptions are even legible on the exterior walls of the Palaestra, acclaiming Lucretius Satrius Valens and Nero (**D37b**; compare **D15** and **D24**). Only part of the awning over the Amphitheatre is represented, to provide a view of the interior of the building. Fights have broken out not just in the arena, but in the seating and outside. We do not know who commissioned the painting, or why, but it may have been intended to celebrate the reopening of the Amphitheatre after the ban or simply the trouncing of the Nucerians.

Plate 4.3 **D37a Painting of the riot (NM inv. 112222)**

D37b *CIL* IV 2993x, y

(Latin) Good fortune to Decimus Lucretius.
(Greek letters) Good fortune to Satrius Valens, Augustus Nero.

Celebration of the Nucerians' defeat (D38)

This graffito drawing itself (from the façade of the House of the Dioscuri, VI.ix.6) – a triumphal gladiator brandishing a palm of victory – does not clearly relate to the riot, but the text beneath it may well be an allusion to the slaughter of Nucerians in the riot. It is unclear exactly who is referred to as Campanians (Campania was the name for the whole region).

Figure 4.6 D38a Celebration of the Nucerians' defeat

CAMPANI VICTORIAVNI
CVMNVCERINIS PERISTIS

D38b *CIL* IV 1293 = *ILS* 6443a

Campanians, in our victory you perished with the Nucerians.

Games during the ten-year ban (D39)

The following notice from AD 62 advertises a show including a hunt and athletics. The games advertised in this notice are most unlikely to have been displayed, given that a massive earthquake struck the town on 5 February. What this notice does seem to indicate, therefore, is that games might be advertised three weeks or so in advance of their presentation. It is unclear why the number 373 appears at the end.

D39 *CIL* IV 7989a, c, in red, Large Palaestra, north external wall

For the well-being of Nero Claudius Caesar Augustus Germanicus, at Pompeii, there will be a hunt, athletics and sprinklings of Tiberius Claudius Verus on 25–26 February. 373.

Good fortune to Claudius Verus.

The judgements of Nero and Poppaea (D40–43)

Eight graffiti from around the town hail 'judgements' of Nero and Poppaea. Poppaea was Nero's mistress and then wife from AD 62 until her death in 65, being granted the title 'Augusta' in 63, following the birth of a daughter. We do not know what these judgements were, but one hypothesis is that, as a result of Poppaea's intervention, Nero revoked the ban on gladiatorial games. Wealthy Poppaei lived in Pompeii during the mid-first century AD and have been tentatively linked with the grand House of the Menander (I.x.4). It is often assumed that the empress Poppaea also originated from Pompeii, and that she owned the magnificent villa at Oplontis. Neither of these hypotheses can be proved, although we can be sure from a wooden tablet at Herculaneum that she did own an estate in the area of Pompeii.

In the light of D42, however, the 'judgements' of Nero seem to have more to do with honorific grants of colonial status than with lifting a ban on gladiators. The emphasis on Pompeii being a 'true colony' may well be a response to Nero's settlement of veterans at Nuceria. Tensions between Pompeians and Nucerians also appear in a graffito found in the area of a brothel, which wishes on the Pompeians the hook used for dragging away the bodies of executed criminals (D43). Compare also *CIL* IV 1329 for an expression of ill will towards Nucerians. Nero made grants of colonial status to the harbour town of Puteoli on the Bay of Naples, his birthplace Antium in Latium, and Tegianum in southern Italy. The writer of this text, therefore, is claiming that Pompeii too has been granted colonial status by Nero.

D40 *CIL* IV 3726 = *ILS* 234, IX.vi, AD 63–65

Good fortune to the judgements of Augustus, father of his country, and of Poppaea Augusta.

D41 *CIL* IV 1074, AD 63–65

Good fortune to the judgements of Augustus and Augusta; while you are safe, we are fortunate for ever.

D42 *CIL* IV 3525 = *ILS* 6444, VI.xv

Good fortune to the judgements of Augustus. Puteoli, Antium, Tegianum, Pompeii: these are true colonies.

D43 *CIL* IV 2183

Good fortune to the Puteolans; good luck to all Nucerians; the executioner's hook to Pompeians.

Gladiatorial Barracks and Training School (D44–50)

See also J11–20.

Figure 4.7 D44 Plan of the Gladiatorial Barracks

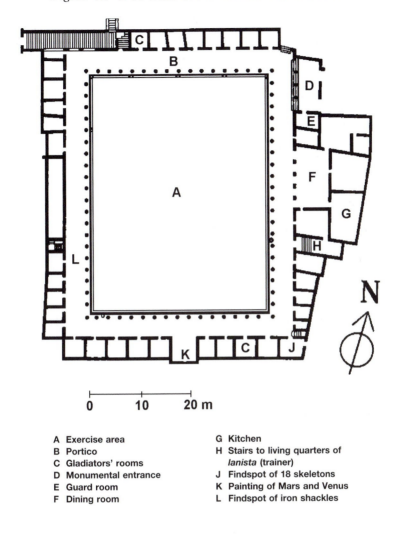

A Exercise area
B Portico
C Gladiators' rooms
D Monumental entrance
E Guard room
F Dining room

G Kitchen
H Stairs to living quarters of
  lanista (trainer)
J Findspot of 18 skeletons
K Painting of Mars and Venus
L Findspot of iron shackles

*Graffiti by Gladiators in the 'House of the Gladiators' (V.v.3)
(D45–50)*

This building – a converted house, with a central peristyle courtyard surrounded by rooms – appears to have served as a training centre for gladiators, possibly until the much larger Barracks behind the Theatre were established in the mid-first century AD (D44). A considerable quantity of graffiti scratched upon the columns of the peristyle provides a vivid picture of the variety of gladiators who performed in Pompeii. Many types of gladiator are mentioned, including the chariot fighter (*essedarius*), Thracian sabre fighter (*traex*), heavily armed fighter, gladiator with fish emblem on helmet (*murmillo*), lightly armed net and trident fighter (*retiarius*) and cavalryman (*eques*). Some graffiti record an individual gladiator's number of

65

fights and victories, and some create the impression that some gladiators were mobbed by their female fans, but these were probably written by the gladiators themselves, so may not be entirely objective records of popularity!

The gladiator Celadus – his triumphs in the arena and beyond (D45–48)

D45 *CIL* IV 4297

Celadus, belonging to Octavus(?), fought 3, won 3.

D46 *CIL* IV 4341

Thracian gladiator Celadus.

D47 *CIL* IV 4342 = *ILS* 5142a

Girls' heart-throb, Thracian gladiator Celadus, belonging to Octavus(?), fought 3, won 3.

D48 *CIL* IV 4345 = *ILS* 5142b

The girls' idol, Celadus the Thracian gladiator.

Victories of Florus (D49)

D49 *CIL* IV 4299

28 July, Florus won at Nuceria; 15 August, won at Herculaneum.

A Roman philosopher (D50)

It is curious to find the name of one of the lone ancient voices critical of gladiatorial combat (Seneca, *Moral Letters* 7) etched up in the *triclinium* of the gladiators' training school. To the right of this name are the beginnings of alphabets in Latin and Greek.

D50 *CIL* IV 4418

Lucius Annaeus Seneca

Theatrical entertainment (D51–70)

Modifications to the Large Theatre in the Augustan era by the Holconii (D51–56)

Two notables, the Holconii (two brothers, or, perhaps less likely, father and son) (**F89** and **H5**), greatly increased the seating capacity by adding a new upper section of seating supported by vaulted passageways, or a 'crypt'. They created two privileged areas of seating, or 'boxes', over the covered corridors leading into the *orchestra* from either side of the Theatre. These modifications may have been inspired by the emperor Augustus' legislation governing the segregation of audience members in theatres, since the new seating arrangements allowed for the spectators to be divided up into more groups than before. Their benefaction was recorded in multiple inscriptions set up in different parts of the Theatre, including two identical inscriptions, both well over 6 metres long, found in the area of the stage (**D51**).

The building work of the Holconii (D51)

D51 *CIL* X 833 and 834 = *ILS* 5638

Marcus Holconius Rufus and Marcus Holconius Celer (built) at their own expense the crypt, boxes and theatre seating.

Commemoration of the architect (D52)

Celebration of an architect is not common, especially a freedman, although more architects are commemorated in Campania than elsewhere. The decision to honour the architect in this way implies that the task of designing and executing the modifications to the Theatre was an extensive one. The same architect's name also appears on another fragmentary building inscription, but its original location is unknown (*CIL* X 807).

D52 *CIL* X 841 = *ILS* 5638a

Marcus Artorius Primus, freedman of Marcus, architect.

Honours for the Holconii and emperor Augustus in the Theatre (D53–56)

D53, honouring Holconius Rufus, is one of very few inscriptions on coloured marble to have survived in Pompeii. **D54** marks the culmination of Holconius Rufus' career, some years after his generosity in the Theatre. Its bronze letters are incorporated into the marble seating on the lowest level of the *cavea* (seating area) just above the broader steps for the double honorific chairs (or *bisellia*), in a central position. To judge from additional holes for metal still visible, something seems to have been fixed above the inscription. Although a small statue may have stood there, it is more likely that an honorific chair was set up here in Rufus' honour, in the place where the best possible view of the stage could be had. It would not necessarily have been a chair for him to sit on, but may have been an honour designed to perpetuate his name after death. He was also honoured with a statue outside the Stabian Baths (**F89**).

D53 *CIL* X 837 = *ILS* 6361, 2/1 BC

To Marcus Holconius Rufus, duumvir with judicial power four times, quin-quennial, military tribune by popular demand, priest of Augustus, by decree of the town councillors.

D54 *CIL* X 838 = *ILS* 6361a, some time between 1 BC and AD 14

To Marcus Holconius Rufus, son of Marcus, duumvir with judicial power five times, twice quinquennial, military tribune by popular demand, priest of Augustus, patron of the colony, by decree of the town councillors.

D55 *CIL* X 840 = *ILS* 6362, AD 13/14

To Marcus Holconius Celer, duumvir with judicial power, quinquennial designate, priest of Augustus.

D56 *CIL* X 842, 2/1 BC

[To Imperator Caesar] Augustus, father [of the fatherland, hailed as victorious general fourteen times], consul thirteen times, chief priest, holder of tribunician power twenty-two times.

The Covered Theatre/Odeion (D57)

The building inscription of the Covered Theatre (**B9**) records that two prominent colonists approved its completion in the 70s BC, and some scholars believe that it was intended to act as a council chamber for the colonists. The following inscription of bronze letters inlaid into the paving was found in 1793, but its letters were gradually pilfered over the years, so that nothing now remains to be seen of it (J26–28). It commemorates the donation of the beautiful multicoloured marble paving by a magistrate. On the expression 'instead of games', see D1–5.

Marble paving for orchestra (D57)

D57 *CIL* X 845

Marcus O[culat]ius Verus, son of Marcus, duumvir, instead of games.

Drama at Pompeii (D58–62)

Theatre tokens?

Over 100 small counters in bone and ivory have been found. Most of them are round, but some are square. They contain images and abbreviated texts. Their function is unclear, but some may have been gaming counters and others theatre tickets. The latter perhaps serve to identify a particular seat in the Theatre, by the name of the section of seating and by number. Aeschylus (**D59b**) was a famous Athenian tragic playwright of the fifth century BC.

D58 *CIL* X 8069.14

Figure 4.8 D58a Theatre token?

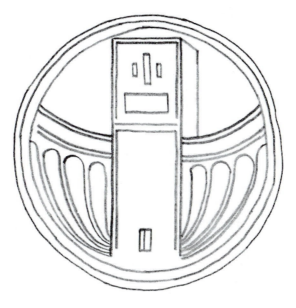

(a) A picture of a curved structure (seating area?) with a tower
(b) Text [Roman numeral, then in Greek]: XI/ Semicircle/ 1A

D59 *CIL* X 8069.16

(a) A picture of some sort of building
(b) Text [Roman numeral, then in Greek]: 12 /Of Aeschylus/ 1B

D60 *CIL* X 8069.13

(a) A picture of a helmeted figure
(b) Text [Roman numeral, then in Greek]: 8/ Athena/ H/ Z [Greek eta and zeta]

D61 *CIL* X 8069.7

(a) A picture of a half-opened door
(b) Text [Roman numeral, then in Greek]: 1/ door/ A

The dramatist Menander (D62)

The Greek poet of New Comedy, Menander, was celebrated in the house that today bears his name (I.x.4). A large portrait of the seated poet is painted in the peristyle. At his feet is his name 'Menander' (*CIL* IV 7350a), and another text in tiny letters on his open book proclaims his achievement (**D62**). His name also appears in a graffito on a column of the nearby peristyle (*CIL* IV 8338).

D62 *CIL* IV 7350b

Menander. He was the first of all to write comedy [. . .] four books.

Actors (D63–70)

Troupes of performers went on tour to different towns in Campania: Actius Anicetus and his troupe of actors inspired a number of graffiti at Pompeii (**D63–65**) and he is also recorded at Herculaneum. A monumental inscription from Puteoli (*CIL* X 1946) records one Gaius Ummidius Actius Anicetus as pantomime actor (a single actor who mimed the whole scenario), and it seems likely that this is the same actor. See Franklin (1987). This is just a selection of the more interesting and identifiable graffiti mentioning an Actius: it is quite possible that some of the others do not refer to the same individual. The actor Paris is also acclaimed in a number of graffiti (**D66–68**), and it even seems that some supporters of a candidate for election to local political office identify themselves as fans of the actor Paris (**D69**). More striking yet is the fact that the actor Norbanus Sorex was publicly honoured with two portrait busts in the town (**D70**).

Actius Anicetus (D63–65)

D63 *CIL* IV 3891, I.ii.6, peristyle

Actius Anicetus, greetings. Horus, greetings.

D64 *CIL* IV 5399, tomb 4 in Fondo Pacifico (near the Amphitheatre)

Actius, master of stage performers.

D65 *CIL* IV 4965, Large Theatre, west wall of stage

Actius, greetings.

Paris (D66–69)

D66 *CIL* IV 3867 = *ILS* 5181a, on façade of tomb 4 in Fondo Pacifico (near the Amphitheatre)

Paris, pearl of the stage.

D67 *CIL* IV 3877, on façade of tomb 6 in Fondo Pacifico (near the Amphitheatre)

Master of the stage, farewell.

D68 *AE* (1985) 288, graffito (combining Latin and Greek) in House of Gaius Iulius Polybius

Unsurpassed Paris, triumph!

D69 *CIL* IV 7919, in black along Street of Abundance, at IX.xii.7

I beg you to make Gaius Cuspius Pansa aedile. Purpurio with the fans of Paris.

Norbanus Sorex (D70)

The actor Norbanus Sorex was honoured with two portrait busts, one found complete with its support in the temple of Isis (NM inv. 4991), the other represented only by the inscribed support, found in the Building of Eumachia (see **E41–45**). He was not necessarily himself an inhabitant of Pompeii: like other actors, he travelled around Italy. He also set up his own portrait bust as a dedicatory offering to the goddess Diana, in her sanctuary at Nemi, in the Alban Hills 25 km to the south-east of Rome, where there was a theatre. He described himself there too as mime actor of second parts. His offering there is one of a group of herms set up by actors, which appear to date to the first half of the first century AD.

D70 *CIL* X 814 = *ILS* 5198

(Portrait) Of Gaius Norbanus Sorex, actor of second parts; the presidents of the Fortunate Augustan Suburban Country District (set this up). Space given by decree of the town councillors.

Literary pastimes (D71–104)
Latin poetry in graffiti (Appendix 2)

Most quotations consist of just a few words, but whole verses or couplets of poetry are sometimes written up on walls. Sometimes the original text is modified for effect, and one particularly accomplished parody on the opening line of the *Aeneid* survives (**D71**). Virgil is by far the most popular source of quotations. A handful of quotations from Greek literature also survive. See Appendix 2 for a table of data.

Parody of Aeneid 1.1 (D71)

This graffito appears on the façade of a house belonging to the fuller Marcus Fabius Ululitremulus, near a picture of Aeneas leading Anchises and Ascanius into safety from Troy. The line is written in the same metre as the *Aeneid* and quotes the most famous opening words in Latin literature: *arma virumque cano* . . . I sing of arms and a man . . . The owl is a symbol of fullers, because of its link with their patroness, Minerva. The parody also puns on the fuller's name (*ululam cano*).

D71 *CIL* IV 9131, IX.xiii.5

Fullones ululamque cano, non arma virumque
I sing of fullers and an owl, not of arms and a man.

Local literary talent (D72–79)

It is against this background of literary consciousness that the preservation of some original verses composed by a named poet, Tiburtinus, seems less surprising. Many other apparently original verses can also be found scratched upon walls, but Tiburtinus is the only identifiable individual poet. His compositions are love elegy – actually some of the earliest Latin love elegy preserved – predating well-known poets such as Catullus, Propertius or Tibullus. Other anonymous poets have also left us some of their verses. The couplet D74 inventively draws inspiration both from Propertius, *Elegies* 1.1.5 and Ovid, *Amores* 3.11.35. It appears a number of times in Pompeii, in different places. Variations on D77 also recur elsewhere (e.g. *CIL* IV 9130, House of Marcus Fabius Ululitremulus).

Verses by Tiburtinus (D72)

A whole series of verses apparently written in the same hand appear on an external wall of the Covered Theatre. They are believed to date from a period shortly after the Covered Theatre was constructed, in the 70s BC. The following is the best preserved sequence.

D72 *CIL* IV 4966, with Solin (1968), 118–20

What is happening? Alas, eyes, first you led me into the fire,
Now of your own accord you give generously to your cheeks.
But tears cannot put out the flame;
They inflame the face and melt the spirit.

Composed by Tiburtinus.

Pompeian love poetry by anonymous poets (D73–79)

D73 *CIL* IV 9123, IX.xiii.4

Nothing can last for all time:
When the Sun has shone brightly it returns to Ocean;
The Moon wanes, which recently was full.
Even so the fierceness of Venus often becomes a puff of wind.

D74 *CIL* IV 1520: *atrium* of VI.xiv.43

Blondie has taught me to hate dark girls.
I shall hate them, if I can, but I wouldn't mind loving them.
Pompeian Venus Fisica wrote this.

D75 *CIL* IV 10241, Tomb 21OS (= 20 Maiuri / 23 Della Corte), necropolis outside the Nucerian Gate

Greetings to Primigenia of Nuceria.
I would wish to become a signet ring for no more than an hour
That I might give you kisses despatched with your signature.

D76 *CIL* IV 5296, IX.viii, in a doorway

Oh, if only I could hold your sweet arms around my neck
In an embrace and place kisses on your tender lips.
Go now, entrust your joys to the winds, my darling,
Believe me, fickle is the nature of men.
Often I have been wakeful in the middle of a wasted night
Thinking these things to myself: many men whom Fortune has
raised up on high,
Now suddenly rush headlong, and fall, overwhelmed by her.
In this way when Venus has suddenly joined together lovers' bodies,
Light parts them and [————]

D77 *CIL* IV 4091, House of Caecilius Iucundus (V.i.26)

Whoever loves, let him flourish.
Let him perish who knows not love.
Let him perish twice over whoever forbids love.

D78 *CIL* IV 5092, IX.v.11, peristyle

If you felt the fires of love, mule-driver,
You would make more haste to see Venus.
I love a charming boy; I ask you, goad the mules, let's go.
You've had a drink, let's go, take the reins and shake them,
Take me to Pompeii, where love is sweet.
You are mine . . .

D79 *CIL* IV 1928, Basilica

Love dictates and Cupid points the way as I write.
I'd rather die than be a god without you.

Improving advice in the House of the Moralist (III.iv.2–3) (D80)

Three couplets are painted upon the walls of the summer dining-room.

D80 *CIL* IV 7698a–c

Let water wash your feet clean and a slave wipe them dry;
Let a cloth cover the couch, take care of our linens.

Remove lustful expressions and flirtatious tender eyes
From another man's wife; may there be modesty in your expression.

[. . .] postpone your tiresome quarrels
If you can, or leave and take them home with you.

Playing with words and images (D81–85)

An architect's signature (D81)

The architect Crescens incorporates his signature into the picture of a ship in a graffito found in the peristyle of the House of Triptolemus (VII.vii.5).

Figure 4.9 D81a An architect's signature

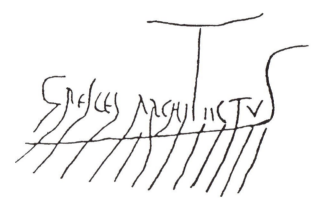

D81b *CIL* IV 4755

Crescens, architect

The snake game (D82)

In this graffito near a house entrance in IV.v, the letters curve around, forming a snake's body, with its head drawn at the start of the text. All four lines of the Latin poem begin with the letter S. It perhaps alludes to some sort of physical exercise requiring great skill at balancing during weaving in and out along a snake-like course.

Figure 4.10 D82a The snake game

D82b *CIL* IV 1595

If anyone has chanced to observe the snake game,
In which young Sepumius has shown his skill,
Whether you are a spectator of the theatrical stage or a devotee of horses,
May you always have balance equal to his everywhere.

The minotaur at Pompeii (D83)

This graffito was found in the peristyle of the House of the Lucretii (IX.iii.5,24).

Figure 4.11 D83a The minotaur at Pompeii

D83b *CIL* IV 2331

Labyrinth. Here lives the minotaur.

Two word squares (D84–85)

Within these word squares any row or column makes a Latin word or name. *Roma* = Rome; *amor* = love; *olim* = once; *Milo* is a man's name; *rotas* = wheels; *opera* = tasks; *tenet* = holds; *Arepo* is possibly a proper name; *sator* = sower. It has been noticed that the letters of the second square (with N being counted twice) can be rearranged to make two times, Pater Noster AO, i.e. 'Our Father, Alpha and Omega'. A Christian presence in Pompeii is possible by AD 79 (Nero had blamed the Christians for the Great Fire in Rome in AD 64), but this square is more likely to be simple word play, like **D84**, later adopted elsewhere as a Christian symbol. See also **E68–71** for Jews.

D84 *CIL* IV 8297

```
R  O  M  A
O  L  I  M
M  I  L  O
A  M  O  R
```

D85 *CIL* IV 8623

```
R  O  T  A  S
O  P  E  R  A
T  E  N  E  T
A  R  E  P  O
S  A  T  O  R
```

Scribbles, messages, crude graffiti and insults (D86–104)

Many other pieces of writing have been found all over Pompeii, both scratched on walls and written with a type of charcoal pen. Volume IV of *CIL*, which collects writings on walls at Pompeii and the surrounding area, has over 10,000 entries. Many of these are what we might nowadays regard as casual scribbling or graffiti: single words, names, messages, sayings, insults or obscenities, some accompanied by drawings. Most of these, not surprisingly, occur in 'public' areas, but such areas might include, for example, the *atria* of private houses, where clients would pay their respects to their patrons.

I was here (D86)

Many Pompeians felt the urge to mark their presence by writing or scratching their names. D86 is noteworthy for obligingly giving the exact date and year (2 October 78 BC), by the usual Roman method of referring to the chief magistrates for the year; 78 BC was soon after the colony was founded.

D86 *CIL* IV 1842, inside the Basilica

Gaius Pumidius Dipilus was here, five days before the *nones* of October when Marcus Lepidus and Quintus Catulus were consuls.

Casual greetings (D87–89)

D87 *CIL* IV 1852, Basilica

Pyrrhus to his colleague Chius: I grieve because I hear you have died; and so farewell.

D88 *CIL* IV 8364

Secundus greets his own Prima everywhere. Mistress, I ask you to love me.

D89 *CIL* IV 1880, Basilica

Lucius Istacidius, I regard as a stranger anyone who doesn't invite me to dinner.

Rivalry of Severus and Successus (D90)

The following exchange was found in a bar (I.x.2–3). There are three messages, the first and third by Severus, the second the reply of Successus, which is clearly written but contains difficult grammar and spelling (*pravessimus*, which he applies to himself, ought to mean something like 'utterly evil' but presumably had a colloquial, positive meaning, like 'wicked').

D90 *CIL* IV 8259, 8258

– Successus the weaver loves the barmaid of the inn, called Iris, who doesn't care for him, but he asks and she feels sorry for him. A rival wrote this. Farewell.

– You're jealous, bursting out with that. Don't try to muscle in on someone who's better-looking and is a wicked and charming man.

– I have written and spoken. You love Iris, who doesn't care for you. Severus to Successus.

D91 *CIL* IV 1820, Basilica

Chios, I hope your piles again become sore,
So that they smart more than they smarted before.

D92 *CIL* IV 5251, IX.viii.11, *triclinium*

Restitutus has often deceived many girls.

'Wit and wisdom' (D93–96)

Latin literature often shows a great liking for *sententiae* – pithy but contentious or thought-provoking sayings. Several such have been found at Pompeii, all of these examples in the form of a line of metrical verse (*senarius*). In **D96** the comment 'I wish' appears in different handwriting.

D93 *CIL* IV 1870 and 1811, Basilica

A small evil becomes very great through being ignored.

D94 *CIL* IV 2069, House of Holconius (VIII.iv.4)

If you want to waste time, scatter millet and gather it up.

D95 *CIL* IV 5112, beside door of IX.v.18

Learn: while I am alive, you, hateful death, are coming.

D96 *CIL* IV 8408

Lovers, like bees, lead a honeyed life.
    I wish.

Toilet humour (D97)

D97 was found in the latrine in what may have been the slave quarters of the huge and beautifully decorated House of the Centenary (IX.viii.6). Martha uses the word for a dining-room, *triclinium*, misspelt as *trichilinium*.

D97 *CIL* IV 5244, Latrine

This is Martha's banqueting room, as she shits in this banqueting room.

Prostitutes (D98–99)

D98 *CIL* IV 1751, just outside the Marine Gate, above a seat

If anyone sits here, let him read this first of all: if anyone wants a fuck, he should look for Attice – costs 4 sesterces.

D99 *CIL* IV 8356, House of the Menander (I.x.4), rear entrance vestibule

At Nuceria, look for Novellia Primigenia near the Roman gate in the prostitutes' district.

Brothel graffiti (D100–102)

The following will give the flavour of over 100 comments (*CIL* IV 2173–296) recorded in graffiti in a brothel (VIII.xii.18–20). A handful are in Greek. Curiously, they even include the first word of *Aeneid* Book 2 (*CIL* IV 2213).

D100 *CIL* IV 2175

Here I fucked lots of girls.

D101 *CIL* IV 2185, 2186

Sollemnes, you fuck well.

D102 *CIL* IV 2192

15 June, Hermeros fucked here with Phileterus and Caphisus.

Graffiti about graffiti (D103–104)

Given the sheer quantity of graffiti in Pompeii, it is hardly surprising to find one particular message repeated several times around the town (D103, also *CIL* IV 1904, 2461 in the Large Theatre, 2487 in the Amphitheatre), as well as various despairing requests to people to refrain from leaving their remarks (D104).

D103 *CIL* IV 1904

I admire you, wall, for not having collapsed at having to carry the tedious scribblings of so many writers.

D104 *CIL* IV 7521

Whoever writes anything here, let him rot and be nameless.

The baths (D105–109)

Stabian Baths (D105)

Their earliest phase was perhaps established during the fifth or at the end of the fourth century BC, with a major phase of modifications during the second century BC. Further alterations were performed in 80–50 BC (**B11**), in the Augustan era, and after AD 62. They preserve features that subsequently disappeared from bath design elsewhere, including individual hip-baths in addition to the communal pools, and the control of the water supply from a well by a water-wheel, rather than via an aqueduct. The sweating-room (*laconicum*) mentioned in **B11** was converted into a cold room (*frigidarium*) in the late first century BC, by incorporating a circular pool. This also happened in the Forum Baths. The addition of a swimming pool in the *palaestra* also occurred at about this time.

Figure 4.12 D105 Plan of the Stabian Baths

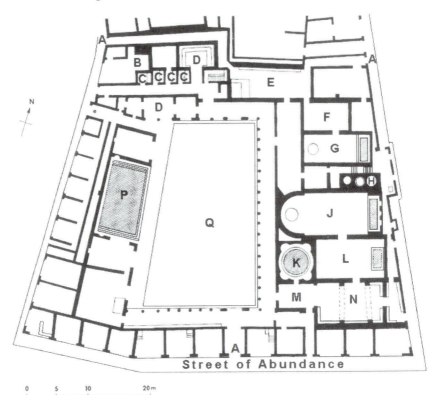

A Entrance	**J** *Caldarium* (men's)
B Well and water-wheel	**K** *Laconicum*, converted to *frigidarium*
C Hip-baths	**L** *Tepidarium* (men's)
D Latrine	**M** Vestibule
E *Apodyterium* (women's)	**N** *Apodyterium* (men's)
F *Tepidarium* (women's)	**P** *Natatio* (swimming pool)
G *Caldarium* (women's)	**Q** *Palaestra*
H Furnace	

Forum Baths (D106–108)

These public baths (with separate sections for men and women) were built during the mid-first century BC, and rebuilt under Augustus. In AD 3–4, the duumvirs had a large marble basin set up in the hot room (*caldarium*), around whose rim was an inscription in bronze letters (**D106**). Some time later, during the mid-first century AD, Marcus Nigidius Vaccula donated three bronze benches and a bronze brazier (heater) to the warm room (*tepidarium*) in these baths, as well as a similar bronze brazier to the Stabian Baths. All of these sported pictorial puns on his last name (*cognomen*), Vaccula, meaning 'little cow'. The legs of the benches terminate at top and bottom with a cow's head and hoof, and his *cognomen* is omitted altogether from the inscription on the braziers, being replaced by a picture of a little cow (**D107–108**).

Marble basin (D106)

D106 *CIL* X 817 = *ILS* 5726

When Gnaeus Melissaeus Aper, son of Gnaeus, and Marcus Staius Rufus, son of Marcus, were duumvirs with judicial power for the second time, they saw to the making of the basin, by decree of the town councillors, at public expense. It cost 5,250 sesterces.

Bronze bench of Nigidius Vaccula (D107)

D107 *CIL* X 818

Marcus Nigidius Vaccula at his own expense.

Bronze brazier of Nigidius Vaccula (D108)

Plate 4.4 D108a Bronze brazier of Nigidius Vaccula

D108b *CIL* X 8071, 48

Marcus Nigidius [picture of little cow] at his own expense.

Baths of Crassus Frugi (D109)

These baths, whose attractions are advertised by an elegantly inscribed marble plaque, must have been located on the sea shore at Pompeii, but remain undiscovered. The inscription had been reused, so its position provides no hint as to the location of the baths. It seems likely that the owner of the baths, Crassus Frugi, is the consul of AD 64. His use of a freedman to run his business is quite usual in Roman society (compare **H21, H23, H26–29, H50, H69, H71–72, H75**). Pliny the Elder (*Natural History* 31.2.5) mentions some exceptional baths of Licinius Crassus near Baiae (further north around the Bay of Naples), which were built in the sea over a natural hot spring.

D109 *CIL* X 1063 = *ILS* 5724

Baths of Marcus Crassus Frugi with seawater and baths with fresh water. Ianuarius, freedman.

For the Baths of Julia Felix, see **H44**.

5

RELIGION

Religion played a central part in Pompeian life right from the sixth century BC, when activity focused upon two sanctuaries, those of Apollo next to the Forum (E1–2) and of (probably) Hercules and Minerva at the 'Doric Temple' in the Triangular Forum. By the end of the second century BC, more public temples had been added to the town, honouring Jupiter (E9–11), Isis (E3–6) and Dionysus (for the suburban Sanctuary of Dionysus, see A15–17; for religion in the Oscan town, see also A12–13). Religious experiences at Pompeii, therefore, drew upon a variety of foreign influences, from Greece and Egypt, at a relatively early date. Some temples in the town and its environs are of disputed identity (such as the so-called 'Temple of Jupiter Meilichios' in the Theatre district, which may have been dedicated to Asclepius), while others, dedicated to Ceres and perhaps Neptune (E14), have yet to be discovered. It also seems plausible that the large temple adjacent to the Basilica was dedicated to Pompeian Venus, but no hard evidence supports this hypothesis.

Public cults attracted dedications from individuals and donations by local magistrates (E2, E4–6, E9–14). Miniature altars and statuettes could be set up in any temple: the deity whose temple it was did not necessarily have to be the one represented. Thus, in the Temple of Isis, statuettes of Venus and Bacchus stood near one of Isis herself (E4–5). Apart from a colossal bust of Jupiter from his temple in the Forum, no cult statues have been found.

The dramatic political change at Rome, with the emergence of the first emperor, Augustus, had an immediate impact upon the cults of Pompeii. Cult officials in charge of the worship of Mercury and Maia first of all included Augustus alongside these deities, but a short time later actually devoted their attentions to Augustus and subsequent emperors alone (E30–31). During the lifetime of Augustus himself, we also find priests of the emperor, even before he had been offically deified (D53–55). In addition, an entirely new cult of Augustan Fortune was introduced to Pompeii by one of the local elite, who donated some of his own land near the Forum as a site for the new temple (E32–37).

Official involvement in the town's public cults mirrored the hierarchical structure of Roman society. Women from the elite were excluded from holding political office, but could become prominent in public life as priest-esses of Ceres and Venus (**E39–50**). Some cults created official posts for freedmen and even slaves. The cults of Mercury, Maia and Augustus, and of Augustan Fortune, as well as the local district cults of the *Lares* (the guardian deities of a district) were entrusted to presidents (*magistri*) and attendants (*ministri*), who were generally freedmen and slaves respectively (**E28–31**, **E34–37**, **E62–64**).

The expression of religious sentiment, however, was far from confined to temples or public cults. Religious dedications, commemorations of vows, and graffiti are found in houses, shops and public areas throughout the town (**E16–18**, **E21–22**, **E25–27**, **E58–60**). One interpretation of the enigmatic frieze in the Villa of Mysteries sees the room in which it was displayed as a place devoted to the cult of Dionysus. Otherwise, cults in the house focused pri-marily upon the *lararium*, or shrine of the household gods (*Lares*) often found in the *atrium* or kitchen, and upon the *genius* of the master of the household (**E51–57**). The large numbers of such shrines indicate widespread religious practices among the inhabitants of Pompeii as a whole, but popular religious feelings are generally difficult to pin down. Some hints emerge from graffiti (**E21–27**) and also from paintings, which seem to invoke a deity's support for an enterprise, such as the picture of Mercury outside a dyer's workshop, shown descending from the steps of a temple carrying a money-bag and his wand.

Finally, alongside various pagan cults, a variety of written evidence shows the presence of Jews at Pompeii.

Temple of Apollo (E1–2)

The Sanctuary of Apollo, to the west of the Forum, was founded by the first half of the sixth century BC. The temple was rebuilt along Hellenistic lines during the second century BC (**A12**). In the early 70s BC, one of the first actions of the Roman veteran colonists on their arrival in the town was to rededicate the temple's main altar, perhaps as a symbol of the change in regime (**B7**). At some point before 2 BC, permission was given for the sanc-tuary to encroach upon neighbouring space (**E1**). There are some signs of structural repair following earthquake damage, perhaps from AD 62 (**C4**), but this was not completed before the eruption. Elegant bronze statues of Apollo and his sister Diana in their guise as archer-gods were found in the sanctuary, as well as an impressive sundial, mounted upon a marble column next to the temple (**E2**).

Modifications to the Sanctuary: end of first century BC, before 2 BC (E1)

This inscription relates to changes either in the sanctuary's relationship with the Forum to the east or with private houses to the west. It gives legal permission for the blocking off of light from space adjacent to the sanctuary. It names the town in formal terms as the *colonia*

Veneria Cornelia. This initially led to the Temple of Apollo, where this was found, being erroneously identified as the Temple of Venus. For Holconius Rufus, see also **D51**, **D53–54**, **F89**.

E1 *CIL* X 787 = *ILS* 5915

Marcus Holconius Rufus, duumvir with judicial power for the third time and Gnaeus Egnatius Postumus, duumvir with judicial power for the second time, in accordance with a decree of the town councillors paid 3,000 sesterces for the right to block off light, and saw to the building of a private wall belonging to the *colonia Veneria Cornelia* as far as the roof.

Dedication of a sundial (E2)

Standing next to the temple podium, this sundial mounted on an Ionic column is accompanied by an inscribed plaque, recording its donation by a pair of magistrates. The same pair of magistrates also donated a seat and sundial in the Triangular Forum (*CIL* X 831).

E2 *CIL* X 802

Lucius Sepunius Sandilianus, son of Lucius, and Marcus Herennius Epidianus, son of Aulus, duumvirs with judicial power, saw to this being made at their own expense.

Temple of Isis (E3–8)

A temple to the Egyptian goddess Isis was probably established in the Theatre district towards the end of the second century BC, reflecting the trading and cultural links between the town and Alexandria. The harbour town of Puteoli (modern Pozzuoli), further north-west on the Bay of Naples, also had a temple to an Egyptian deity, Serapis, by 105 BC, and evidence for the cult of Isis has been found in the nearby towns of Herculaneum and Stabiae.

Following earthquake damage, the small temple, set within an enclosure, had been completely rebuilt by the son of a freedman from a prominent Pompeian family (**C5**). The opportunity was also taken at this time to take over part of the adjacent Samnite Palaestra. The popularity of the cult is reflected in the discovery of statuettes of Isis and several cult-rattles (*sistra*) in private houses. Furthermore, some twenty household shrines (*lararia*) were decorated with images of Isis, and several individuals donated statuettes within the sanctuary enclosure (**E4–6**). In addition, the actor Norbanus was honoured with a portrait bust in the sanctuary, perhaps in connection with his appearances in the adjacent Theatre (**D70**). The notion that the cult's popularity was the result of some kind of religious crisis, with the rise of a belief-based cult requiring initiation at the expense of 'traditional' public cults, is no longer tenable, although the cult was regarded with suspicion at Rome until the first century AD. The reference to 'worshippers of Isis' in electoral notices (**E7–8**), however, certainly implies that some at least of her adherents had a sense of group identity not found with other cults.

The discovery of the temple in the 1760s, early on in the excavation of Pompeii, caused a great stir and captured visitors' imaginations. Their interest was aroused not only by the unusual discovery of an 'Egyptian' temple in Italy, but also by the vividness of the remains uncovered in the sanctuary. These included carbonized remains in pits and on the altar, a dead body (presumed to be the priest), statuettes and well-preserved paintings (cut away from the walls, and transferred to the royal collection) (**J6–10**). Much of the sanctuary's decoration was calculated to emphasize the foreignness of the goddess. For example, a tablet inscribed with genuine hieroglyphs was discovered in front of the temple itself, and paintings depicted Egyptian gods, including the dog-headed Anubis, Bes, Osiris, Harpocrates and Isis herself, and Egyptian landscapes peopled with strange creatures, such as the crocodile, ibis and pygmies. Finally, a small structure (*purgatorium*), with steps leading down to a well, was believed to have provided purifying water for the religious ceremonies.

Figure 5.1 E3 Plan of Temple of Isis

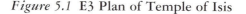

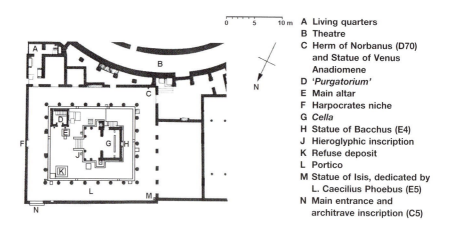

A Living quarters
B Theatre
C Herm of Norbanus (D70) and Statue of Venus Anadiomene
D *'Purgatorium'*
E Main altar
F Harpocrates niche
G *Cella*
H Statue of Bacchus (E4)
J Hieroglyphic inscription
K Refuse deposit
L Portico
M Statue of Isis, dedicated by L. Caecilius Phoebus (E5)
N Main entrance and architrave inscription (C5)

Statuette of Bacchus (E4)

The marble statuette (NM inv. 6312) depicts Bacchus with a panther, as a version of the Egyptian god Osiris. It was displayed in a small niche incorporated into the rear wall of the temple, which had ears in stucco on either side, a symbol of the deity's responsiveness to prayer. Its dedication, inscribed upon its plinth, reveals that it was set up by the father of the child who had nominally rebuilt the temple.

E4 *CIL* X 847

Numerius Popidius Ampliatus, father, at his own expense.

Statuette of Isis (E5)

The marble statuette (NM inv. 976), executed in an archaizing style, depicts the goddess holding a *sistrum* (the rattle used in her worship) in her right hand, and the key of the Nile in her left. Traces of gilding can still be seen on the marble.

E5 *CIL* X 849

Lucius Caecilius Phoebus erected (this statue); space granted by decree of the town councillors.

Dedication to Isis of a statuette (E6)

This inscribed pilaster, which once supported a (now lost) statuette, was removed from the site into a private collection. Consequently, its original location is unknown, but it may have come from the temple.

E6 Tran Tam Tinh (1964), 176 no. 148

To Augustan Isis. Manilia Chrysa [fulfilled] her vow [willingly to the deserving deity].

Electoral notices of the worshippers of Isis (E7–8)

Both of these notices date from the last decade before the eruption. E7 was displayed on the road outside the Temple of Isis, E8 on the Stabian Street, some 50 metres from the temple.

E7 *CIL* IV 787 = *ILS* 6420b

All the worshippers of Isis call for Gnaeus Helvius Sabinus as aedile.

E8 *CIL* IV 1011 = *ILS* 6419f

Popidius Natalis, his client, with the worshippers of Isis, call for Cuspius Pansa as aedile.

Jupiter (E9–13)

See also J40.

Dedication to Jupiter in Greek by an Alexandrian, April 3 BC (E9)

A marble plaque was found in the temple of Jupiter in the Forum, which bears two inscriptions, the earlier one (E9) from 3 BC on one side in Greek, and a later Latin one (E10) on the other side. The name of the dedicator, Hephaistion, and his use of the Greek language and Egyptian dating system evoke the cultural and religious customs of Alexandria. (Compare the presence of another Alexandrian at Pompeii in H80.) The date is 23 April 3 BC, using an Egyptian month and an era starting from Octavian's final victory over Antony and Cleopatra in 30 BC; the 'Emperor's day' in each month was the day on which he was born.

E9 *CIL* X 796

Gaius Iulius Hephaistion, son of Hephaistion, priest of the community of Frigi, dedicated to Jupiter Frigio in the 27th year of Caesar, in the month of Pharmouthi, on the Emperor's day.

Dedication to Jupiter on behalf of the emperor Gaius Caligula (E10)

Although the vast majority of inscriptions relating to the emperor Gaius Caligula in the Roman world as a whole were destroyed or had his name erased from them following his murder, he had clearly been popular at Pompeii during his reign. He was also nominated as an honorary magistrate there (F107–108). This inscription in the temple was engraved on the reverse side of E9.

E10 *CIL* X 796, AD 37

To Jupiter Best and Greatest. For the well-being of [Gaius] Caesar Augustus Germanicus, hailed as victorious general, chief priest, holder of tribunician power, consul, [. . .]octus at his own expense.

A dedicatory base (E11)

This small marble base originally supported a statue in the temple. It can be dated by its use of the digamma, a letter of the alphabet revived by the emperor Claudius for a short time.

E11 *CIL* X 797 = *ILS* 5004, AD 47–54

Spurius Turranius Proculus Gellianus, son of Lucius, grandson of Spurius, great-grandson of Lucius, of the Fabian tribe; staff officer twice; prefect of the curators of the Tiber channel; prefect with the powers of a praetor in charge of jurisdiction in the city of Lavinium; 'father' of the deputation of the Laurentine people in charge of concluding the treaty with the Roman people in accordance with the Sibylline books, which relates to the rites concerned with the origins of the Roman people, the Quirites, and of the people of the Latin name, which are observed among the Laurentines; priest of Jupiter; priest of Mars; leading member of the Salii priesthood; augur and pontiff; prefect of the Gaetulian cohort; military tribune of the tenth legion (dedicated this). Space granted by decree of the town councillors.

Other dedications to Jupiter, original context unknown (E12–13)

E13 was found during the construction of the Sarno aqueduct at the end of the sixteenth century. For Pompeian Venus see **E15–20**.

E12 *CIL* X 926

Quintus Lollius Scylax and Calidia Antiochis his mother and Marcus Calidius Nasta, to Jupiter, fulfilled their vow willingly to the deserving god.

E13 *CIL* X 928 = *ILS* 3180

By command of Venus Fisica, Antistia Methe, wife of Antistius Primigenius (dedicated this) to Jupiter Best and Greatest, by decree of the town councillors.

Neptune (E14)

This inscription was found outside the town, towards the shore, perhaps where there was once a temple to the sea-god.

E14 *CIL* X 8157

Sextus Pompeius Ruma, freedman of Sextus, to Neptune, willingly fulfilled his vow.

Pompeian Venus (E15–20)

Venus held a special place at Pompeii, as its guardian deity, and was integral to the colony's identity as *Colonia Cornelia Veneria*. Pompeian Venus is sometimes given the unique cult title Venus Fisica, which perhaps alludes to her links with nature. The title Fisica seems to be derived from Oscan, and is otherwise found elsewhere describing the obscure Oscan deity Mefitis. Venus is invoked to help with various endeavours, whether electoral or in matters of the heart (**E15–18**). The significance of the cult is also indicated by the imperial gifts mentioned in two graffiti (**E19–20**). Compare also **D74** and **E13**.

E15 *CIL* IV 26 = *ILS* 6399, Republican date

I ask you to elect Numerius Barcha as duumvir, a good man, and may Pompeian Venus [be favourable] to your offerings.

E16 *CIL* IV 4007, I.iii.30

May you, my darling, thrive, and may you have the goodwill of Pompeian Venus.

E17 *CIL* IV 2457, Theatre corridor

Methe, slave of Cominia, from Atella, loves Chrestus. May Pompeian Venus be dear to both of them and may they always live in harmony.

E18 *CIL* IV 538 = *ILS* 5138

[On the margin, underneath a picture of the beginning and end of the fight between two gladiators]:

Whoever harms this, may he leave behind an angry Pompeian Venus.

Offerings to Pompeian Venus by Nero and Poppaea (E19–20)

Two graffiti from the House of Iulius Polybius (IX.xiii.1–3) appear to record gifts sent to the town's guardian goddess by the emperor and his wife. Poppaea is said to have sent jewels including a beryl (an aquamarine gemstone from India), while Nero (referred to here as Caesar and Augustus) sent gold. On Poppaea's possible connections with Pompeii, see notes to **D40–43**.

E19 *AE* (1985) 283

Poppaea sent as gifts to most holy Venus a beryl, an ear-drop pearl, and a large single pearl.

E20 *AE* (1985) 284

When Caesar came to most holy Venus and when your heavenly feet brought you there, Augustus, there was a countless weight of gold.

Popular views of the gods (E21–27)

Unspecific gods sometimes appear in graffiti (**E21–22**). **E23** gives the names of the various deities associated with the days of the week (compare **H3**). The symbol of a phallus (erect male organ) is commonly found in Pompeii in what seem to modern eyes as unexpected places, such as on wall plaques at street corners, or above an oven in a bakery (**E24**). Although it can simply be a symbol of sex, it is more often a symbol of fertility and prosperity, or of hopes for good fortune. **E26** is a graffito upon a bar counter in an inn (I.xi.2). The final graffito (**E27**) shows a disappointed lover turning against the goddess Venus.

E21 *CIL* IV 6815, VI.xvi.4–5

May god always make Felix Aufidius felicitous.

E22 *CIL* IV 5370

He who disdains life will easily despise god.

E23 *CIL* IV 5202 (in Greek)

The gods' days:
Of Kronos
Of the Sun
Of the Moon
Of Ares
Of Hermes
Of Zeus
Of Aphrodite

E24 *CIL* IV 1454, in a bakery, above an oven

Here lives [phallus] good fortune.

E25 *CIL* IV 7716, III.v.1

Shitter, be on your guard against evil, or else, if you disregard this, may you
incur the wrath of Jupiter.

E26 *CIL* IV 8417

The good god lives here in the house of Act[. . .].

E27 *CIL* IV 1824, Basilica

Whoever is in love, let him come; I wish to break the ribs of Venus
With sticks and maim the goddess's loins;
If she can perforate my tender heart,
Why can I not break her head with a stick?

Cult of Mercury and Maia, and Augustus (E28–31)

Mercury and his mother Maia were worshipped somewhere in Pompeii by
an association of freedmen and slaves, under the authority of the local town
council. Inscribed plaques, which can be dated to 14 BC and then 2 BC, show
how the emperor gradually infiltrated the cult during this period. First of
all, Mercury and Maia appear by themselves, then Augustus appears alongside them, and finally Augustus is named by himself. For later dedications,
see also *CIL* X 891 (AD 1), X 892 (AD 3), X 895 (AD 23), X 899 (AD 32),
X 901 (AD 34), X 902 (AD 34).

E28 *CIL* X 885, 14 BC

[Marcus] Sittius Papia, freedman of Marcus, (set this up as) sacred to Mercury and Maia in accordance with a decree of the town councillors, by command of Marcus Melsonius, son of Aulus, for the second time, and Publius Rogius Varus, son of Publius, duumvirs with judicial power; and of Numerius Paccius Chilo, son of Numerius, and Marcus Ninnus Pollio, son of Marcus, duumvirs in charge of streets, sacred and public buildings, in the consulship of [Marcus] Crassus and Gnaeus Lentulus.

E29 *CIL* X 886 = *ILS* 6389, 14 BC

Marcus Sittius Serapa, freedman of Marcus, (set this up as) sacred to Mercury and Maia in accordance with a decree of the town councillors, by command of Publius Rogius Varus, son of Publius, and Marcus Melsonius, son of Aulus, for the second time, duumvirs with judicial power; and of Numerius Paccius Chilo, son of Numerius, and Marcus Ninnus Pollio, son of Marcus, duumvirs in charge of streets, sacred and public buildings, [in the consulship of] Marcus Crassus and Gnaeus Lentulus.

E30 *CIL* X 888 = *ILS* 6390

Gratus, slave of Arrius; Messius Arrius Inventus; Memor, slave of Istacidius, attendants of Augustus, Mercury, and Maia, [in accordance with a] decree of the town councillors, by command of [. . .]

E31 *CIL* X 890 = *ILS* 6391, 2 BC

Aulus Veius Phylax, Numerius Popidius Moschus, Titus Mescinius Amphio, Primus, slave of Marcus Arruntius, attendants of Augustus, in accordance with a decree of the town councillors, by command of Marcus Holconius Rufus, for the fourth time, and Aulus Clodius Flaccus, for the third time, duumvirs with judicial power, and of Publius Caesetius Postumus and Numerius Tintirius Rufus, duumvirs in charge of streets, sacred and public buildings, in the consulship of Imperator Caesar for the thirteenth time and [Marcus Plautius] Silvanus.

Temple of Augustan Fortune (E32–37)

At the start of the first century AD, a member of the local elite, Marcus Tullius, paid for the building of a temple to Augustan Fortune on land owned by him near the centre of the town, just north of the Forum. Together with the erection of a monumental arch just beside it and a portico along the street leading up to it, the overall effect was of extending the monumental centre of the town beyond the Forum itself. He marked off the land that still remained his private property by means of a small tufa marker beside the temple, to the south. At the end of his life, Tullius' contribution to the town was acknowledged by the councillors, who set up a seat-tomb to him just outside the Stabian Gate (G6).

The cult provided a focus of loyalty towards the imperial regime by freedmen and slaves, who served as its presidents (*magistri*) and attendants (*ministri*), in a similar way to the organization of the cult of Mercury, Maia and Augustus, and of district shrines (E28–31, E61–67). An inscription reveals that it was a requirement of the cult's regulations that the attendants (*ministri*) set up a statue (of what, is not clear), perhaps each year. As with the cult of Mercury, Maia and Augustus, the town councillors had overall authority for the cult. Many of the cult's bases have been found reused in various parts of the town, but some were found in the temple itself.

The construction of the temple, c.AD 3 (E32–33)

E32 is the temple's dedicatory inscription; E33 is the boundary marker of volcanic stone, dividing off land donated by Marcus Tullius to the town from his private property.

E32 CIL X 820 = ILS 5398

Marcus Tullius, son of Marcus, duumvir with judicial power three times, quinquennial, augur, military tribune by popular demand, (built) the Temple of Augustan Fortune on his own land and at his own expense.

E33 CIL X 821 = ILS 5398a

Private land of Marcus Tullius, son of Marcus.

Bases dedicated by the attendants of Augustan Fortune (E34–37)

The first two bases were found in the temple itself. E34 is the earliest statue base set up by attendants (*ministri*) of the cult, in AD 3. E35, which does not conform to the pattern of the others, refers to a 'law', the regulations laid down for the cult when it was first established. It is rather poorly inscribed, with several errors in its carving: in the consular date, for instance, the text gives 'Platilio' instead of 'Plautio'. On the upper surface of the base is a hollow in the shape of a foot, indicating that it originally bore a metal statue. Other bases were found reused in different parts of the town (E36–37).

E34 CIL X 824 = ILS 6382, AD 3

Agathermus, slave of Vettius; Suavis, slave of Caesia Prima; Pothus, slave of Numitor; Anteros, slave of Lacutulanus, the first attendants (*ministri*) of Augustan Fortune, by command of Marcus Staius Rufus and Gnaeus Melissaeus, duumvirs with judicial power, in the consulship of Publius Silius and Lucius Volusius Saturninus.

E35 *CIL* X 825 = *ILS* 6385, AD 45

During the consulship of Taurus Statilius and Tiberius Plautius Aelianus, Lucius Statius Faustus instead of the statue which in accordance with the law of the attendants (*ministri*) of Augustan Fortune he was required to set up, on the proposal of Quintus Pompeius Amethystus, quaestor, they decreed that he should set up two marble bases instead of a statue.

E36 *CIL* X 826 = *ILS* 6383, AD 56

Martialis, slave of Gaius Olius Primus; Manius Salarius Crocus; Primigenius, slave of Gaius Olius Primus, attendants of Augustan Fortune; by command of Quintus Postumius Modestus and Gaius Vibius Secundus, duumvirs with judicial power, and of Gaius Memmius Iunianus and Quintus Bruttius Balbus, aediles, in the consulship of [Lucius D]uvius and Publius Clodius.

E37 *CIL* X 827 = *ILS* 6384

Lucius Numisius Primus, Lucius Numisius Optatus, Lucius Melissaeus Plocamus, attendants of Augustan Fortune; in accordance with a decree of the town councillors, by command of Lucius Iulius Ponticus and Publius Gavius Pastor, duumvirs with judicial power, and of Quintus Poppaeus and Gaius Vibius, aediles, in the consulship of Quintus Futius and Publius Calvisius.

Emperor-worship (E38)

A small temple on the east side of the Forum has been identified as a temple for emperor-worship on the basis of the iconography of its marble altar (**E38**). It displays images closely associated with the emperor Augustus, and probably dates from his reign, although a Flavian date has also been suggested for it in the past. See further Dobbins (1992).

It is possible that the attendants of the cult of Augustus that developed out of the cult of Mercury and Maia (**E30–31**) were the assistants to the priests of Augustus. Holconius Rufus and Holconius Celer were both priests of Augustus during the emperor's lifetime (**D53–55**), and other imperial priests for later emperors are also known, including Lucretius Satrius Valens (perpetual priest of Nero when designated successor, **D11–15**) and Alleius Nigidius Maius (priest of ?Vespasian, **D23**). Otherwise, the tombs of several wealthy individuals emphasize their role as *Augustales* (**G36–49**), who were probably also involved in emperor-worship, but whose meeting place remains unidentified at Pompeii.

Altar for the Emperor in the Forum (E38)

This altar is probably Augustan. Its main (west) scene (**E38a**), facing the entrance to the sanctuary, portrays a sacrifice of a bull, an animal often used in emperor-worship. In detail, what
we see is a priest with veiled head offering a libation (liquid offering) at a tripod altar, accompanied by attendants (including a flute-player and the slave who actually does the killing –
victimarius – carrying an axe), leading the bull to sacrifice in front of a temple with four
columns, which is partially covered by drapery. On the altar's east side is a 'civic crown', a
wreath made up of oak leaves, awarded at Rome for saving citizens' lives, upon a shield,
flanked by laurel trees. This scene reflects the honours granted by the Senate to Augustus in
27 BC. On the north and south sides are depicted sacrificial implements and priestly symbols
beneath garlands of fruit hanging from skeletal ox-heads (*bucrania*); on the north, a libation
dish (*patera*), ladle (*simpulum*) and jug (*urceus*); on the south (**E38b**), a hand-towel (*mantele*),
incense-box (*acerra*), and curved augur's staff (*lituus*).

Plate 5.1 **E38a Altar for the Emperor: scene of bull sacrifice**

Plate 5.2 **E38b** Altar for the Emperor: sacrificial paraphernalia

Public priestesses (E39–50)

Public priestesses associated with the cults of Venus and Ceres acted as generous benefactors towards the town. Two of them – Mamia (**E39–40**) and Eumachia (**E41–47**) – made particularly significant contributions to the development of the east side of the Forum. A Holconia (possibly the daughter of Holconius Rufus or Celer) was honoured publicly with a statue (**E48**). Alleia, the daughter of Alleius Nigidius Maius, was a public priestess in the Neronian period (**E49**) and has been suggested as a candidate for a statue of this period found in the market, or Macellum (**E50**). For the family of Alleia Decimilla, see **F87**.

Mamia (E39–40)

Temple building (E39)

This large inscription commemorating the construction of a building is thought to belong to the temple adjacent to Eumachia's Building on the east side of the Forum, often called the 'Temple of Vespasian'. The temple in question has long been interpreted as being that of the *genius* of Augustus, but Gradel (1992) has argued that instead the temple was dedicated to the *genius* of the colony.

E39 *CIL* X 816

Mamia, daughter of Publius, public priestess, [built this] to the *genius* [of the colony/of Augustus] on her own land and at [her own] expense.

Tomb (E40)

At her death, Mamia was honoured with a seat-tomb outside the Herculaneum Gate (tomb 4 left). This imposing type of monument – designed to allow the passer-by to sit down for a while – was exclusively granted at Pompeii by the town council to public benefactors in recognition of their services to the town. Compare G4–9.

Plate 5.3 E40a Mamia's tomb

E40b *CIL* X 998 = *ILS* 6369

To Mamia, daughter of Publius, public priestess, a place for burial was given by decree of the town councillors.

Eumachia (E41–47)

Eumachia's Building in the Forum (E41–45)

Eumachia built a grandiose building on the east side of the Forum. This replaced some shops and private houses flanking the Forum. She recorded her benefaction in two dedicatory inscriptions, one found complete at the back entrance to the building on the Street of Abundance (**E42**), the other (a much grander inscription incorporated above the portico, overlooking the Forum) preserved only in fragments (*CIL* X 811). The back-door inscription is itself a substantial chunk of marble, which had previously been used for an inscription (*CIL* X 959), but it was recut so that its reverse could be used for Eumachia's text.

The date of the building is the early first century AD, in the late Augustan or Tiberian period, perhaps after the rededication of the Roman Forum's Temple of Concord to Augustan Concord at Rome in AD 10. A Marcus Numistrius Fronto was duumvir in AD 3 (*CIL* X 892), but he is more likely to have been Eumachia's husband, who was perhaps deceased by the time of the building, than her son, who is mentioned in the inscription.

A statue of Eumachia was found complete with its inscribed base in a purpose-built niche towards the rear of her building (**E43**). It depicts her dressed in tunic, *stola* and cloak, with an idealizing portrait (NM inv. 6232).

The function of the building is disputed. Its inscription shows that the building was dedicated to Augustan Concord and Piety, perhaps in imitation of Livia, who built a temple dedicated to Concord in honour of her husband Augustus at Rome. The statue bases of Aeneas (**E44**) and Romulus (**E45**) also imitate monuments at Rome, namely the statues set up in the Forum of Augustus. The iconography of these statues was apparently familiar at Pompeii, appearing in paintings on the Street of Abundance. Romulus was depicted brandishing the *spolia opima* (an award made to a general who had killed in battle the leader of the enemy), and Aeneas leading his family to safety from Troy, holding his son Ascanius by the hand, while carrying his father Anchises on his shoulders. This family group was even parodied in a painting showing them as human figures with dogs' heads, and large phalluses. The highly elaborate door-frame, with its acanthus scrolls inhabited by tiny animals, which recalls the frieze on the Altar of Augustan Peace at Rome, was actually put in place here in modern times. It does not fit this particular entrance, and may in fact belong to the adjacent temple. Even without this, the Augustan programme of decoration is still fairly extensive. Fragments of a statue of Augustan Concord were found in the large central niche opposite the building's main entrance from the Forum. The discovery of Eumachia's statue set up by the fullers has led some to argue that her building served as headquarters for the fullers. It seems unlikely that the rather noxious fulling process itself took place in such a grand edifice, despite the claim that basins were found in the building's courtyard. If these basins did exist, they may well have been related to the rebuilding work in progress in AD 79 (**J46**). No clear picture emerges of what the building was used for, and indeed it may well have served a variety of functions.

Figure 5.2 E41 Plan of Eumachia's Building

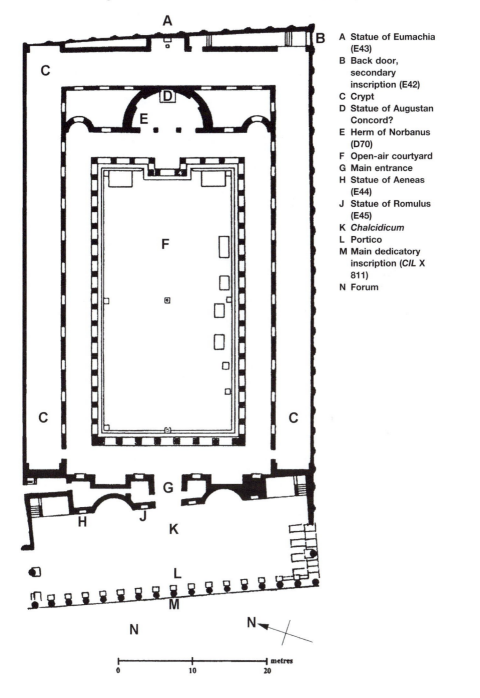

A Statue of Eumachia (E43)
B Back door, secondary inscription (E42)
C Crypt
D Statue of Augustan Concord?
E Herm of Norbanus (D70)
F Open-air courtyard
G Main entrance
H Statue of Aeneas (E44)
J Statue of Romulus (E45)
K *Chalcidicum*
L Portico
M Main dedicatory inscription (*CIL* X 811)
N Forum

E42 *CIL* X 810 = *ILS* 3785

Eumachia, daughter of Lucius, public priestess, in her own name and that of her son, Marcus Numistrius Fronto, built at her own expense the chalcidicum, crypt and portico in honour of Augustan Concord and Piety and also dedicated them.

Plate 5.4 E43a Statue of Eumachia

E43b *CIL* X 813 = *ILS* 6368

To Eumachia, daughter of Lucius, public priestess; the fullers (set this up).

E44 *CIL* X 808 + 8348 = *ILS* 63

Aeneas, [son] of Venus and Anchises, [led] into Italy the Trojans who had survived when Troy was captured [and burnt . . . [three lines lost here] . . .], founded [the town of Lavinium and reigned there] for three years; in the Laurentine war he did not disappear, and [was called] Father Indigens, and was received among the company of the gods.

E45 *CIL* X 809 = *ILS* 64

Romulus, son of Mars, founded the city of Rome and reigned for 38 years; he was the first general to dedicate the enemy spoils (*spolia opima*) to Jupiter Feretrius, having slain the enemy's general, King Acro of the Caeninenses, and, having been received among the company of the gods, was called Quirinus.

Another gift by Eumachia (E46)

An inscribed plaque records another gift to the town by Eumachia, but we know neither the nature of the statue nor its original context.

E46 *AE* (1992), 277

Eumachia, daughter of Lucius, (set up this) statue.

Eumachia's tomb (E47)

Eumachia's tomb inscription is deceptively unprepossessing, given that it belongs to the biggest tomb found so far. The tomb was architecturally lavish, and reproduced the basic arrangement of a seat-tomb (see E40, G4–9), but on a much larger scale (see further, G15–19).

E47 D'Ambrosio and De Caro (1983) 11OS

Eumachia, daughter of Lucius, for herself and her family.

Holconia (E48)

This inscription accompanied an honorific statue to Holconia, which was probably part of an arch honouring her family, at the crossroads outside the Stabian Baths, where a statue base and statue in honour of Holconius Rufus were also found (F89).

E48 *CIL* X 950/1

To Holconia, daughter of Marcus, public priestess.

101

Alleia (E49)

E49 *EE* VIII 855

Alleia, daughter of Maius, priestess of Venus and Ceres, to herself, in accordance with a decree of the town councillors, with [public] money.

Statue of a local priestess, from the Macellum (E50)

Although the identity of this woman is unknown, her position as a priestess is indicated by her veiled head, her olive-wreath and her holding a libation-dish (*patera*) and an incense-box. Her hairstyle suggests a Neronian date. In another niche of the same building was found a heroic semi-nude statue of a young man.

Plate 5.5 E50 Statue of a local priestess

Cults in the home (E51–57)

Shrine of the household gods (lararium), House of the Vettii (E51)

Many houses had a shrine in their main reception room (*atrium*) or kitchen. This example, from the House of the Vettii is particularly lavish; it is located in a secondary *atrium* next to the kitchen. In the pediment can be seen a libation dish (*patera*) at the centre, a knife to the right, and a skeletal ox-head to the left. Below, in the painting, at the centre appears the figure of the *genius*, dressed in a toga, with veiled head. He is carrying a libation dish (*patera*) in his right hand and incense-box in his left. On either side of him the *Lares* (household gods) appear as youthful male figures dressed in tunics, carrying drinking-horns and a wine bucket. At the bottom a snake slithers towards offerings upon a small altar.

Plate 5.6 E51 House of the Vettii, *lararium*

Vows on household shrines (E52–53)

These vows were probably all offered by slaves or freedmen. E52 accompanies an elaborately painted shrine, which depicts a *genius* sacrificing at an altar, around which a snake entwines itself. On either side appear *Lares*. E53, a painted inscription inside a placard, appears on a household shrine in a kitchen. Painted upon the shrine are a figure praying, the *Lares* pouring libations and a snake.

E52 *AE* (1985) 285, House of Gaius Iulius Polybius (IX.xiii.1–3)

For the well-being, return, and victory of Gaius Iulius Philippus. Publius Cornelius Felix and Vitalis, slave of Cuspius, made a vow here to the household gods.

E53 *CIL* IV 9887, II.iv.13

Felix [made] a vow to the household gods (*lares*).

The genius of the household's master (54–57)

In addition to worshipping the household gods, members of the household also made offerings to the *genius* (divine spirit) of the master of the household (*paterfamilias*). E54 is inscribed upon a marble plaque incorporated into the household shrine. A herm (portrait bust set upon a short marble column) located in the main reception room (*atrium*) or the household shrine itself might provide a focal point for such ceremonies (E55–57).

E54 *CIL* X 861 = *ILS* 3641, IX.i.20

To the *genius* of our Marcus and to the Lares. The two Diadumeni, freedmen (set this up).

Herm of Lucius in the House of Caecilius Iucundus (E55)

Two herms were found in the *atrium* of the House of Caecilius Iucundus (V.i.26), one on either side of the doorway into the *tablinum*, opposite the main entrance to the house. One of these was found together with its bronze portrait bust still intact, and bronze genitalia beneath (NM inv. 110663). The portrait depicts an ageing man, with a prominent wart, and is thought to date from the Augustan period. His identity is problematic. It could be the father of the banker Lucius Caecilius Iucundus, whose name was Lucius Caecilius Felix, and who was alive in the Augustan era. Alternatively, the freedman Felix who set up the portrait might himself be the banker's father. In this case, we should imagine that Felix was a favoured freedman who eventually became his ex-master's heir. For other finds from this house, see C3, D77, F17, H69–82.

Plate 5.7 E55a Herm of Lucius

E55b *CIL* X 860 = *ILS* 3640

To the *genius* of our Lucius. Felix, freedman (set this up).

E56 *CIL* X 864, VIII.ii.14–16

To Gaius Cornelius Rufus.

E57 *CIL* X 865, VI.xiv.20

To our Primus. Anteros, treasurer (set this up).

Visions and vows (E58–60)

Individuals might choose to set up monuments to commemorate particular religious experiences. **E58** is a thin marble plaque affixed to an altar in a shop, IX.1.25. **E59** was inscribed upon a small marble altar. **E60** accompanied a painting of Isis.

E58 *CIL* X 930

Pacuvius Erasistratus, after a vision.

E59 *CIL* X 863, VII.xii.26

Antiochus fulfilled his vow.

E60 *CIL* IV 882

Pilo[ca]lus fulfilled his vow willingly to the deserving deity.

Crossroad shrines to the *Lares* (E61–67)

Pompeii was divided up into districts, each of which had a shrine to the guardian gods of the neighbourhood (the *Lares*). These shrines are generally located at street corners on main roads, or at junctions onto main roads. Over thirty such shrines have been identified in the town. The cults were tended by low-status individuals appointed annually, often freedmen presidents (*magistri*) and their slave attendants (*ministri*). The actual shrine can consist of any combination of an altar, niche and chapel. Most often, remains are found of the paintings accompanying the shrine. Typical themes include the *Lares* holding up drinking-cups, four figures (probably the *magistri*) carrying out a sacrifice, a snake representing the location's divine spirit (*genius loci*) and attendants of the sacrifice, such as a flute-player or incense-carrier. Inscriptions alongside shrines are more rarely found, but can include lists of the neighbourhood's officials presiding over the cult.

Plate 5.8 E61 District shrine on street corner,
between I.xi and I.ix

Lists of local district officials (E62–64)

E62 is an inscription painted on a house front along the Street of Abundance near the Forum. It gives the names of the neighbourhood officials in charge of the crossroad cult for the years 47 and 46 BC. It may originally have been situated next to an altar, but no trace of one remains. It is painted in small black letters on a block of tufa covered by plaster and was not visible in AD 79. After excavation, however, once the plaster became exposed to the elements, it gradually peeled off, eventually revealing this inscription beneath. It is highly unusual for such an old painted inscription to be preserved. Other partially preserved lists of names of neighbourhood presidents have also been found painted at crossroads (*CIL* IV 7807, 7425, 7855).

E63 is written with charcoal inside a placard, above an altar fixed to a wall situated at the corner of I.xi. It gives the names of the local district officials, or more probably their attendants, in charge of the cult. Below the text were pictures relating to the cult, with two snakes below, and above two *Lares* with drinking-cups next to a figure sacrificing. Its excavators could discern five layers of painting, which indicates that the shrine's painting was renewed over a period of some years. On the upper surface of the altar itself were found considerable quantities of ash and wood, perhaps the remnants of burnt offerings.

E64 is a painted placard containing the names of the presidents of this crossroad cult, who appear to be slaves. It accompanies an altar and painting on a corner of the Street of Abundance. The painting depicts a snake below, approaching offerings, and a sacrifice by the cult's officials at an altar, flanked by two *Lares*. Above appears the inscription in a placard.

E62 *CIL* IV 60 = *ILS* 6375

During the year when Gaius Julius Caesar was dictator for the second time and Marcus Antonius was master of the horse [47 BC], the presidents of the neighbourhood and of the crossroads: Marcus Blattius, son of Marcus; Marcus Cerrinius, son of Marcus; Marcus Sepullius [. . .]; [. . .]; Quintus Pra[. . .]; Gaius Corne[lius . . .]; [. . .]; Publius Ro[. . .]ius, slave of [. . .]; Salvius E[. . .]ro, slave of Marcus.

During the consulship of [Gaius Caes]ar and Marcus Lepidus [46 BC]: [. . .] Blattius, son of Marcus; Gaius Ermatorius, son of Publius; Marcus Titius Plutus, freedman of Marcus; Marcus Stronnius Nic[. . .]o, freedman of Marcus; Marcus Oppius Aes[. . .], freedman of Spurius; Gaius Cepidius [. . .] of Gaius; [. . .].

E63 *CIL* IV 7425, II.i

Primigenius, slave of Caesetia; Stalbnus, slave of Numerius Maro; Chius, slave of Gaius Virius Primigenius.

E64 *CIL* IV 7855

Successus, Victor, Axclepiades, Cosstas.

Dedications and requests (E65–67)

As well as lists of cult officials, some crossroad shrines have preserved various dedications and requests. **E65** is painted above an altar at a street corner, where there is a painting of two horns-of-plenty and a garland. **E66** (see also **Plate 5.8**) appears to the left of a street-corner shrine, where a painting of a *Lar* and a snake can still be faintly seen. On top of the altar were found the carbonized remains of a sacrifice of a chicken. **E67** is inscribed upon a bronze plaque, which was originally affixed to a wall.

E65 *CIL* IV 3774 = *ILS* 3822, IX.viii.8

Sacred to Well-being.

E66 *CIL* IV 8426, I.xi

By the sacred Lares, I ask you . . .

E67 *CIL* X 927

Agathemerus and Heracla presidents of the Lares, gave as a gift.

Jews (E68–71)

An inscription written in Hebrew (**E68**) seems to record the sale of something by three men to a fourth. An inscription in Greek letters on an *amphora* (**E69**) records a slave of a master known as Judaicus (i.e. 'The Jew' / 'from Judaea'). Jewish names appear in contexts which suggest Jewish slave-girls: a Maria is listed among a group of textile workers (*CIL* IV 1507) and supporting Helvius Sabinus (**F58**), and a Martha at **D97**.

Pottery has also been found with labels which probably indicate kosher food. Pliny the Elder (*Natural History* 31.95) tells us that special (*castimoniarum*) garum is made from fish without scales for religious and Jewish rites. Several pottery vessels labelled '*garum cast*' have been found (**E70**). Finally, **E71**, inscribed in large letters, before Pompeii's destruction, was written by someone with knowledge of the Old Testament (*Genesis* 13.13 and 18–19), perhaps in criticism of the morality of Pompeii. The story in *Genesis* culminates in 19.24 with 'Then the Lord rained upon Sodom and Gomorrah brimstone and fire from the Lord out of heaven.' Some of the evidence mentioned here (and see also note to **D85**) could apply to early Christians, but no unequivocal evidence has been found of Christianity at Pompeii.

E68 *CIL* IV 8010 = *CIJ* 562

Sold by Kar[. . .], Jesus, Shadani(ham?) son (?) of Lenanath, to Vergaz . . . what is beneath the baths.

E69 *CIL* IV 6990 (*amphora*)

Felix, slave of Judaicus.

E70 *CIL* IV 2569 (two *amphorae*)

Kosher garum.

E71 *CIL* IV 4976 (IX.i.26, Street of Abundance)

SODOM[A] GOMORA

6

POLITICS AND
PUBLIC LIFE

The colony of Pompeii was governed on a system modelled on that of Republican Rome. Magistrates were elected for a period of one year to lead a town council made up of men who had previously served as magistrates. An anecdote about the Roman author and politician Cicero (**F1**) represents him commenting favourably on democracy at Pompeii. The point of Cicero's comment was that in the 40s BC, Julius Caesar as dictator appointed men directly to the Senate at Rome, whereas no such direct patronage operated at Pompeii: someone wishing to become a councillor had to stand for democratic election, though exceptions did occur later (see **C5, G21, G24**). The members of the town council (equivalent of the Senate at Rome) were all freeborn male citizens, of good character and reputable profession (e.g. not gladiators, actors or public executioners). Councillors had to live in the town or its immediate surroundings. A minimum level of property was required, but we do not know what this was at Pompeii. Membership of the council was for life. Councillors enjoyed various privileges, including the best seats at public shows in the theatres and Amphitheatre. The council as a whole controlled civic finances and public religion, and had authority over areas of public space (notably the Forum, but also streets of tombs). It would grant honorific tombs and statues to the town's most important benefactors in specific areas of public space (**B12, E40, E49?, F87, F91, G4–12; D70, F89, F93–95, F102–103**). It supervised the construction of new public buildings and also the implementation of standard weights and measures (**H64**). For evidence of individual magistrates' activities, see **F86**.

Each year, elections for two aediles and two duumvirs were held in March, with the newly elected magistrates beginning their year in office on 1 July. There were two junior magistrates each year, known as aediles, or sometimes called 'duumvirs in charge of streets, sacred and public buildings' (**E28–29, E31**). There were also two senior magistrates, known as duumvirs (literally 'two men', the equivalent of the consuls at Rome). They had to have held the post of aedile already, usually three to five years earlier. They presided over meetings of the council and were in charge of fulfilling decrees passed by the council. Prefects were appointed in exceptional cases (like the *dictator* at Rome) (see **D6**, **D36**, **F107–108**). In the early years of the colony, the two pairs of duumvirs and aediles were collectively known as quattuorvirs ('board of four men') (**B7**). Important members of the elite might be elected as *duumvir* on more than one occasion (exceptionally, Marcus Holconius Rufus was elected five times **D54**, **F89**). The most important magistracy was elected only every five years. This office was the quinquennial (literally 'five-yearly'), whose task it was to revise the roll of citizens (census) and update the membership list of the town council. Again this was a local equivalent of the censors at Rome.

One of the unique phenomena of the historical record preserved at Pompeii is the huge quantity of painted notices relating to local elections (**F2–85**). Around 2,800 examples have been found on the outside walls of houses and public buildings, clustered along major roads and at busy junctions. Tombs on the roads leading out of the town also displayed such notices, sometimes relating to towns other than Pompeii (**F82–85**). Most of the notices were produced by professional sign-writers (**F74–81**). The vast majority of notices date from the final years of Pompeii's existence, but some earlier ones have also been traced, often preserved underneath more recent notices. A few very fragmentary ones are even in Oscan. Most of the notices recommend an individual for election to a particular magistracy. A few denigrate a candidate (**F11–13**, **F65**). Generally, the content of the notices is fairly formulaic and brief. In some cases they simply give the candidate's name and the office being sought (**F31**). In others they give the name of his supporters, which may be an individual or apparently a whole group, usually of traders (**F14–28**, **F35–64**). Sometimes the supporter is also the resident or owner of the property upon whose façade the notice is posted (**F17–19**). A surprising number of supporters are women, even though they could not actually vote (**F51**, **F54**, **F56–58**). A few give some indication of the candidate's personal qualities (strong and honourable) (**F4–9**, **F31–33**). Political parties in the modern sense did not exist. In addition to painted notices canvassing support for candidates before elections, one was apparently acclaimed after his success too (**F73**).

This exceptional documentation of elections at Pompeii has yielded some interesting insights into the functioning of local politics. It was quite usual for electoral notices of one year to be whitewashed over, and for the next year's notices to be painted on top of them. By studying the relative layering of notices, Franklin (1980) reconstructed a list of candidates at Pompeii for the last nine years before the eruption.

In addition to these notices, our other main sources of information about local politics and career patterns are monumental inscriptions, chiefly honorific inscriptions on statue bases (**F89**, **F90**, **F92–95**) and epitaphs upon tombs (**F87–88**, **F91**, **G4–5**, **G24**). These tend to give an outline of the individual's career. The most important area in the town where honorific statues were placed was the Forum, the centre of civic life. The size and shape of the bases indicate whether they originally supported an equestrian or pedestrian statue. Forty-one bases survive for standing statues and sixteen for equestrian statues, but few of these preserve their inscriptions. In fact, of these fifty-seven bases we can only identify with any certainty six members of the local elite who were honoured with a statue (or in the case of Marcus Lucretius Rufus with two statues) (F90–95). Some of these bases may have originally displayed honorific statues of members of the imperial family.

Men of rather humbler backgrounds appear to have played prominent roles in the Fortunate Augustan Suburban Country District. An inscription of 7 BC (F97) records the names of the first slave attendants (*ministri*) who supported the work of the presidents (*magistri*), implying that administration in the District was radically reorganized at this time, perhaps in imitation of Augustus' reorganization of the city of Rome in the same year. Despite the location of this district beyond the town's walls, its officials acted as public benefactors in the heart of the town, paying for seating in the Amphitheatre (see also D1). One of its presidents (*magistri*), though a mere freedman (and, as such, excluded from becoming a town councillor) even laid claim to the symbols of the highest Roman political authority upon his tomb (F98). Inhabitants of country districts appear in other inscriptions, but may not belong to this particular district (F96, F99, G12, G18).

The Senate and emperor at Rome could also impose their authority upon the local council, but apparently did so only rarely, such as when the Roman Senate imposed a penalty upon the Pompeians following the riot in the Amphitheatre (D34–36). This was in response to a particular local crisis. By contrast, the other major intervention from Rome – the recouping of public lands – occurred on an empire-wide scale under Vespasian (F109). The town was, naturally enough, always eager to secure the support of the reigning emperor, even of an emperor condemned by later history as a madman (F107–108), since the town council elected Gaius Caligula an honorary duumvir twice. Another sign of enthusiasm for the current regime was to vote an honorific statue to the emperor or a member of his family. What survives can only be a tiny fraction of the original number of honorific imperial inscriptions (F100–104).

Politics at Rome and Pompeii compared (F1)

F1 Cicero, quoted in Macrobius' *Saturnalia* 2.3.11

On another occasion, Cicero openly mocked Julius Caesar's willingness to appoint people to the Senate. For when he was asked by his host Publius Mallius to hasten his stepson's entry to the town council (*decurionatum*), he replied in front of a great many people, 'he shall have it at Rome, if you wish; at Pompeii it is difficult'.

Election notices (F2–85)

Typical brief examples (F2–3)

F2 *CIL* IV 7620

I beg you to elect Satrius quinquennial.
  (See also **Plate** 4.1.)

F3 *CIL* IV 880

Sabinus asks you to elect Marcus Holconius aedile.

Candidates' qualities (F4–10)

The oldest notices, from the Republic, tend also to be the simplest, recommending someone as a 'good man' (**F4**). This was so common as to be usually abbreviated to 'VB' (*virum bonum*). The following expressions were also used to recommend candidates: 'excellent young man', 'honest young man' (**F5**), 'young man of integrity', 'outstanding youth', 'extremely honourable', 'worthy of public office', 'young man deserving every good', 'young man of blameless age', 'very deserving young man'. The Latin word *iuvenis* translated here as 'young man' actually meant anyone up to 45 years old, so we should not necessarily imagine a town council dominated by twenty-somethings. Occasionally, a more unusual and elaborate recommendation is made, with some even being composed in verse (**F6–7**). Only rarely do the notices actually allude to what we might call the candidate's manifesto (**F8–10**). The reference to good bread perhaps refers to bread distribution already made by Polybius or to one promised after his election. A wall painting, often misleadingly given the caption 'baker's shop', apparently depicts a figure in a toga – possibly a candidate or magistrate – handing out loaves of bread from a platform. In addition to notices relating to votes for an individual, some notices are simply expressions of goodwill towards a candidate. For the recommendations made for one particular candidate, see further **F29–72**.

F4 *CIL* IV 67 = *ILS* 6398b

I beg you to elect Publius Furius duumvir, a good man.

F5 *CIL* IV 3741

I ask you to elect Claudius Verus duumvir with judicial power, an honest young man.

F6 *CIL* IV 6626 (next to F24) = *ILS* 6422b

If integrity in life is thought to be of any use,
  This man, Lucretius Fronto is worthy of great honour.

F7 *CIL* IV 7201

Gaius Cuspius for aedile.
   If glory is to be given to someone who lives modestly,
   To this young man ought the glory he deserves be given.

F8 *CIL* IV 429 = *ILS* 6412e

I beg you to elect Gaius Julius Polybius aedile. He brings good bread.

F9 *CIL* IV 3702 = *ILS* 6405

Genialis asks for Bruttius Balbus as duumvir. He will preserve the treasury.

F10 *CIL* IV 4999

Marcus Casellius Marcellus, a good aedile and great giver of games.

Negative campaigning (F11–13)

One particular candidate during the Flavian period, Marcus Cerrinius Vatia, seems to have been the butt of ironic electioneering. These notices appear clustered together on one stretch of the 'Street of the Augustales'. Ironic supporters of other candidates include 'all the runaway slaves' (*CIL* IV 7389) and dice-throwers (**F65**).

F11 *CIL* IV 575 = *ILS* 6418e

All those asleep and Macerius ask for Vatia as aedile.

F12 *CIL* IV 576 = *ILS* 6418f

The little thieves ask for Vatia as aedile.

F13 *CIL* IV 581 = *ILS* 6418d

The late drinkers all ask you to elect Marcus Cerrinius Vatia aedile. Florus and Fructus wrote this.

Types of supporters (F14–28)

The humour of the examples **F11–13** plays on the fact that many notices identify individuals or groups as a candidate's supporters. Individuals might include a candidate's clients (**F14**; see also **E8**) or freedmen (**F15**). Other supporters might be fellow candidates or fellow magistrates (**F16**). Sometimes, an electoral notice appears on the façade of the house where the supporter lives or works (**F17–19**). **F18** appeared to the left of the entrance to the inn run by the innkeeper Euxinus; for Euxinus and Amarantus, see further **H9–11**. The case of

115

Suedius Clemens, the emperor's representative, whose name endorses the candidature of Marcus Epidius Sabinus, is an exceptional example of influence upon local politics wielded by an outsider (F110–114).

The most common type of group to recommend a candidate is a group of tradesmen. Their notices might be painted up outside their place of work, as is the case with the fullers' recommendations on the façade of the fullery of Stephanus (I.vi.7) (F20). A wide variety of tradesmen participate in expressing their opinions, and incidentally provide valuable insight into Pompeii's commercial life (see H51). We find bread-bakers, carpenters, chicken-keepers, dyers, fruiterers, fullers, goldsmiths, grape-pickers, mule-drivers, ointment sellers and porters. Recommendations are also made by inhabitants of a particular district in the town, or by a candidate's neighbours (F21–25). Some candidates, however, boasted of the support of all citizens living in the town (both Pompeians and outsiders) or of the town council (F26–27, F111–113). Other unusual groups include worshippers of Isis (E7–8), spectators at the games (F28, on the external wall of the Large Palaestra, adjacent to the Amphitheatre) and fans of the actor Paris (D69). For an overview of the supporters of one particular candidate, see F29–72.

Individuals (F14–19)

F14 *CIL* IV 933

Thalamus, his client, elects Publius Paquius Proculus duumvir with judicial power.

F15 *CIL* IV 910

Ceratus, freedman, asks for Publius Vedius Numm[ianus] as aedile.

F16 *CIL* IV 98

Julius Polybius, his colleague, elects Postumius [. . .].

F17 House of Caecilius Iucundus (V.i.26), *CIL* IV 3433 = *ILS* 6404a

We, Quintus and Sextus Caecilius Iucundus, ask for Ceius Secundus as duumvir.

F18 Inn of Euxinus (I.xi.10–11), *CIL* IV 9851

Euxinus asks you to elect Quintus Postumius and Marcus Cerrinius aediles, together with Iustus. Hinnulus wrote this.

F19 Inn of Amarantus (I.ix.11), *CIL* IV 9829a

Amarantus Pompeianus asks you to elect Quintus Postumius Proculus aedile. Papilio (wrote this).

Occupational groups (F20)

F20 Fullery of Stephanus (I.vi.7), *CIL* IV 7164

The fullers all ask for Holconius Priscus as duumvir.

Town districts and neighbours (F21–25)

Four groups in electoral notices are probably the inhabitants of different districts: the *Forenses* (Forum-district: F21), the *Campanienses* (area next to the 'Campanian Gate', i.e. today's 'Nolan Gate': F22), the *Urbulanenses* (next to the 'Urbulanian Gate', i.e. today's 'Sarno Gate': F23) and the *Salinienses* (around the 'Salt Gate', i.e. today's 'Herculaneum Gate'; for its Oscan name see B5: F24).

F21 *CIL* IV 783

The *Forenses* ask for [. . .]

F22 *CIL* IV 470 = *ILS* 6438a

The *Campanienses* ask for Marcus Epidius Sabinus as aedile.

F23 *CIL* IV 7667 (next to F6)

The *Urb†u†lanenses* ask you to elect Lucius Ceius Secundus duumvir, worthy of public office.

F24 *CIL* IV 128 = *ILS* 6418a

The *Salinienses* ask for Marcus Cerrinius as aedile.

F25 *CIL* IV 6625 (next to F6)

We neighbours ask for [Marcus] Lucretius Fronto as aedile.

Larger groups in the population (F26–28)

F26 *CIL* IV 9918

We the town's citizens and resident aliens ask for Gaius Ateius Capito as aedile.

F27 *CIL* IV 1045

The people ask for Lucius Popidius Secundus as aedile.

F28 *CIL* IV 7585

The spectators in the amphitheatre ask for Holconius Priscus as duumvir with judicial power.

The campaign of Helvius Sabinus, AD 79 (F29–72)

The candidature of Gnaeus Helvius Sabinus for aedile is one of the best attested, with over 100 electoral notices discovered. This, and the fact that none of the notices concerning him seems to have been painted over by subsequent notices, make it likely that he stood for election in AD 79. Helvius can therefore be taken as an example of the sorts of electoral notices written on the walls of Pompeii.

Findspots of electoral notices supporting Helvius Sabinus

F29 shows the findspots of electoral notices in support of Helvius Sabinus. Not surprisingly, the notices occur most frequently along the busiest streets. The fact that fewest notices have been found in Regions VII and VIII may be explained partly by the fact that these areas, the first to be excavated, are the least accurately recorded. For example, two notices (F45 and F33) were discovered and copied in 1814, but their findspots are recorded so vaguely that little more can be said about their original location than that they were somewhere on streets near the southern end of the Forum.

F29 Findspots of electoral notices supporting Helvius Sabinus

See **Figure 6.1**.

Basic electoral notices (F30)

The majority of electoral notices concerning Helvius Sabinus simply give his *nomen* (family name – Helvius), with or without his *praenomen* (first name – Gnaeus, in the standard abbreviation, Cn.) and *cognomen* (additional or nickname – Sabinus). The post he is running for – aedile, abbreviated to AED – may also be given. One or more standard phrases of endorsement of the candidate may also be included: most of these are so standard as to be given in abbreviated form: *V(irum) B(onum)* – a good man; *D(ignum) R(ei) P(ublicae)* – worthy of public office; *O(ro) V(os) F(aciatis)* – I beg you to elect. Thus, for example, 'I beg you to elect Cn. Helvius Sabinus aedile, a good man, worthy of public office' is 'CN HELVIUM SABINUM AED VB DRP OVF.'

The candidate's name appears in large letters (usually 20 cm high, sometimes 60 cm). The endorsement, if there is one, is in smaller letters, on the line or two lines below. Because of the abbreviations used, the name of the candidate almost always takes up more room than the whole of the rest of the notice. For an example of an electoral notice see **Plate 4.1** on page 49.

F30 Basic types of notices supporting Helvius Sabinus

The following give the basic types of notices found in support of Sabinus, and their frequency.

(a) Helvius for aedile (4)
(b) Cn. Helvius for aedile (1)

Figure 6.1 F29 Findspots of electoral notices supporting Helvius Sabinus

(c) Helvius Sabinus (2)

(d) Cn. Helvius Sabinus (9)

(e) Cn. Helvius Sabinus for aedile (7)

(f) Cn. Helvius Sabinus for aedile, a good man (1)

(g) Cn. Helvius Sabinus for aedile, worthy of public office (3)

(h) I beg you to elect (Cn.) Helvius Sabinus aedile (17)

(i) I beg you to elect Cn. Helvius Sabinus, worthy of public office, aedile (18)

(j) I beg you to elect Cn. Helvius Sabinus, worthy of public office, a good man, aedile (6)

(k) I beg you to elect Helvius Sabinus, worthy of public office, aedile in charge of public roads and sacred buildings (3)

(l) Cn. H. S. (4)

(m) Cn. H. S. aedile (6)

(n) I beg you to elect Cn. H. S. aedile (2)

Endorsements of Helvius (F31–34)

On a few occasions, a less common phrase of endorsement is written out in full. Helvius'
description as a young man need not imply exceptional youth: see introductory notes to F4–10.

F31 *CIL* IV 1145 (Estate of Julia Felix, Street of Abundance)

Cn. Helvius Sabinus, an honest young man for aedile.

F32 *CIL* IV 6684, VI.xvi.38 and *CIL* IV 7754, III.vi.1 (Street of Abundance)

Helvius Sabinus an honest young man.

F33 *CIL* IV 706 = *ILS* 6420a

I beg you to elect Cn. Helvius Sabinus, a thoroughly deserving young man,
worthy of public office, aedile.

F34 *CIL* IV 9859

Cn. Helvius Sabinus, aedile for sacred matters.

Personal endorsements of Helvius Sabinus (F35–59)

On other occasions, the endorsement is made more personal by including the name of a particular person or group. Sometimes, a person states his intention of making Helvius aedile
(FAC(it) – he elects) (F43). In one case the past tense (FECIT) is used, which perhaps implies
that Helvius was elected, though it may just mean that the person voted for him (F35).
Endorsements also come from people who did not have the vote, for example, women (F51,
F53, F56–58). Some of these simply ask people to vote for Helvius, but others use the endorsement *FAC(it)* as if they had the vote.

F35 *CIL* IV 935d (IX.ii)

Balbus elected Cn. Helvius Sabinus aedile.

F36 *CIL* IV 7708 (III.iv.3, Street of Abundance)

Epidius with his household want and support Cn. Helvius Sabinus as aedile.

F37 *CIL* IV 3450 (V.ii west side)

Crescens asks for Cn. Helvius Sabinus as aedile.

F38 *CIL* IV 7595 (III.i.2, Street of Abundance)

Pacuvius eagerly asks for Cn. Helvius as aedile.

F39 *CIL* IV 3640 (IX.ii.25–27)

I beg you to elect Cn. Helvius Sabinus aedile, worthy of public office. Thyrsus votes for him.

F40 *CIL* IV 7525 (II.v.2, Street of Abundance)

I beg you to elect Helvius Sabinus aedile. Astylus wants it.

F41 *CIL* IV 3522 (VI.xv.1)

[. . .] Restitutus asks for [. . .] Sabinus as aedile

F42 *CIL* IV 3477 (VII.i.7/8, Street of Abundance)

Vesonius Primus asks for Cn. Helvius Sabinus, worthy of public office, as aedile.

F43 *CIL* IV 3482 (VI.xii.34)

Primus and his household elect Cn. Helvius Sabinus aedile.

F44 *CIL* IV 357 (IX.v.11, Street of Nola)

The Poppaei ask for Helvius Sabinus to be elected aedile.

F45 *CIL* IV 705

The Popidii ask for Helvius Sabinus as aedile.

F46 GC10 (I.xiv.11)

Equitius with his household asks for Cn. Helvius Sabinus as aedile, worthy of public office.

F47 *CIL* IV 7191 (I.vi.15)

Infantio with his household asks for Cn. Helvius Sabinus as aedile.

F48 *CIL* IV 7340 (I.x.4)

Infantio desires Helvius Sabinus as aedile.

F49 *CIL* IV 7213 (I.vii.1, Street of Abundance)

Amandio with his household asks for Cn. Helvius Sabinus as aedile, worthy of public office.

F50 *CIL* IV 9919 (I.xiv.7)

Porcellus with his household asks for Cn. Helvius Sabinus as aedile, worthy of public office.

F51 *CIL* IV 923 (IX.ii.9–10, Stabian Street)

We ask for Cn. Helvius Sabinus as aedile. Caprasia votes for him.

F52 *CIL* IV 9885 (II.iv.12, Nucerian Street)

Biri(us) with Biria ask you to elect Helvius Sabinus aedile, a good man, worthy of public office: Onomastus, vote for him eagerly.

F53 *CIL* IV 3403 (V.i.17/18, Stabian Street)

Parthope and Rufinus ask for Helvius Sabinus as aedile.

F54 GC 35 (III.iv.F, Nucerian Street)

Martialis, Pucta asks you to elect Helvius Sabinus aedile, worthy of public office.

F55 GC 27 (III.iv.E, Nucerian Street)

Sodala asks for Cn. Helvius Sabinus as aedile.

F56 *CIL* IV 1168 (in Naples Museum, findspot unknown)

Iunia asks for you to elect Cn. Helvius Sabinus aedile.

F57 *CIL* IV 7886 (IX.xi.1, Street of Abundance)

I beg you to elect Cn. Helvius Sabinus aedile, worthy of public office. Aegle asks this.

F58 *CIL* IV 7866 (IX.xi.2, Street of Abundance)

I beg you to elect Cn. Helvius Sabinus aedile, worthy of public office. Maria asks this.

F59 *CIL* IV 7733 (III.v.1, Street of Abundance)

Loreius, vote for Cn. Helvius Sabinus, an honest man, as aedile, and he will vote for you.

Endorsements by groups (F60–65)

On other occasions, the endorsement apparently comes from a group; see also **E7** for support from the worshippers of Isis. For the *Urbulanenses* (**F61**), see **F23**. He also seems to have fallen victim to negative campaigning (see also **F11–13**), being endorsed by dice-throwers (**F65**). The *caudati* of Masculus (*CIL* IV 7747), who supported him, remain unidentifiable.

F60 *CIL* IV 7273 (I.viii.7)

The millers ask for and desire Cn. Helvius Sabinus as aedile, together with his neighbours.

F61 *CIL* IV 7747 (III.vi.1)

The *Urbulane†n†ses* ask for Cn. Helvius Sabinus as aedile.

F62 *CIL* IV 241 (VI.xii.7)

Hermes with the chicken-keepers asks for Cn. Helvius as aedile.

F63 *CIL* IV 852 (IX.iii.30, Stabian Street)

His neighbours elect Cn. Helvius Sabinus aedile.

F64 *CIL* IV 7928 (IX.xiii.1)

His neighbours ask for Cn. Helvius Sabinus, an honest man, as aedile.

F65 *CIL* IV 3435 (VI.xiv.28)

The dice-throwers ask for Cn. Helvius Sabinus.

Multiple election notices (F66–70)

Finally a few electoral notices exist in which other candidates for aedile or duumvir are also recommended. This does not imply that Helvius stood for election on a 'joint ticket' with any other candidate; indeed three different duumviral candidates are mentioned with Helvius.

F66 *CIL* IV 447 (middle section of Street of Nola, north side)

I beg you to elect Cn. Helvius Sabinus, worthy of public office, aedile, and Suettius and Epidius duumvirs with judicial power.

F67 *CIL* IV 1083 (I.iv)

I beg you to elect Cn. Helvius Sabinus aedile and L. Ceius Secundus duumvir, Recepta and also Thalamus.

F68 GC11 (I.xvii.3)

I beg you to elect L. C. Secundus duumvir and Sabinus aedile, an honest man.

F69 GC4 (I.xiv.11)

Equitius asks you to elect Ceius duumvir and Helvius Sabinus aedile.

F70 *CIL* IV 6616 (V.iii.11) and *CIL* IV 6628 (V.iv.c)

I beg you to elect Cn. Helvius Sabinus and M. Samellius Modestus aediles, worthy of public office.

Other notices (F71–72)

The Latin word *dormis* (literally 'you sleep' or 'do you sleep?') appears on several electoral notices, including one for Helvius (**F71**). It seems to imply that someone should wake up and vote for a candidate. **F72** almost certainly is a mistake by the writer: Marcus Epidius Sabinus was a candidate for duumvir in the same year as Helvius Sabinus was candidate for aedile, which presumably confused the writer of the notice.

F71 *CIL* IV 2993t (I.iv. south side)

Wake up and vote for Helvius Sabinus for aedile.

F72 *CIL* IV 7034 (V.vi.b/c)

Cn. Helvius Sabinus for [duum]vir.

Acclamation after an election (F73)

This notice, on an internal wall of the Amphitheatre, appears to broadcast the recent election of Paquius Proculus.

F73 *CIL* IV 1122 = *ILS* 6406a

All Pompeians have elected Publius <P>aquius Proculus duumvir with judicial power, worthy of public office.

The notice-writers (F74–81)

Most of the electoral notices were the work of the same specialist sign-writers who produced the notices for games (D9–24). Sign-writers worked in teams at night. One team appears to have consisted of at least four men (F74; see also F13). (For night-time, see D11 and F75.) The team members subdivided the tasks according to individual expertise, with, for example, one man preparing the background of whitewash and another the actual lettering. Sometimes they signed a notice or added their support for a candidate. Some twenty-seven sign-writers have been identified. In one case, the sign-writer was also a fuller (F76); his comment appears beside a notice endorsing Marcus Pupius Rufus. See also F18.

Teamwork (F74–77)

F74 *CIL* IV 230

[. . .] asks for Marcus Cerrinius Vatia as aedile, worthy of public office [. . .]. Infantio wrote this with Florus and Fructus and Sabinus here and everywhere.

F75 *CIL* IV 7621

Lantern carrier, hold the ladder.

F76 *CIL* IV 3529 = *ILS* 6408b

The fuller Mustius elects and whitewashes. Unico writes, without the rest of the team on the *Nones*.

F77 *CIL* IV 222 = *ILS* 6434

I beg you elect Publius Paquius Proculus duumvir, a good man, worthy of public office; Aulus Vettius Caprasius Felix duumvir, a good man, worthy of public office; they are worthy. I beg you to elect Quintus Marius [Rufus], Marcus Epidius Sabinus aediles in charge of streets, sacred and public buildings; they are worthy [. . .] Onesimus was the whitewasher.

The sign-writer Aemilius Celer (F78–81)

One sign-writer, Aemilius Celer, identifies himself on both types of notices (D11 and F78–79), which cluster around IX.viii, near where he himself lived. His name shows that he was a citizen; he even added his own voice as a neighbour in one notice supporting a candidate for duumvir (F79). His name also appears three times in IX.ix.[a], a house near where several of his notices are found (F80–81).

F78 *CIL* IV 3820 (IX.viii.4) = *ILS* 6407b

Neighbours beg you to elect Tiberius Claudius Verus [duumvir] with judicial power. Aemilius Celer wrote this.

F79 *CIL* IV 3775 (IX.vii.8) = *ILS* 6409

Neighbours beg you to elect Lucius Statius Receptus duumvir with judicial power, a worthy man. Aemilius Celer wrote this, a neighbour. You jealous one who destroys this, may you fall ill.

F80 *CIL* IV 3790 (IX.ix.[a])

Publius Aemilius Celer.

F81 *CIL* IV 3794 (IX.ix.[a])

Aemilius Celer lives here.

Beyond Pompeii: electioneering for Munatius Caeserninus of Nuceria (F82–85)

The candidature of Munatius Caeserninus for the office of quinquennial at nearby Nuceria was promoted in notices painted on the façades of several tombs outside the Nucerian Gate of Pompeii. One notice even reminds Nucerian voters of the games he has already provided for them (F83).

F82 *CIL* IV 3875 = *ILS* 6445c and *AE* (1990) 176

I beg you to elect Lucius Munatius Caeserninus quinquennial duumvir at Nuceria, a good man.

F83 *CIL* IV 9939

Lucius Munatius Caeserninus for quinquennial, Nucerians: you have watched the boxers.

F84 *CIL* IV 9942

I beg you to elect Lucius Munatius quinquennial and [Lucius] Magius Celer duumvir, good men.

F85 *CIL* IV 9959

I beg you to elect [Lucius Munatius C]ae[se]rninus quinquennial, Nucerians.

Magisterial duties (F86)

In many respects the magistrates of the Roman colony continued the administrative duties of the Oscan magistrates who preceded them (**A8–12, A16–17, A22, A24**). The town's duumvirs and aediles between them were responsible for civic finances, public religion (**E5, E11, E13, E28–31, E34, E36–37**) and public space (**D1–3, D5**). A decree of the council would authorize the duumvirs in office to negotiate a contract for building work, which they were then responsible for seeing to its satisfactory completion (**B7–9, B11, D106, E1**). For the obligation of magistrates to pay for building work or for games during their year in office, see **B11, D16, D19–20, D57**. An inscription found outside the Stabian Gate (**F86**) records road-building of duumvirs outside the town itself, into Pompeii's territory. For the supervision of weights and measures, see **H64**. The aediles supervised the markets: for their control of stalls around the Amphitheatre, see **H65**.

F86 *CIL* X 1064 = *ILS* 5382

Lucius Avianius Flaccus Pontianus, son of Lucius, of the Menenian tribe, and Quintus Spedius Firmus, son of Quintus, of the Menenian tribe, duumvirs with judicial power, paved the road at their own expense from the milestone to the station of the carriage drivers, where it is in Pompeii's territory.

Careers (F87–95)

Under-age town councillors (F87)

Numerius Popidius Celsinus was appointed to the town council when only 6 years old in return for his restoration of the Temple of Isis, probably after the earthquake in AD 62 (**C5**). It is likely that his father, Popidius Ampliatus, paid for the reconstruction in his son's name since he himself, as a freedman, was excluded from membership of the town council. Nevertheless, it is now apparent that the co-option of the child Celsinus was not just a tactic to deal with a family whose adult member was excluded from the council. The recent discovery of the family tomb of the Lucretii Valentes shows that at least two other children were made town councillors (**G21, G24**). Unlike Popidius Celsinus, these boys belonged to one of the most prominent families of the Neronian and Flavian periods. Marcus Alleius Libella, who was only 17 at the time of his death, had already been made a town councillor too (**F87**).

Tomb of the Alleii outside the Herculaneum Gate (F87)

A large altar-tomb outside the Herculaneum Gate illustrates the problems encountered by the elite in ensuring their family's survival. This tomb was set up by Alleia Decimilla to her husband and son. Marcus Alleius Luccius Libella, quinquennial in AD 25/26 (*CIL* X 896), had been adopted by a Marcus Alleius, and had married his daughter Alleia Decimilla.

F87 *CIL* X 1036 = *ILS* 6365

To Marcus Alleius Luccius Libella, father, aedile, duumvir, prefect, quinquennial; and to Marcus Alleius Libella, son, town councillor, (who) lived
17 years; a place for the monument was given publicly; Alleia Decimilla,
daughter of Marcus, public priestess of Ceres, saw to this being done for her
husband and son.

Premature deaths – Gaius Vestorius Priscus, aedile (F88)

The tomb of Gaius Vestorius Priscus is located just outside the Vesuvian Gate. His epitaph
appears on an eye-catching tomb, which is set inside a rectangular enclosure, and topped by
an altar. Inside the enclosure, the tomb's walls display scenes in stucco and painting. These
include a table covered with silver banqueting vessels and a combat between a pair of gladiators (probably alluding to games presented by Vestorius). Vestorius himself perhaps features
in another scene opposite the tomb's entrance, which would have greeted visitors to the tomb.
This shows a man entering a room, where there are writing implements and money on tables,
and slippers beneath a couch. A smaller figure, probably a slave, stands in attendance to one
side. Elsewhere, a seated figure raised up on a podium, surrounded by standing figures below,
may depict Vestorius executing some of his public duties as aedile. He was probably a candidate for the post of aedile in AD 75/76. Given the public honours granted to Vestorius after
his death, it seems likely that he died while holding office as aedile.

F88 *AE* (1913) 70

To Gaius Vestorius Priscus, aedile. He lived 22 years. His burial place was
granted along with 2,000 sesterces for his funeral by decree of the town councillors. Mulvia Prisca, his mother, set this up at {her own} expense.

An outstanding career – Marcus Holconius Rufus (F89)

Marcus Holconius Rufus enjoyed a long and prominent career in public life, from the 20s BC
to the early first century AD, accumulating an unparalled sequence of magistracies, and being
selected as one of the few men known to have been the colony's patron. This was an important role, since the task of a patron was to protect the town's interests at Rome. Formally
selected by the town council, patrons could be prominent locals or important figures at Rome,
even members of the imperial family. Other patrons of Pompeii included Publius Sulla (nephew
of the dictator Sulla, charged with establishing the new colony) (**B15**), Marcellus, the emperor
Augustus' nephew and son-in-law (**F101**), and an otherwise unknown Sallustius (**F90**).

Holconius Rufus was of equestrian rank, but his statue (NM inv. 6233) appropriated status
symbols more correctly belonging to others. His statue shows him in military dress, complete
with tunic, breastplate and cloak; this alludes to his post of military tribune, even though he
did not actually serve in the army in this role! He is depicted wearing the sandals of a senator,
and the design on his breastplate imitates that of the famous cult statue of Mars the Avenger
in the Forum of Augustus in Rome. Colouring was visible when the statue was first found
in 1853: his tunic was white, edged with yellow, his cloak red, and shoes black. The tree
trunk supporting the statue was green. His hair, irises and eyebrows were also coloured. The
statue stood on an inscribed base just outside the main entrance to the Stabian Baths, at the
foot of the pillar of a large arch, which punctuated a major crossroads on the Street of
Abundance. This arch is thought to have honoured other members of his family too, including
a Holconia (**E48**). For his generosity and honours in the Large Theatre, see **D51**, **D53–54**.
On sources for his wealth, see **H49**.

Other Holconii were also prominent in public life, and not just his partner in public works, Marcus Holconius Celer (**D51**, **D55**, **F96**). Further generations continued to prosper: Marcus Holconius Gellius was duumvir under Tiberius (*CIL* X 895); Marcus Holconius Macer stood in for the emperor himself, as prefect with judicial powers under Caligula (*CIL* X 904); and Marcus Holconius Priscus was a candidate for election as aedile and then as duumvir during the last years of the town (**F20**, **F28**).

Plate 6.1 **F89a Statue of Marcus Holconius Rufus**

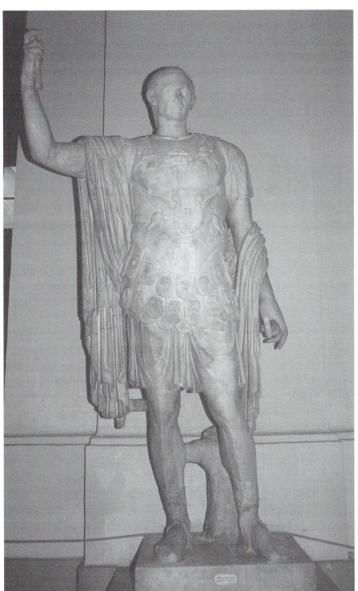

F89b *CIL* X 830 = *ILS* 6361b

To Marcus Holconius Rufus, son of Marcus, military tribune by popular demand, duumvir with judicial power five times, quinquennial twice, priest of Augustus Caesar, and patron of the colony.

Statues in the Forum (F90–95)

For the equestrian statue of a Lucretius Valens, possibly also set up in the Forum, see G24.

A patron's equestrian statue (F90)

F90 *CIL* X 792

To Quintus Sallustius, son of Publius, duumvir with judicial power, quinquennial, patron. By decree of the town councillors.

A commercial success (F91)

This epitaph reveals that Aulus Umbricius Scaurus the younger had been granted an equestrian statue in the Forum, of which no trace has been found. The inscription has been attached to the wrong tomb since 1813, after it was found in pieces in the street in front of the line of tombs outside the Herculaneum Gate (J29). For this family's fish sauce business, see H20–29.

F91 *CIL* X 1024 = *ILS* 6366

To Aulus Umbricius Scaurus, son of Aulus, of the Menenian tribe, duumvir with judicial power. The town councillors voted for him a site for his monument, 2,000 sesterces for his funeral, and an equestrian statue to be set up in the Forum. His father Scaurus dedicated this to his son.

Pedestrian statues (F92–95)

Marcus Lucretius was probably honoured in the Augustan period, and the Cuspii Pansae under Nero. See further D6–7 for the Cuspii Pansae in the Amphitheatre.

F92 *CIL* X 788 = *ILS* 6363b

To Marcus Lucretius Decidianus Rufus, duumvir three times, quinquennial, priest, military tribune by popular demand, staff officer. Marcus Pilonius Rufus (set this up).

F93 *CIL* X 789 = *ILS* 6363c

To Marcus Lucretius Decidianus Rufus, duumvir three times, quinquennial, priest, military tribune by popular demand, staff officer. By decree of the town councillors after his death.

F94 *CIL* X 790

To Gaius Cuspius Pansa, son of Gaius, duumvir with judicial power four times, quinquennial. By decree of the town councillors, at public expense.

F95 *CIL* X 791

To Gaius Cuspius Pansa, son of Gaius, son, priest, duumvir with judicial power. By decree of the town councillors, at public expense.

Country district officials (F96–99)

Several inscriptions mention presidents (*magistri*) or attendants (*ministri*) of country districts. These were the rural equivalent of the presidents and attendants of urban districts (**E62–64**). Like them, these men tended to be freedmen and slaves respectively, and were thus excluded from membership of the local town council. Although we do not have any direct evidence for their carrying out religious duties, it is likely that they did so, as part of their local administrative responsibilities. By acting as officials of a country district, they could gain prestige and status, as well as acting as public benefactors. Such men clearly took some pride in their positions, commemorating their status upon their tombs (**F98**). The epitaph of Marcus Obellius Firmus (**G12**) reveals that the inhabitants of a country district (*pagani*) had a formal system for meeting and passing decrees, much like the town council did. This also lies behind the dedication of an honorific statue to Marcus Holconius Celer by *pagani* (**F96**).

Honorific dedication of a statue by pagani (F96)

This statue base was found reused in one of the buildings at the south end of the Forum; its letters had been erased with a chisel, but it was still possible to read the text.

F96 *CIL* X 944

To Marcus Holconius [Celer], son of Marcus, duumvir with judicial power, quinquennial [designate, priest] of Augustus; the inhabitants of a country district (set this up).

Fortunate Augustan Suburban Country District (F97–99)

One particular district, the Fortunate Augustan Suburban Country District, is prominent in the historical record: it was apparently reorganized in 7 BC, perhaps related in some way to that year's reorganization of the city of Rome by Augustus into regions, wards and neighbourhoods. The presidents of this district also acted as benefactors in the town itself, paying for part of the Amphitheatre's stone seating (**D1**).

The first attendants (F97)

F97 illustrates a sense of hierarchy even between slaves, since the slave of a member of the imperial household is given prominence at the start of the list. 'Agrippa Minor' is Agrippa Postumus (grandson of Augustus), aged 5 in 7 BC. He nominally owned a villa somewhere near Pompeii, and also a roof-tile workshop, revealed by roof-tiles of 11 BC stamped with the inscription 'workshop of Agrippa Minor'.

F97 *CIL* X 924 = *ILS* 6381, 7 BC

Dama, slave of Agrippa Minor, Manlianus slave of Lucretius, Anteros slave of Staius Rufus, Princeps slave of Mescinius, the first attendants of the Fortunate Augustan Suburban Country District set this up, in the consulship of Tiberius Claudius Nero for the second time and Gnaeus Calpurnius Piso.

Tomb of a president (F98)

This epitaph was found on a tomb outside Herculaneum Gate, accompanied by a relief showing two *fasces* with axes, symbols of authority more normally associated with consuls at Rome or local magistrates.

F98 *CIL* X 1042 = *ILS* 6378

Marcus Arrius Diomedes, freedman of a woman, (set this up) to himself and his family to their memory; president of the Fortunate Augustan Suburban Country District.

Tomb of a country district dweller (F99)

This inscription was found outside the Herculaneum Gate. As well as acting as an epitaph, it regulates the dimensions of the tomb enclosure.

F99 *CIL* X 1027 = *ILS* 6379

To Numerius Istacidius Helenus, inhabitant of the Augustan Country District; to Numerius Istacidius Ianuarius; to Mesonia Satulla. 15 feet deep, 15 feet broad.

The impact of Rome (F100–114)

Imperial honours (F100–104)

Statue of Augustus (F100)

This inscription was not itself found, but only the impression left by its letters, where it had fallen. It can be dated to 9/8 BC from Augustus' titles.

F100 *CIL* X 931

To Imperator Caesar Augustus [son of the deified, hailed as victorious general] thirteen times, in his fifteenth year of tribunician power, father of his country, [consul eleven times].

Statue of Marcellus (F101)

Marcellus was nephew and son-in-law to Augustus. This inscribed marble base for a pedestrian statue was found in a prominent location, opposite the main entrance to the Triangular Forum. For patrons of Pompeii, see notes on **F89**.

F101 *CIL* X 832 = *ILS* 898

To Marcus Claudius Marcellus, son of Gaius, patron.

Statue of Julia Augusta (Livia) (F102)

This honorific inscription was found in the Forum, near the Temple of Jupiter. It belongs to the period after Augustus's death and deification in AD 14.

F102 *CIL* X 799 = *ILS* 122

To Augusta Julia, daughter of Drusus, (wife) of the deified Augustus. By decree of the town councillors.

Statue of Nero as Caesar (F103)

This statue was voted to the future emperor, Nero, after he had been adopted by Claudius, but before he himself had become emperor, i.e. AD 51–4. Compare **D12–15** for a priest of Nero as Caesar.

F103 *CIL* X 932 = *ILS* 224

To Tiberius Claudius Nero Caesar, son of Tiberius Claudius Caesar Augustus Germanicus, father of his country. By decree of the town councillors.

Statue of Agrippina the Younger (F104)

This inscription commemorates the Younger Agrippina (Nero's mother) as wife of Claudius, so presumably belongs to the same period as **F103**.

F104 *CIL* X 933

To [Julia] Agrippina, daughter of Germanicus Caesar, (wife) of [Tiberius] Claudius Caesar Augustus.

Good wishes for rival imperial wives in graffiti (F105–106)

Neither of these graffiti is well preserved, but the following texts have been suggested for them. Both appear on exterior walls of private buildings. For more graffiti regarding Nero and Poppaea, see D40–42, E19–20.

F105 *CIL* IV 8277

Octavia, wife of Augustus. Good wishes and good health to you.

F106 *CIL* IV 10049

Good fortune to Poppaea Augusta. Good fortune.

The emperor Gaius Caligula as honorary magistrate of Pompeii (F107–108)

The future emperor Gaius Caligula was honoured by being nominated twice as the town's duumvir: in AD 34, when he was still Tiberius' heir (F107–108), and in AD 40/41 when emperor (*CIL* X 904). This was an honorific position only: the real work was done by a prefect in each of those years, Marcus Lucretius Epidius Flaccus and Marcus Holconius Macer. In common with inscriptions bearing his name throughout the Roman world, his name is erased from an inscription set up by the attendants of Augustus in AD 34, indicated below by brackets [[. . .]], but, unusually, his name is preserved in another similar inscription.

F107 *CIL* X 901 = *ILS* 6396

[. . . Phroni]mus slave of Messius Faustus; [Pl]acidus, slave of Veius Fronto; Aulus Arellius Graecus, attendants of Augustus by decree of the town councillors by command of [[Gaius Caesar and]] Marcus Vesonius Marcellus, duumvirs with judicial power and Marcus Lucretius Epidius Flaccus, prefect, and of Lucius Albucius and Decimus Lucretius, duumvirs in charge of streets, sacred and public buildings; in the consulship of Paullus Fabius and Lucius Vitellius.

F108 *CIL* X 902

Phr[onimus, slave of Messius Faustus]; Placi[dus slave of Veius Fronto]; Aulus Are[llius Graecus], attendants [of Augustus, by decree of the town councillors, by command of Marcus Vesonius Marcellus, duumvir with judicial power and of Marcus L]ucretius Epidius Flac[cus, prefect with judicial power] of Gaius Caesar; and of Lucius Albucius Celsus and Decimus Lucretius Valens, duumvirs in charge of the streets, sacred and public buildings, in the consulship of Paullus Fabius and Lucius Vitellius.

The intervention of Vespasian's agent, Suedius Clemens
(F109–114)

Reclaiming public lands (F109)

Following his accession in AD 69, after traumatic civil wars (including the so-called 'Year of the Four Emperors'), the emperor Vespasian was particularly concerned to stabilize the empire's finances. The actions of his agent at Pompeii, who undertook to investigate the usurpation of public lands by individuals and to reassign them to the town, was typical of Vespasian's initiatives as a whole. Multiple copies of this inscription documenting the intervention of Suedius Clemens were set up: examples have been found outside the Herculaneum, Vesuvian and Nucerian Gates.

F109 *CIL* X 1018 = *ILS* 5942

By the authority of Imperator Caesar Vespasian Augustus, Titus Suedius Clemens, tribune, made an inquiry into public lands appropriated by private individuals, carried out a survey, and restored them to the Pompeian state.

Electoral influence (F110–114)

Suedius Clemens' influence extended beyond his judicial business on behalf of the emperor into the realm of local politics, with his support being cited in several electoral notices favouring the candidature of Marcus Epidius Sabinus. One of these, at the major crossroad junction by the Stabian Baths, is unusually long and detailed (F111). Others reveal that Epidius Sabinus also enjoyed the support of the town council itself, a unique claim, but hardly surprising given the circumstances (F111–113).

F110 *CIL* IV 791 = *ILS* 6438b

I beg you to elect Marcus Epidius Sabinus duumvir with judicial power, in accordance with the opinion of Suedius Clemens.

F111 *CIL* IV 768 = *ILS* 6438d

I beg you to elect Marcus Epidius Sabinus duumvir with judicial power. He is worthy. May you elect one who is a protector of the colony according to the opinion of Suedius Clemens, the worshipful judge, and by agreement of the whole council on account of his merits and his honesty, worthy of public office. Sabinus, the theatre official, elects him with applause.

F112 *CIL* IV 7605

Trebius, his client, asks you to elect Epidius Sabinus duumvir with judicial power, with the support of the most venerable council.

F113 *CIL* IV 7579

I beg you to elect Marcus Epidius Sabinus duumvir with judicial power, a most worthy young man. The venerable council is electing him. Good fortune to Clemens, venerable judge.

F114 *CIL* IV 1059 = *ILS* 6438c

We beg you to elect Marcus Epidius Sabinus duumvir with judicial power, a worthy young man. Suedius Clemens, most venerable judge, elects him at the request of his neighbours.

7

TOMBS

The tombs lining the streets leading away from the town provide a curious picture of Pompeian society. The streets beyond the Herculaneum and Nucerian Gates have been extensively explored, but much more still remains undiscovered beyond the other gates. The tombs show how people wished to be remembered after their deaths. Writing inside and outside tombs, pictures that have been painted or created in stucco or in sculpted relief, as well as the physical form of the overall tomb enclosure and individual monument, often projected a carefully calculated image of a single individual or of a family as a whole. At first glance, the same people dominated the landscape outside the town as inside: the grandest tombs commemorated the wealthy elite whose statues and buildings dominated the town (**G4–12, G15**). Nevertheless, sections of society who did not commonly appear in monumental inscriptions within the town's walls – freedmen and freedwomen (**G1, G27–35**), children (**G54–55**), the lower classes (**G56–58**), even slaves (**G42–46, G51**) – had more prominence outside the town.

An overall survey of the town's tombs will not, however, give us an accurate picture of the town's population. Although they do appear, children and slaves are under-represented, while freedmen and freedwomen are over-represented. We also know little about the town's population before the colony was established: only a glimpse is provided by the discovery of a family burial ground beyond the Stabian Gate, which was apparently used continuously by the same family from pre-Roman times onwards (**G1–3**), and by Samnite burials outside the Herculaneum Gate. This confirms that it was Roman colonists who introduced monumental tomb architecture to the town, which was then gradually adopted by local families too. Also, most of the last generation of Pompeians is not represented, for obvious reasons: a few Flavian tombs exist, but most date from Augustan to Neronian times.

With these caveats in mind, we can still mine the tombs for information about society and funerary customs, tracing family relationships and social mobility (e.g. **G27–32**), political careers (**F87–88, F98, G4–5, G7–8, G12**) and occupations (**H52, H60**). Some non-Pompeians who had the misfortune to die away from home are also found (**G66–69**), while others died having

137

migrated to live in Pompeii (G61–65). By studying the inscriptions in context, looking not just at the epitaph, but also at the actual burial and structure of the tomb, we can recreate some of the religious rites performed at the graveside (notes to G12–14, G66). Most of the tomb enclosures contained multiple burials, in the form of cremations. Ashes were placed in urns, which were either stored in niches inside a tomb, or buried underground beneath a herm, a form of funerary monument common only in this part of Campania: see G16a. This was a small upright stone carved into a generalized human head shape, with only the hairstyle at the back indicating a male or female figure. The herm itself would thus mark the actual point of burial, and would often be connected to the urn below by a pipe, which allowed for the pouring of libations onto the ashes. Not all herms were inscribed, but many display simple texts recording the deceased's name and age. Despite their humble appearance, they might be used for magistrate and child, male and female, slave and free alike. Another local type of tomb was the so-called 'exedra' or 'seat-tomb' (E40, G4–9). These were large monuments, consisting of a masonry seat (usually semicircular) capable of accommodating at least eight weary passers-by. All tombs of this type at Pompeii are situated just outside a gate, and all were granted as a public honour to the deceased.

Fondo Azzolini necropolis (G1–3)

A necropolis was found by chance in 1911, about 500 metres beyond the Stabian Gate. In an area (*c.*400 square metres) enclosed by a wall, 44 inhumations from the fourth to second centuries BC were discovered, and, including the Roman burials above the Samnite ones, there were over 160 burials in all. Almost all the pre-Roman tombs are non-monumental, with only one (Tomb X) containing two small burial chambers preceded by a vestibule. Among the few grave goods were some coins minted at Naples, metal strigils (used by bathers to clean themselves), bronze bracelets and silver earrings. Tomb XVII contained the remains of a dog. There were 119 Roman-period cremations, with herms commemorating members of the Epidii family. Two lead curse-tablets were found (one damning a victim's face, hair, brain, lungs and kidneys, *CIL* IV 9251) and a coin from the reign of Claudius. It seems that the whole area was a family burial-ground, belonging to the Epidii – a notable family at Pompeii from Oscan times down until AD 79 (A17, F107–108, F110–114) – where burial practices changed over time.

G1 *NSc* (1916) 303

Mythus, freedman of Epidius Flaccus, lived 75 years.

G2 *Pompei oltre la vita* no. 19, herm

Epidia Agate.

G3 *NSc* (1916) 303

Vibia Pelagia, lived 40 years.

Public tombs: honouring the elite (G4–12)

Seat-tombs (G4–9)

Outside the Herculaneum Gate (G4)

G4 *CIL* X 996 (tomb 2 left)

To Aulus Veius, son of Marcus, duumvir with judicial power twice, quinquennial, military tribune by popular demand. By decree of the town
councillors.

See **E40** for Mamia (Tomb 4 left).

Outside the Nolan Gate (G5)

This tomb is Tiberian/Claudian in date. In the middle at the back of the semicircular seat is
a column with an Ionic capital, supporting a marble vase.

G5 *AE* (1911) 71

Numerius Herennius Celsus, son of Numerius, of the Menenian tribe,
duumvir with judicial power twice, staff officer, to Aesquillia Polla, daughter
of Gaius, his wife. She lived 22 years; a burial place was given publicly by
decree of the town councillors.

Outside the Stabian Gate (G6–8)

G6–7 had both ceased to be looked after by AD 79, since rubbish was found dumped in them,
including other funerary inscriptions. For Marcus Tullius, see also **E32–33**. Further on from
them was a variation on the seat-type of tomb, which was rectilinear in plan rather than semicircular (G8). A large marble relief was found with it, depicting a procession, gladiatorial
games and beast hunts.

G6 *EE* VIII no. 330

To Marcus Tullius, son of Marcus, by decree of the town councillors.

G7 *EE* VIII no. 318

To Marcus Alleius Minius, son of Quintus, of the Menenian tribe, duumvir
with judicial power; a place for burial was given publicly by decree of the
town councillors.

G8 *CIL* X 1065

To Gnaeus Clovatius, son of Gnaeus, duumvir with judicial power, military tribune; [burial] place [given in accordance with a decree of the town councillors].

Outside the Vesuvian Gate (G9)

Arellia Tertulla was possibly the wife of Marcus Stlaborius Veius Fronto, a prominent magistrate, who was quinquennial in AD 25/6.

G9 *NSc* (1910) 405

To [Ar]ellia Tertulla, daughter of Numerius, wife of Veius Fronto. To her the town councillors gave a burial place after her death and decreed a funeral at public expense.

Other public tombs (G10–12)

Not all people honoured with public tombs were prominent magistrates, benefactors or priestesses, or married to such. Although granting a seat-tomb appears to have been the highest public acknowledgement for an individual after his or her death, other degrees of public honour were also granted to individuals. Some of these individuals were young men who had started upon their careers in public life, but had died before advancing far. It is likely that these young men were honoured as much for the prominence of the family they had just departed as for any achievements of their own. See also **F87–88**, **F91**.

Outside the Vesuvian Gate (G10)

G10 is displayed on a high podium supporting a column, which perhaps originally bore a vase, like the tomb of Aesquillia Polla (**G5**). For another honorific tomb in this area, see **F88**.

G10 *AE* (1913) 71

To Septumia, daughter of Lucius. Granted by decree of the town councillors a burial place and 2,000 sesterces for the funeral. Antistia Prima, daughter of Publius, her daughter, built (this monument).

Outside the Herculaneum Gate (G11)

A Titus Terentius Felix appears as a witness in Tablet 80 from the Iucundus archive (*CIL* IV 3340.80, undatable), so if this is the same man, as seems likely, he may have died some time after AD 62 (the date of the latest tablet). A glass urn was found underneath a small altar to the left of the entrance to his tomb enclosure. Nearby were the urns of other family members.

G11 *CIL* X 1019 (tomb 2 right)

To Titus Terentius Felix Maior, son of Titus, of the Menenian tribe, aedile. To him publicly a place given and 2,000 sesterces. Fabia Sabina, daughter of Probus, his wife.

Outside the Nolan Gate (G12)

The tomb of Marcus Obellius Firmus was discovered in 1975. The recent date of its excavation has ensured a more detailed examination of the burial as a whole, not just of the tomb's architecture and inscriptions. It consists of a rectangular enclosure around the burial place, which is marked by an uninscribed herm. Fragments of a light-blue cinerary jar with handles and lid were uncovered *c*.20 cm beneath the surface. A terracotta pipe for libations led from the ground surface beside the herm to the subsoil next to the urn. This contained the remains of the funerary pyre, not just ash, but also fragments of half-burned decorative bone, possibly from the funerary couch, which had been burned together with the body. The exterior façade of the tomb's enclosure displays several painted inscriptions and graffiti, including an announcement of games. The funerary inscription is high up in the centre, on the front of the tomb. The grant of 5,000 sesterces is significantly higher than the sum of 2,000 mentioned in other funerary inscriptions. See F96–99 for comment on the inhabitants of the country district.

G12 De Franciscis (1976) 246

To Marcus Obellius Firmus, son of Marcus, aedile, duumvir with judicial power. The town councillors decreed him a burial place and 5,000 sesterces for his funeral; the inhabitants of the country district decreed him 30 pounds of frankincense and a shield, and their attendants 1,000 sesterces for perfumes, and a shield.

Cult of the dead (G13–14)

Both of these inscriptions were found on herms outside the Herculaneum Gate. The *Iuno* was the female equivalent of the *Genius* (see E54–57), the divine spirit or guardian believed to occupy every individual. Offerings to the departed spirit would have been poured down a clay pipe leading from the herm to the ashes below (see G12).

G13 *CIL* X 1009 = *ILS* 8055

To the *Iuno* of Melissaea Amyce.

G14 *CIL* X 1023 = *ILS* 8053

To the *Iuno* of Tyche, (slave) of Julia Augusta, worshipper of Venus (?).

Eumachia's tomb: changes over time (G15–19)

The tomb (11OS, outside the Nucerian Gate) of the public priestess and benefactor, Eumachia, was exceptionally grand, the largest tomb discovered so far. It consisted of three parts: a large terrace, raised up above street level, which led to a huge seat area, with finally an enclosure behind, where burials were placed. This was framed at the rear by a tall frontage, topped by a frieze of an Amazon fight. Its façade was 13.9 metres long, and it extended back 13.09 metres. Entrance to the tomb was via a locked door, which gave access to the seven steps up to the terrace. G15 (Plate 7.1) shows the terrace with the seat, and herms found in situ.

Unlike other major benefactors, Eumachia was not the recipient of a public seat-tomb. The tomb which she built for herself, however, incorporated a huge seat area, 13.55 by 5.65 metres, much bigger than any of the seats granted by the council. Much of the tomb's decoration had been plundered before it was excavated, probably largely during late antiquity, given finds of late-Roman objects there.

Eumachia's own funerary inscription was a simple epitaph divided in two across the main façade of the tomb (E47). Ten herms were found on the terrace, but six do not bear inscriptions. From the four inscribed herms (G16–19), it is possible to trace how use of the tomb was extended from Eumachia and her immediate family in Tiberian times to the family of the prominent Alleius Nigidius Maius (on whom, see D19–24 and H50), by Neronian times or later. The herms record the burial here of his adoptive mother and some of his freedmen. This implies that the two families had become linked, perhaps by adoption. Judging from his name, Alleius Nigidius Maius himself had been born a Nigidius, and then been adopted by the Alleii. The possibility that his adoptive mother may have been a freedwoman (again, judging from her name) suggests that his career may have been one of striking social mobility. The other herms, of his freedmen (G18–19), show how they too basked a little in his reflected glory.

Plate 7.1 G15 Eumachia's tomb

Plate 7.2 G16a Herm of Eumachius Aprilis

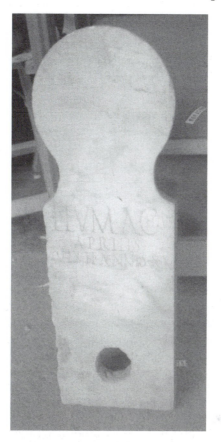

G16b D'Ambrosio and De Caro (1983) 11OS no. 7

Lucius Eumachius Aprilis, lived 20 years.

G17 D'Ambrosio and De Caro (1983) 11OS no. 13

Pomponia Decharcis, wife of Alleius Nobilis, mother of Alleius Maius.

G18 D'Ambrosio and De Caro (1983) 11OS no. 10

To Gnaeus Alleius Eros, freedman of Maius, appointed as *Augustalis* free of charge, to whom the *Augustales* and inhabitants of the country district decreed 1,000 sesterces for his funeral rites. Lived 22 years.

G19 D'Ambrosio and De Caro (1983) 11OS no. 12

Gnaeus Alleius Logus, deserving of all colleges.

Tomb of the Lucretii Valentes: fight for survival of a family name (G20–26)

Many more tombs still remain to be uncovered along the roads leading further out into countryside beyond the town. A recent discovery gives some idea of what may yet be found elsewhere. The tomb of the Lucretii Valentes is located in the modern district of Scafati, to the south-east of Pompeii. It consists of an enclosure containing seven burials and a commemorative plaque honouring another member of the family, buried elsewhere. One possible reconstruction of the family's relationships and development is given in **Figure 7.1**, but there is much scope for confusion and alternative interpretations, given the repeated occurrence of individuals called Decimus Lucretius Valens.

The Lucretii Valentes were a prominent family, whose lavish gladiatorial shows are known from painted notices (**D11–15**). The joint presentation of games (thirty pairs of gladiators) by father and son is highly unusual, but the new evidence from this tomb shows that another father and son from this family had also done exactly the same thing some time earlier (**G24**). The reason for this unusual pattern may lie in another unusual achievement, revealed by the epitaphs, which was the fact that at least two members of the family had been nominated to the town council as children (**G21** and **G24**). We may suppose, then, that the presentation of games by father and son may have marked the child's nomination, and may explain why the son did not sponsor the games on his own. What their family tomb also allows us to see in more detail is how the family had to fight for survival in the face of premature deaths, and how adoption was one weapon by which a family name might be perpetuated.

Two tufa herms without inscriptions may date from the Augustan era. Four herms bunched together in a single part of the tomb appear to represent the immediate family of Decimus Lucretius Valens (aedile in AD 33/34). The largest herm, with female characteristics, could be his wife, but its inscription has been erased by weathering. The second largest herm is of Decimus Lucretius Valens himself (**G20**); then two increasingly smaller herms represent his two sons, both of whom died young, Decimus Lucretius Valens (**G22**) and Decimus Lucretius Iustus (**G21**). The commemorative plaque on the tomb's façade may have honoured another son of his, perhaps also called Decimus Lucretius Valens, who (the tone of the inscription implies) may have died in his twenties (**G24**). This plaque reveals many surprises: it shows that in addition to the town councillors, the *Augustales* and inhabitants of the country district (all of whom are recorded as having

144

voted honours in other epitaphs), and other groups too voted him honours at his untimely demise. The *nates*, *scabiliari* and *fore<n>ses* voted him shields (i.e., his portrait carved within a shield for public display). The *scabiliari* are probably the group who beat time using clappers (*scabilla*) for dancers in the theatre, and the *nates* may be cushion-sellers there. The *fore<n>ses* are probably the inhabitants of the Forum region, and also occur in an electoral notice (**F21**), but the other groups are otherwise unheard of in Pompeii. It also records that this member of the family had received equestrian status from the emperor Claudius.

On this interpretation, Decimus Lucretius Valens had three sons; one died as a small child, another survived only into his teens, and the third perished as a young adult. It seems that these circumstances prompted him to adopt a new, adult heir, Decimus Lucretius Satrius Valens (perpetual priest of Nero Caesar). His herm stands apart, in a separate part of the enclosure (**G23**). Decimus Lucretius Satrius Valens himself had a son called Decimus Lucretius Valens (a Flavian candidate for aedile), so the family name would have been perpetuated, had not Vesuvius intervened. The existence of this last individual is revealed by some graffiti in the family home (II.vi.3) (**G25–26**), which also mention his otherwise unknown mother Iusta and sister Valentina (see **Figure 7.1**).

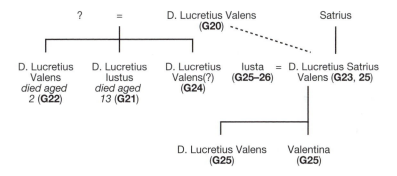

Figure 7.1   A hypothetical family tree

G20 *AE* (1994) 396

To Decimus Lucretius Valens, son of Decimus, of the Menenian tribe.

G21 *AE* (1994) 395

To Decimus Lucretius Iustus, son of Decimus, of the Menenian tribe. Nominated onto the town council free of charge. Lived for 13 years.

G22 *AE* (1994) 394

To Decimus Lucretius Valens, son of Decimus. Lived for 2 years.

G23 *AE* (1994) 397

To Decimus Lucretius Satrius Valens, son of Decimus, of the Menenian tribe.

G24 *AE* (1994) 398

[To Decimus Lucretius Valens, son of Decimus, of the Menenian tribe . . .], honoured by Tiberius Claudius Caesar Augustus with a public [horse]; nominated onto the town council free of charge, aged eight [. . .]. Together with his father, he presented thirty-five pairs of gladiators with a regular hunt. On account of his generosity, the town council (decreed) that he be given a [funeral] and a burial-place, that he receive a public eulogy, and that an equestrian statue be set up at public expense. The *Augustales* and inhabitants of the country district also decreed him pedestrian statues, and their attendants, the cushion-sellers and clapper-beaters, and inhabitants of the Forum region decreed him shields. He lived for [. . .] years.

G25 *CIL* IV 9888

Good fortune to Satrius. Good fortune to Iusta. Good fortune to Valentina. Good fortune to D(ecimus) L(ucretius) V(alens).

G26 *CIL* IV 9889

Good fortune to Decimus, Iusta, and their children.

Freedmen and freedwomen (G27–35)

Freedmen and freedwomen – slaves who had been freed by their masters – were a distinctive feature of Roman society, and became increasingly prominent from the Augustan period onwards, until Caracalla granted universal citizenship to the inhabitants of the Empire in AD 212. Such individuals were particularly keen to celebrate their achievement in becoming Roman citizens. They could do this through the medium of their tomb and its inscription, and consequently are perhaps over-represented in the funerary record. After their release, ex-slaves became clients of their patron and retained close connections with their original household. They might still live in the same house, and might be buried in the household's tomb at their death (G27–28, G40–41). Some freedmen and freedwomen promoted their patron's commercial interests (D109, H21, H23, H26–29, H69).

Some of their epitaphs provide intriguing glimpses of the success with which they and their families were integrated into Roman citizen society after their manumission. We can see how two slaves of the same master could marry after having received their freedom (slaves could not formally marry) (G30–33). Once freed, ex-slaves could possess slaves and build up a network of freedmen and freedwomen for themselves (see G38–47). It was also the case that children born to a freedman after his manumission were full Roman citizens (G32).

Freedmen were excluded from reaching the ranks of the governing class, but could achieve positions of importance and act as benefactors of the community at a lower level, in certain religious cults (E28–31, E34–37, E62–64, G33) and as *Augustales* (G48) or officials in their country district (F96–99). Imperial freedmen and freedwomen – slaves freed by the emperor or by a member of the imperial family – were regarded as being of higher status than normal ex-slaves (G34–35; compare F97).

Integration of a freedwoman into an elite household (G27–29)

G27 is on a marble plaque in the centre of the tomb's façade (Tomb F, north: Nucerian Gate necropolis). G28–29 are on marble herms inside the tomb enclosure, marking actual burials.

G27 *AE* (1990) 179a

To Gaius Veranius Rufus, son of Quintus, duumvir; Verania Clara, freed-woman of Quintus, to her excellent patron, for herself and her household.

G28 *AE* (1990) 179b

Verania Clara, freedwoman of Quintus.

G29 *AE* (1990) 179c

Gaius Veranius Rufus, son of Quintus, aedile.

Marriage of ex-slaves (G30–31)

G30 is on a limestone plaque on the façade of Tomb D north, Nucerian Gate necropolis; G31 is on a marble tablet on the façade of another in the same necropolis. See also G32 and G33.

G30 *AE* (1990) 177a

Caecilia Agathia, freedwoman of Lucius, in her lifetime constructed (this) for herself and for Lucius Caecilius Dioscurides, freedman of Lucius, her husband.

G31 *EE* VIII no.326 (Fondo Pacifico)

To Publius Mancius Diogenes, freedman of Publius, in accordance with his will, at the discretion of Mancia Doris, freedwoman of Publius.

A freedman's freeborn citizen son (G32)

This epitaph shows another case of the marriage of two ex-slaves freed by the same master. Since their son was born after his father had been freed, he is of freeborn status, and this is emphasized by reference to his citizen tribe.

G32 *NSc* (1893) 333

[Marcus Pe]tacius Dasius, freedman of Marcus. [To Marcus Pe]tacius Severus, son of Marcus, of the Menenian tribe, his son; to Petacia Vitalis, freedwoman of Marcus, freedwoman.

Ex-slaves of status (G33–35)

G33, an inscribed marble slab, was found *c.*400 metres from the Villa of Mysteries, on the road from Pompeii to Oplontis, 5 metres below the current ground level. It belongs to a small funerary chamber. Its lettering suggests that it is of a Republican or early Augustan date. The post of 'president of Mercury' probably alludes to this freedman's position in the cult of Mercury and Maia (E28–29).

G34 (a reused inscription) and G35 (a herm outside the Stabian Gate) commemorate two of the many ex-slaves freed by the imperial family, the first a freedman of Livia (wife of Augustus), the second a freedwoman of the emperor Claudius(?). The imperial household of slaves, freedmen and freedwomen was huge, and its members would travel in order to accompany the emperor and his family, or to look after their economic interests.

G33 *AE* (1992) 285

Publius Ancarsulenus Philadelphus, freedman of Publius, president of Mercury, Ancarsulena Eleutheris, freedwoman of Publius, freedwoman.

G34 *CIL* X 1076

Nardus, freedman of Livia.

G35 *EE* VIII no. 319

To Claudia Laudica, freedwoman of Augustus. Lived 55 years.

Augustales (G36–49)

Traditionally, *Augustales* have been regarded as priests involved in emperor-worship. The position of *Augustalis* was granted to freedmen and freeborn; consequently, it is not always clear whether an individual is a freedman or not. They had to pay an entrance fee to the public treasury on joining the group, and might act as public benefactors (**D18**). Their meeting place has yet to be identified at Pompeii. Prominent *Augustales* received honours, including a *bisellium*, a double-width honorific chair for use at public shows. This sign of public recognition sometimes found its way onto their tombs too (**G37** and **G47**). Some of the most eye-catching tombs at Pompeii belong to *Augustales*, who were apparently keen to commemorate their status.

Public honours for an Augustalis (G36)

This inscription is inscribed twice, on a small altar (at the base of which are the ashes) and on a short pillar. Cerrinius Restitutus is one of the witnesses on tablets of Caecilius Iucundus (*CIL* IV 3340.70 and 76), which indicates that he was alive in Neronian times. His tomb is located just outside the Herculaneum Gate (Tomb 1 left). Seats beside the tomb may have accommodated visitors to the tomb at times of festivals honouring the dead.

G36 *CIL* X 994–5

Marcus Cerrinius Restitutus, *Augustalis*. Place given by decree of the town councillors.

A prominent Augustalis*: Gaius Calventius Quietus (G37)*

This is a particularly elaborate tomb of the Neronian period (Tomb 20 left, outside the Herculaneum Gate), designed to give the impression that the deceased was a leading man of his generation. His name also appears in witness lists in the archive of Caecilius Iucundus (*CIL* IV 3340.50–1, 87). His tomb consists of an altar, raised up on several steps, in the centre of an enclosure. It is of marble with sculpted reliefs depicting a *bisellium* and footstool (on the front), and each side has an oak wreath with ribbons. A candidate of the same name, standing as duumvir during the late Neronian/Flavian era, may be his son.

Plate 7.3 **G37a** Tomb of Calventius Quietus

G37b *CIL* X 1026 = *ILS* 6372

To Gaius Calventius Quietus, an *Augustalis*. Because of his generosity, the honour of a *bisellium* was given him by decree of the town councillors and by agreement of the people.

Double commemoration for Munatius Faustus (G38–47)

During the late Neronian era, the *Augustalis* Munatius Faustus built himself a tomb outside the Nucerian Gate (Tomb 9ES), for him to share with his wife, Naevoleia Tyche (a freed-woman) (**G38**). Inside this tomb were a number of herms, marking the burials of himself and members of his household (both freed and slave) (**G39–46**). His wife, however, evidently not satisfied with what he had done, built another, much more elaborate monument outside the Herculaneum Gate (Tomb 22 left) (**G47**). This monument is similar to the adjacent **G37**, an altar raised up on steps within the centre of an enclosure, decorated with sculptural reliefs, which represent highlights of his career. These depict on one side a *bisellium* and footstool, and on the other a ship. On the front is a detailed scene, showing a ceremony of some sort, perhaps a distribution (of money or grain?) made by the deceased to the people of Pompeii. Above this scene and the inscription appears a woman's head peering out from a window, probably none other than Naevoleia Tyche herself, surveying the monument she had commissioned. Munatius Faustus was not actually buried here, however, although a herm of a Gaius Munatius Atimetus was found here (*CIL* X 1031).

G38 D'Ambrosio and De Caro (1983), Tomb 9ES

Gaius Munatius Faustus, *Augustalis* and Country District Dweller by decree of the councillors, to himself and to his wife, Naevoleia Tyche.

G39 D'Ambrosio and De Caro (1983), Tomb 9ES, no. 1

To Gaius Munatius Faus†t†us.

G40 D'Ambrosio and De Caro (1983), Tomb 9ES, no. 2

To Lucius Naevoleius Eutrapelus.

G41 D'Ambrosio and De Caro (1983), Tomb 9ES, no. 3

Munatia Euche.

G42 D'Ambrosio and De Caro (1983), Tomb 9ES, no. 4

Helpis, lived 3 years.

G43 D'Ambrosio and De Caro (1983), Tomb 9ES, no. 5

Primigenia, lived 9 months, 5 days.

G44 D'Ambrosio and De Caro (1983), Tomb 9ES, no. 6

Arsinoe, lived 3 years.

G45 D'Ambrosio and De Caro (1983), Tomb 9ES, no. 7

Psiche, lived 3 years, 6 months.

G46 D'Ambrosio and De Caro (1983), Tomb 9ES, no. 8

Atimetus, lived 26 years.

Plate 7.4 G47a Tomb of Munatius Faustus outside the Herculaneum Gate

G47b *CIL* X 1030 = *ILS* 6373

Naevoleia Tyche, freedwoman of Lucius, for herself and for Gaius Munatius Faustus, *Augustalis* and Country District Dweller, to whom the town councillors with the consent of the people decreed an honorific chair (*bisellium*) for his merits. Naevoleia Tyche had this monument made in her lifetime for her own freedmen and freedwomen and those of Gaius Munatius Faustus.

A cautionary tale (G48–49)

Three figures are represented on this tomb outside the Nucerian Gate (Tomb 23OS) by statues: the woman in the centre is the deceased's patron, Vesonia, daughter of Publius, whereas the two men are the deceased Publius Vesonius Phileros together with his 'friend' Marcus Orfellius Faustus. Vesonius erected the tomb during his lifetime (and had to add *Augustalis* later on). He had a life of ups and downs if we are to take seriously the message inscribed on the podium: this message is a curious variation on customary entreaties to a passer-by to stay awhile in order to read an epitaph.

G48 *AE* (1986) 166a

Publius Vesonius Phileros, freedman of a woman, *Augustalis*, built this monument for himself and his kin in his lifetime, for Vesonia daughter of Publius, his patron, and for Marcus Orfellius Faustus, son of Marcus, his friend.

G49 *AE* (1964) 160

Stranger, delay a brief while if it is not troublesome, and learn what to avoid. This man whom I had hoped was my friend, I am forsaking: a case was maliciously brought against me; I was charged and legal proceedings were instituted; I give thanks to the gods and to my innocence, I was freed from all distress. May neither the household gods nor the gods below receive the one who misrepresented our affairs.

Slaves (G50–51)

Unlike freedmen and freedwomen, the status of slave is rarely explicitly recorded on tombstones at Pompeii. Two exceptions appear below. G50 is inscribed on a marble plaque from a tomb outside the Nucerian Gate, beneath which was a terracotta jar containing bones and a low denomination coin (*as*) of the Republic. G51 is inscribed on a herm. Otherwise, where the deceased has a single name, of a type typical of slaves, we may suppose this to be his or her status. See the household tomb of Munatius Faustus (G38–46).

G50 *EE* VIII 332

Conviva, slave of Veia, lived 20 years.

G51 D'Ambrosio and De Caro (1983), Tomb 19ab OS

Helle, slave-girl, lived 4 years.

Children (G52–55)

A few notices of births have been found. The mother's name in G52 suggests that she was a slave, whereas the baby boy is a citizen in G53 (from front door of I.vii.7). G52 was found in a bedroom off the *atrium* of III.ii.1. Considering the rate of infant mortality in Roman times, children are certainly under-represented in funerary inscriptions, but it is characteristic of those who are commemorated as infants that their ages at death are recorded in more detail than is usual for adults: G54, from outside the Marine Gate; G55 from Tomb A South outside the Nucerian Gate. For what seems to be a sequence of deaths among young slave children in a single household, see G42–45.

G52 *CIL* IV 8820

23rd January, Ursa gave birth on a Thursday.

G53 *CIL* IV 8149

Cornelius Sabinus born.

G54 *CIL* X 1059

Saturninus lived 1 year, 7 months.

G55 *AE* (1990) 182a

Lucius Nonius Celer lived 1 year, 4 months.

Burials of the poor? (G56–58)

A series of inscriptions (*CIL* X 8349–61), which appear to be epitaphs, are inscribed directly upon the masonry of the town walls between the Sarno and Nolan Gates, rather than upon separate tombstones. Nearby were found thirty-eight cinerary urns containing cremations. They perhaps represent burials of the poorer inhabitants of Pompeii.

G56 *CIL* X 8349

Alleia Calaes; Al(leia) Nu(m)phe

G57 *CIL* X 8350

Gaius Cosidius

G58 *CIL* X 8353

Fausta Iulia

Latest discovery of a necropolis (G59)

A previously unknown area of tombs was discovered in the late 1990s, *c*.80 metres east of the Amphitheatre, but only one of its fifty-plus herms bears a clearly legible inscription.

G59 D'Ambrosio (1998a)

Curtia Phyle lived for 30 years.

Non-Pompeians (G60–69)

All Roman citizens born at Pompeii were enrolled in the voting tribe Menenia. Individuals from other voting tribes, therefore, must have originated from some other town (**G60**: Tomb 23 left, outside the Herculaneum Gate).

G60 *CIL* X 1033

To Gnaeus Vibrius Saturninus, son of Quintus, of the Falernian tribe. Callistus, freedman (set this up).

The Tillii family (G61–65)

G61–65 are the epitaphs inscribed together on a single plaque of marble across the façade of Tomb 17OS outside the Nucerian Gate. They show the migration, possibly during the Caesarian period, of a whole family to Pompeii from the area of Arpinum, where they had held public office. Having moved to Pompeii, the family became office-holders here too: Gaius Tillius Rufus, son of Gaius (possibly the same as G62) is known to have been duumvir twice at Pompeii (*CIL* X 8148). Three generations are commemorated by inscriptions on the tomb, set up by the youngest member of the family, whose name is not fully preserved at the start of the inscription (G61).

G61 D'Ambrosio and De Caro (1983), Tomb 17OS, inscription A

[Gaius? Tillius,] son of Gaius, of the Cornelian tribe; [military tribune] of the 10th Cavalry Legion, duumvir with judicial power.

G62 D'Ambrosio and De Caro (1983), Tomb 17OS, inscription B

To Gaius Tillius Rufus, son of Gaius, of the Cornelian tribe, father, duumvir with judicial power twice, aedile with judicial power at Arpinum, augur at Verulae.

G63 D'Ambrosio and De Caro (1983), Tomb 17OS, inscription C

To Gaius Tillius, son of Lucius, of the Cornelian tribe, grandfather.

G64 D'Ambrosio and De Caro (1983), Tomb 17OS, inscription D

To Fadia, daughter of Gaius, mother.

G65 D'Ambrosio and De Caro (1983), Tomb 17OS, inscription E

To Gaius Tillius Rufus, son of Gaius, of the Cornelian tribe, brother, military tribune in the 10th Legion, augur at Verulae.

Burials of Praetorians (G66–69)

The praetorian guard was the emperor's personal bodyguard. The names of various praetorians from different cohorts appear in graffiti at Pompeii, which suggests that praetorians were present in the town on a number of different occasions (**H59**). In addition, one of the wax tablets of Caecilius Iucundus (**H79**) documents a transaction with a member of the guard stationed at Nuceria. Four (probably) of the guard were buried together in a line just outside the Nolan Gate, possibly on public land (**G66–68**); this may have been an honour reserved for those who died in public service. Their monuments are stone markers with rounded tops, a type of funerary monument similar to ones found elsewhere in Italy, but they are the only ones of their type so far discovered at Pompeii. Perhaps the physical form of their monuments was intended to distinguish these burials at a glance as being those of outsiders. By contrast, the burial of a praetorian from Pompeii is marked by a herm, the funerary monument typical of the region (**G69**). It is also located away from the other praetorians, outside the Stabian Gate. **G66** is inscribed on a marble slab with a rounded top, fixed in the ground, where a terracotta lidded jar containing the remains of the cremation is buried. Next to this were the remains of the funeral pyre, including fragments of decorative bone, perhaps from a funerary couch.

G66 De Caro (1979) no. 1

Lucius Betutius Niger, son of Quintus, of the Oufentinan tribe, soldier in the 2nd praetorian cohort. Lived for 20 years, performed military service for 2 years.

G67 De Caro (1979) no. 3

Lucius Manlius Saturninus, son of Quartus, of the Romilian tribe, Ateste his hometown, bodyguard, performed military service for 5 years, lived for 24 years. His brother set this up.

G68 De Caro (1979) no. 4

Sextus Caesernius Montanus, son of Spurius, of the Velinan tribe, from Aquileia, bodyguard, performed military service for 11 years, is buried here.

G69 *NSc* (1897) 275

Gaius Caelius Secundus, soldier of the 8th cohort. Lived for 28 years, served for 14.

8

COMMERCIAL LIFE

Pompeii offers us a unique opportunity to appreciate the energy with which the occupants of a small harbour town engaged in commercial activities. Pompeii was ideally situated to act as an intermediary for inland areas towards Nuceria (H2). It also hosted one of the region's weekly markets (H3–4). Some of the inhabitants expressed their enthusiasm for making money, as can be seen in floor mosaics displayed prominently in their houses (H20, H36–37), and there was no shortage of opportunities for doing so. Inscriptions of many kinds (electoral notices, tombstones and graffiti) reveal a wide range of occupations practised in the town (H51–63). Money-making took many forms, from trade to renting out property, from education to prostitution (H38–50). It is also possible to uncover the distribution pattern of fountains, bars and bakeries in much of the town, which (much like the distribution of electoral notices, F29) gives an impression of the relative levels of activity in different parts of the town (H83).

The region's natural fertility made an important contribution to its productivity and prosperity (H1). Innovative archaeological investigation by Jashemski (1979, 1993) has transformed our picture of land use within the town's walls. When trees and plants died in the aftermath of the eruption, their roots decayed, so that gradually the cavities left behind became filled by volcanic debris. When excavating, the debris is removed for several metres until the ancient ground level is reached. Cavities filled with volcanic debris then become visible on the surface. These can be carefully cleared of debris and then filled with cement. When this hardens, the soil from around the cast is removed, and often the shape of the root can be identified as being that of a specific plant. Her work has uncovered commercial market gardens and vineyards (note to H10–11), as well as domestic gardens. Some of the locally produced wine was exported (see notes on H47–48), but much of it would have been consumed in the neighbourhood. Pottery transport containers (*amphorae*) found on the site show that large quantities of wine were also brought into the town, to cater for the market for wines of different taste, quality and price (H6–8).

Pompeii's fish sauce, however, was of world-class quality. According to Pliny the Elder, the town was famous for its production of fish sauce (*garum*) (**H18**). The sites where it was produced on a large scale are still unidentified, probably because they were on the coast or along the river. These areas are still not as yet fully excavated and remain disguised by changes inflicted upon the local landscape by the eruption. The area could certainly provide the necessary ingredients: fish from the sea, salt from the Salt District outside what is now known as the Herculaneum Gate (**B5** and **F24**) and fresh water from the Sarno River. Fish sauce tended to be stored in *urcei*, clay vessels smaller than those used for wine. The containers of one particular producer, Umbricius Scaurus, far outnumber those of any other producer, and a detailed picture of his business can be built up from these containers and from other finds (**H20–29**).

Although *amphorae* were primarily transport containers for fluids, especially wine and olive oil, their inscriptions show a far greater variety of contents. They might contain a whole variety of goods for sale, from edibles such as fruit, nuts and pulses to lotions and medicines (**H31–34**). The prices of some of these goods are revealed by graffiti (**H15–17**).

The local authorities were in charge of regulating trade and commerce in the town. The standardization of public measures in the Forum was undertaken by the duumvirs during the Augustan period, apparently adapting the pre-existing Oscan system by erasing the earlier measurements inscribed in Oscan and modifying the measuring holes within the table itself (**H64**). A series of paintings found in the estate of Julia Felix vividly illustrate other aspects of commercial life in the Forum (**H66–68**).

Finally, the wax tablets of the banker Lucius Caecilius Iucundus (**H69–82**) give an impression of the variety of business transactions conducted by individuals. Some also relate to his collection of local taxes on behalf of the town. The discovery of two other wax tablets in the Palaestra Baths (**H38**), which relate to a business deal between two women, shows that such tablets must have been in common use, and were not just the professional apparatus of the banker.

A regional perspective (H1–4)

The fertility of Campania (H1)

This description comes in Florus' summary of the Samnite War (see **A7**), part of his abridgement (epitome) of Roman history. Liber (Bacchus) and Ceres are associated with wine and cereal respectively. Compare **A6**. For a map of the Bay of Naples, see **A4**.

H1 Florus, *Epitome* 1.16

Of everything not just in Italy, but in the whole world, the region of Campania is the most beautiful. Nothing is more temperate than its climate:

indeed, its spring flowers blossom twice. Nothing is more fertile than its land: consequently there is said to be a competition between Liber and Ceres. Nothing is more welcoming than its sea: here are those famous harbours of Caieta, Misenum and Baiae with its warm springs, the Lucrine Lake and Avernus, some of the pleasures of the sea. Here are the mountains which befriend the vine – Gaurus, Falernus, Massicus and, most beautiful of them all, Vesuvius, imitator of Etna's fire. Here are the coastal cities of Formiae, Cumae, Puteoli, Naples, Herculaneum, Pompeii and that chief of cities, Capua, once reckoned among the three greatest.

Pompeii's port (H2)

The eruption changed the landscape so thoroughly that no clear sign remains of the original course of the River Sarno nor of Pompeii's port, although recent excavations are believed to have located part of the town's ancient harbour front, beyond the Marine Gate. Compare A5.

H2 Strabo, *Geography* 5.4.8

Nola, Nuceria and Acherrae have as their port Pompeii on the River Sarno, which transports goods in both directions.

Market days (H3–4)

Graffiti recording the pattern of markets in the region show that Pompeii was one of the towns to host a regular regional market. These graffiti also illustrate the difficulties of dealing with the Roman calendar.

Although the calendar in use today is essentially that created by Julius Caesar in terms of the lengths of months and leap years, the Romans used a different system for days of the month, looking forward to one of three named days in the month (Kalends = 1st, Nones = 5th or 7th, Ides = 13th or 15th). Thus our 30th December was called 'three days before the Kalends of January' (counting inclusively: 30th, 31st, 1st). Official calendars marked days in an eight-day cycle, but the Romans also imported from Egyptian astrologers the idea of a seven-day week with each day sacred to a particular planet. (Names of days of the week in English, French, Italian and Welsh preserve some or all of these names, e.g. Satur(n)day; Mar(s)di etc.) Some dates at Pompeii (e.g. H4) also include the number of days since the last new moon.

The writer of H3, found on the wall of a shop (III.iv.1), seems to have thought in terms of a seven-day week, and noted the venue of local markets. If the writer was intending the table to be of general use, rather than covering a particular week, the local markets must have operated on a regular seven-day cycle, not the eight-day cycle recorded as part of official Roman calendars. Above the table are various numbers and calculations. The table is not clearly aligned: the eight place-names are written slightly smaller and occupy the space of the first six days only. Three further columns to the right of the table list the dates between the day after the Ides of one month and the Ides of the next. However, whichever months are taken, the list is incorrect. Three more columns list the numbers between 1 and 30.

H4 also contains confusion over dates of market days: 6 February AD 60 was not a Sunday but a Wednesday. Neither day seems to agree with H3, which records markets at Cumae on Monday ('Moon') and at Pompeii five days later.

159

H3 *CIL* IV 8863

Day	Markets
Saturn	Pompeii
	Nuceria
Sun	Atella ~~Cumae~~
	Nola
Moon	Cumae
Mars	Puteoli
Mercury	Rome
Jove	Capua
Venus	

H4 *CIL* IV 4182, AD 60

In the consulship of Nero Caesar Augustus and Cossus Lentulus, son of Cossus, 8 days before the *Ides* of February {i.e., 6th February}, Sunday, 16th (day of the new) moon, market at Cumae, 5 (days before the *Ides* of February), market at Pompeii.

Wine production and selling (H5–11)

Literary sources provide a little information about Pompeian wine production (**H5**), and pioneering excavations by Jashemski since the 1960s have uncovered some commercial vineyards within the town. Most of our archaeological evidence, however, relates to the selling and consumption of wine. It is possible to deduce the origin of an *amphora* from its shape, material and labels, and this information reveals how diverse the orgins were of the wine drunk in the town. A case study of the *amphorae* found on the premises of a wine dealer adds more detail to this picture of diversity by tracing the geographical distribution of one wine-seller's suppliers. Graffiti and paintings cast further light upon aspects of the everyday consumption of wine and of the choice available to the drinker.

Types of vine (H5)

Columella, *On Agriculture* 3.2.27, also mentions the Horconian and 'Pompeian' Murgentine vines. It is possible that 'Horconian' is a manuscript variant for 'Holconian', and that this type of vine may have been named after the Pompeian family of the Holconii (see D51, D53–55, F89).

H5 Pliny the Elder, *Natural History* 14.35

For around Vesuvius is the Murgentine vine, a very strong species from Sicily, which some call Pompeian, productive only in fertile soil, like the Horconian variety, which is grown only in Campania.

Information from pottery storage and transport vessels (amphorae) (H6–8)

In literature, we hear of wine-jars labelled with the name of the wine and the consular year in which it was produced. In fact, only a few consular dates have been found (*CIL* IV 2552–61) and often labels simply say 'Red' or 'Vintage Red' (rarely white). (Compare A25 for Oscan practice.) Somewhat more frequently, the names of the wines are found. Not surprisingly, the majority of these are local, from Vesuvius, Sorrento (H6), Capua, Cumae, Telesia, Trifolinus (near Naples) and Falernus in Campania. The last two were well known in Rome, Falernian being a byword for good wine in literature and a graffito in a bar (H12). Faustinum wine (H7) was a very good type of Falernian according to the Elder Pliny. Also renowned was wine from Setia (40 miles south-east of Rome, but 100 miles from Pompeii), found at Pompeii. Perhaps more surprising are the *amphorae* labelled as containing wine from Tauromenium (modern Taormina) in East Sicily, which are as numerous as those from any named local vine-yard. It is possible, however, that at least some local wines were moved around in skins or in barrels rather than in the pottery containers suitable for sea travel. Several *amphorae* from the Greek island of Cos have also been found (H8 seemingly imported to Rome first), and individual examples from Crete and from Cnidos (south-west Asia Minor/Turkey).

H6 *CIL* IV 5521 and 5522, *tablinum* of IX.viii.6, *amphora* Mau XII/Dressel 2–4

(Wine from the farm of) Fabius at Sorrento. When Vespasian was consul for the second time {i.e. AD 70}.

H7 *CIL* IV 2553, *amphora* Mau XII/Dressel 2–4

(Wine from) Faustinum in the fourth consulship of Claudius and the third of L. Vitellius {i.e. AD 47}.

H8 *CIL* IV 2565, *amphora*

Coan (wine from) ?Granianus' (farm). Workshop at Rome of Aterius Felix.

Wine-selling: a case study (H9)

I.ix.11–12 ('House of Amarantus') was used as a wine shop during the town's last years of existence. The owner's name appears in an electoral notice on the western façade of House 11 (F19). His name was also recently found on two *amphorae* in the garden (H9). Other *amphorae* found there vary in shape and size, and many bear inscriptions, several in Greek. Consequently, their places of origin can be traced, revealing a surprising range of contacts for a relatively small-scale business.

Excavations during the 1990s and archive work investigating its first excavation in 1952–1953 have also revealed not just the findspots of the *amphorae*, but also how they were found, and what they were being used for. Three *amphorae* in the *atrium* (room 2) of I.ix.12 were full of lime mortar, and were accompanied by a pile of blue pigment, and two *amphorae* in another part of the same room contained cocciopesto (a type of mortar). In the same room, used empty *amphorae* were cast aside in what looks like an *impluvium* (although curiously, it has no water cistern beneath), while full containers of wine were stacked upright in a corner. Also found was a group of broken *amphorae*, including over thirty Cretan wine *amphorae*. Other *amphorae* were carefully stacked upside down, probably in two tiers, in a corner of the garden in I.ix.11. These were mostly local Campanian Dressel 2–4 *amphorae* for wine, with a few Cretan, two Aegean and one rare *amphora* from Gaza. This case study thus illustrates the limitations of the vast majority of *amphora* finds on the site, which have tended to end up in storerooms divorced from their contexts.

H9 Berry (1997) 122

Of Sextus Pompeius Amarantus

The Inn of Euxinus (I.xi.10–11) (H10–11)

Outside this inn is a painted sign depicting a phoenix and two facing peacocks. A short text wishes good fortune to its customers (**H11**). The name of the innkeeper Euxinus appears in an electoral notice painted on its façade (**F18**), and three *amphorae* bear labels instructing their delivery to his address (**H10**). Excavation revealed that thirty-two vines were planted in the garden, in irregular rows. Their grapes could have been fermented on the premises in two large pottery vessels (*dolia*), found partially embedded in the ground. Each of these had a capacity of about 100 gallons. Presumably Euxinus made available to his customers a range of wines, both home produced and imported.

H10 *AE* (1967) 86d

At Pompeii, near the Amphitheatre, to the innkeeper Euxinus.

H11 *CIL* IV 9850, with Solin (1968) 123–4

The phoenix is lucky; may you be too.

Consumption: food and drink (H12–17)

H12 was written in the bar to the left of the entrance to house VII.ii.45. Two paintings from another bar (VI.x.19.1) include what amount to 'speech bubbles' spoken by characters in the pictures. They depict everyday scenes: the first picture (**H13**) shows a soldier being served wine by a slave; the second (**H14**), a man in a toga holding out his cup for a refill.

H12 *CIL* IV 1679

Hedone says, 'You can drink here for one *as*, if you give two, you will drink better; if you give four, you will drink Falernian.'

H13 *CIL* IV 1291

Give a drop of cold.

H14 *CIL* IV 1292

Another cup of Setinan (wine).

Lists of food (H15–17)

H15, a long list of products, was found in the *atrium* of IX.vii.24–5, which was connected by a doorway to a bar with a serving counter. The list (written in three unequal columns), which is divided up into individual days, records food either sold or bought. The numbers are probably prices in *asses*, except where the symbol for *denarius* (= 16 *asses*) occurs. Several other lists have been found; H16–17 clearly record expenditure from an individual. H16, from VII.ii.30, is one of two adjacent graffiti (with *CIL* IV 4889) in a bedroom, listing expenses.

H15 *CIL* IV 5380

7 days before the *Ides*, cheese 1
  bread 8
  oil 3
  wine 3
6 days before the *Ides*
  bread 8
  olive 5
  onion 5
  cooking pot 1
  bread for slaves 2
  wine 2
5 days before the *Ides*, bread 8

  bread for slaves 4
  porridge 3
4 days before the *Ides*, wine {unknown type} 1 *denarius*
  bread 8, wine 2, cheese 2
3 days before the *Ides*
  {unintelligible}
  bread 2
  female? 8
wheat 1 *denarius*
  beef? 1, dates 1
  incense 1, cheese 2
  small sausage 1
   soft cheese 4
   oil 7

For Servatus
[unknown item]
oil 1 *denarius*, 8
bread 4, cheese 4

leek 1, for a small plate 1
[two unknown items]

2 days before the *Ides*, bread 2
  bread for slaves 2

1 day before the *Ides*, bread for slaves 2
  plain bread 2
  leek 1

On the *Ides*
plain bread 2
oil 5
porridge 3
whitebait 2

H16 *CIL* IV 4888

firewood	
steward/land-agent?	4
bread	6
cabbage	2
beetroot	1
mustard	1
mint	1
salt	1

H17 *CIL* IV 8561 (Large Palaestra, II.vii)

Pompeii	
[. . .]	3½ *asses*
p(ound?) of lard	3 *asses*
wine	1 *as*
cheese	1 *as*
oil	1 *as*
bread	2½ *asses*
pork	4 *asses*

Fish sauce (*garum* and *hallex*) (H18–30)
Pompeii's fame (H18–19)

See also **E70** for kosher fish sauce.

H18 Pliny the Elder, *Natural History* 31.93–94

Furthermore, there is another type of choice fluid, called *garum*, produced from the guts of fish and anything else which would have been discarded, steeped in salt – in other words, it is the fermentation of decaying matter . . . These days, the most popular *garum* is made from the mackerel in the fisheries of New Carthage (it is called *garum* of the allies), and around twelve pints costs 1,000 sesterces. Almost no fluid except for perfume begins to fetch a greater price, bringing fame to the countries of origin . . . Clazomenae too is praised for its *garum*, as are Pompeii and Leptis . . .

The waste product of *garum*, its dregs, neither processed nor strained, is *hallex*. It has begun to be produced separately from a tiny fish of no other use . . . Then it became a luxury and has increased into countless types, just as *garum* can be diluted to the colour of old honeyed wine and to such a pleasant taste that it can be drunk.

H19 GC no. 227, painted on an *amphora*

First-rate mackerel sauce of Marcus Acceius Telemachus

Umbricius Scaurus' fish sauce (H20–29)

A local producer, Aulus Umbricius Scaurus, dominated the market for fish sauce (*garum*) at Pompeii from Neronian times until the eruption. Inscriptions painted upon small one-handled pottery vessels (*urcei*) containing the sauce reveal that he ran a number of workshops. These were managed by members of his household: legible names include freedmen Umbricius Abascantus and Umbricius Agathopus, freedwoman Umbricia Fortunata, and a slave Eutyche (**H21, H23, H26–27, H29**). Over fifty of these containers have been found in Pompeii itself and its environs (e.g. the villas at Boscoreale and Boscotrecase). A unique choice of decorative scheme in his *atrium* also allows us to identify his house, a luxurious property (with a private bath-suite) to the west of the town overlooking the sea (VII, Ins. Occ. (*Insula Occidentalis*) 12–15). Around his *impluvium* were found four larger-than-life black and white mosaic depictions of fish sauce vessels bearing promotional inscriptions (**H20**). Although others also included similar painted inscriptions on their vessels (**H19**), Scaurus took a bold step in representing them through art in one of the main reception areas of his house. His repeated claims for his sauce's excellence seem almost a modern style of advertising, which appears to have paid dividends. Around 30 per cent of inscriptions on fish sauce containers in Campania relate to his workshops. One fish sauce container inscribed with his name has even been found at Fos-sur-mer in southern France. Despite his commercial success, he suffered a blow in the early death of his son (of the same name), honoured by the town council (**F91**).

Mosaic fish sauce vessels (H20)

Plate 8.1 H20a Mosaic fish sauce vessel from Scaurus' house

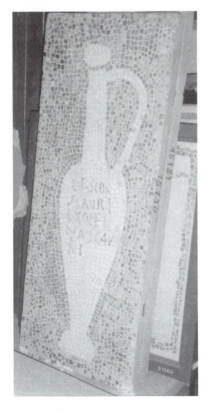

H20b *AE* (1992) 278a–d

Scaurus' finest mackerel sauce from Scaurus' workshop
Finest fish purée
Scaurus' finest mackerel sauce
Best fish purée from Scaurus' workshop

Inscriptions painted on fish sauce containers (H21–29)

H21 *CIL* IV 5671 = *ILS* 8599d

Finest fish sauce by Umbricius Abascantus

H22 *CIL* IV 5682

Scaurus' finest mackerel sauce

H23 *CIL* IV 5689 = *ILS* 8599a

Best finest mackerel sauce from the workshop of Aulus Umbricius Abascantus

H24 *CIL* IV 5694 = *ILS* 8599b

Scaurus' finest mackerel sauce from Scaurus' workshop

H25 *CIL* IV 5711

Best fish purée of Aulus Umbricius Scaurus

H26 *CIL* IV 2576

Scaurus' finest mackerel sauce by Scaurus' Eutyche

H27 *CIL* IV 5712, found in kitchen of IX.vii.16

Best essence, to Aulus Virnius Modestus from Agathopus

H28 *CIL* IV 9406 (found in an inn)

Scaurus' finest mackerel sauce from Scaurus' workshop by Martial, imperial freedman

H29 *CIL* IV 5675

Finest fish sauce from Umbricia Fortunata, belonging to Veturinus Iulianus

H30 *CIL* IV 5717–18 = *ILS* 8598

Finest *hallex*.

Other products (H31–35)

H31 Table showing labelled contents of pottery vessels

Product	Pot size	Location	CIL IV	Notes
Barley	Large	various houses	5745–60	Baked and salted
Bay	Large	?	6048	
Chick peas	Large	?	5728–9	
Dried lees of wine	Medium	VI.xv.8	5730	Used as condiment or medicine
Fennel	Small	?	5731	
Figs	Small	?	2568	
Honey	Small	I.ii.23	10288	'Corsican 2 pounds'
Lentils	Large	VII.v–vi.15	6580	Label in Greek
Lupins	Large	I.vii.7 (under-stairs)	9420	Used as fodder and in medicine
Nuts	Small	VIII.v.9	5761	
Olives	Large	VII.ii.16	5598b	
	Small	II.iv.4	10292	'In water'; found under *lararium*
Pepper	Small	VIII.v.9	5763	
Pickling brine	Small	IX.viii.6 and V.iii.4 (garden)	5721–2	

Lotions and potions (H32–34)

Various pots carry labels showing they contained some sort of medicine. Gavia Severa perhaps specialized in this trade: as well as **H33–34** three other vessels have been found with her name, but no other description of contents. Utica was a town on the North African coast.

H32 *CIL* IV 5738 = *ILS* 8596, *urceus* in peristyle of VIII.ii.14

Best lotion from donkey's milk from Utica

H33 *CIL* IV 5737, *urceus*

Lotion of Gavia Severa

H34 *CIL* IV 5741, *amphora* fragment in peristyle of VII.vii.5

Honey of Gavia Severa from bees fed on thyme

Price of mills at Pompeii (H35)

Marcus Porcius Cato Censorinus, 234–149 BC, was the leading politician and writer of his age. His only surviving work, *On Agriculture*, is intended as practical advice to the owner of a medium-sized estate. In **H35**, Cato discusses the expenses involved in buying an olive mill at Pompeii, later adding (135.2) that Pompeii is the best place to buy such an item.

H35 The Elder Cato, *On Agriculture* 22.3

An olive mill is bought at Pompeii with its equipment for 384 sesterces; transporting it costs 280 sesterces; it is better for it to be prepared for use and assembled at home, which costs 60 sesterces: total cost is 724 sesterces.

Money-making (H36–50)

H36 is a paving inscription, prominently displayed in the entranceway to a house (VII.i.46). It is a frank acknowledgement of the desirability of making money. A similar expression appears in the *atrium* of a house in VI.xiv (**H37**).

Plate 8.2 H36a *Salve lucrum* (Hail, profit)

H36b *CIL* X 874

Hail, profit.

H37 *CIL* X 875

Profit, joy.

Money-lending and usury (H38–41)
Tablets of Poppaea Note (H38)

Two wax tablets (*CIL* IV 3340.154–5) wrapped up in cloth were found, together with some silver vessels weighing about 3 kg in all, in the furnace-area of the Palaestra Baths (VIII.ii.23–4). They relate to a business deal between two women dating to AD 61. A freed-woman, Poppaea Note, has borrowed money from Dicidia Margaris. As security, she has temporarily transferred ownership of two slaves to her creditor, on condition that if she defaults on paying back the loan by a certain date, then Dicidia Margaris can sell the slaves at auction. The second tablet (**H38**) relates to the temporary transferral of the slaves. The careful preser-vation of the tablets implies that Poppaea Note did default on payment, and that Dicidia Margaris kept the record of the original transaction to prove that she had acted legally in selling the slaves.

H38 *CIL* IV 3340.155

Poppaea Note, freedwoman of Priscus, has sworn that the slaves Simplex and Petrinus (or whatever their names are) are hers and that she owns them, and that these slaves are not pledged to anyone else, nor does she share them with anyone else; Dicidia Margaris has bought these slaves, each priced indi-vidually, for [1,450] sesterces and has received formal ownership of them from Popp†a†ea [Note, freedwoman] of Priscus, through the agency of her guardian Decimus Caprasius Ampliatus . . .

[. . . Dicidia Margaris made an agreement with] Poppaea [Note, freed-woman] of Priscus, as follows: these slaves [. . . which Poppaea Note, freedwoman of Priscus,] has sold [to me, are to be returned to her, on condi-tion that the money] loaned against the two [slaves in question is paid beforehand] in full to myself or to my heir, [or that she return it to me] in the course of events. If this [whole] sum [is not paid to me or to my heir] on 1st November next, [it is permitted to me or to my heir to sell] these slaves [in question] on the 13th December next [. . .] at Pompeii in the Forum publicly in the daytime; and [neither] myself nor my heir [is to be held liable] to you because of that, unless it is then thought that this sale has been conducted with fraudulent intent.

If these slaves in question are sold for a lesser sum, [the balance, once the price has been deducted from the initial sum,] will be owed to myself or to my heir.

[But if] these slaves in question are sold [for a higher sum, the excess will be returned to you or to your] heir [. . .]

It is agreed between us that these slaves [are to be kept from henceforth] at your expense, cost, and risk [. . . Dicidia] Margaris, Poppaea Note, freed-woman of Priscus, [through the agency of] guardian {Decimus Caprasius Ampliatus}.

In addition to these things, they agreed between them [the things which have been agreed upon] separately between themselves. Transacted at Pompeii, [. . .] in the consulship of Lucius Iunius Caesennius [Paetus] and Publius Calvisius Ruso {i.e. AD 61}.

Usury (H39–41)

Usury is the practice of lending money at interest. Three records survive relating to a money-lender called Faustilla, which give us a picture of how the practice worked. The first records the usury (interest) to be paid on two modest sums. The second and third add the details that items of some value had to be deposited with the money-lender, who could sell them if the borrower defaulted. One *denarius* was worth 16 *asses*. The rate of interest in the first transaction was 3.75 per cent; in the third, 3.125 per cent. These figures are probably monthly rates of interest. The graffiti were perhaps intended to remind the debtor of what had been pawned, when, and how much interest was being charged.

H39 *CIL* IV 4528 (Inn, VI.xiv.28)

8 February. Vettia, 20 *denarii*: usury 12 *asses*. 5 February from Faustilla, 15 *denarii*: usury 8 *asses*.

H40 *CIL* IV 8204 (in south-east corner of bedroom, I.viii.13)

4 July. Hooded cloak and small cloak [deposited with Fau]stilla. Per 50 [. . .] usury [. . .] 14½ [. . .] 8 *asses*.

H41 *CIL* IV 8203 (to the right of H40)

15 July. Earrings deposited with Faustilla. Per two *denarii* she took as usury one copper *as*. From a total? 30.

Theft (H42–43)

H42 is a graffito of Republican date. *Cave canem* (H43) appears on a black and white mosaic next to an image of a fierce-looking dog, on the threshold at the main entrance to the House of the Tragic Poet (VI.viii.3). Mosaic dogs guard the entrances to other houses, too, such as the House of Caecilius Iucundus (V.i.26), and a plaster-cast has captured the struggles of a chained-up dog trying to escape during the eruption.

H42 *CIL* IV 64

A bronze urn has disappeared from the shop.
If anyone returns it, he shall be given 65 sesterces.
If he brings the thief [. . . the rest illegible]

H43 *CIL* X 877

Beware of the dog.

Property rental (H44)

The large town-block (*insula*) near the Amphitheatre (II.iv.2), which is now occupied by the 'Estate of Julia Felix', was originally taken up by two *insulae* roughly equal in size. During the last years before the eruption, the area was completely reshaped, and it was at this time that the bath complex advertised in H44 was built. For other private baths, see D109. Along with H50, this rental notice shows how income could be derived from urban property. The final phrase is highly abbreviated (with only the initial letters of each word), and its meaning not certain, but likely from the context.

H44 *CIL* IV 1136 = *ILS* 5723 (II.iv.2)

To let, in the estate of Julia Felix, daughter of Spurius: elegant baths for respectable people, shops with upper rooms, and apartments. From the 13th August next to the 13th August of the sixth year, for five continuous years. The lease will expire at the end of the five years.

Schooling (H45–46)

The following were found on one of the columns of the Large Palaestra (II.vii, column 18). They imply that this was the location of a school, H45 being the earliest known set of school Aims and Objectives and H46 a list of boys who had paid their fees. Horace (*Satires* 1.6.75) suggests that schoolboys would pay 8 *asses* each month.

H45 *CIL* IV 8562

Whoever has paid me the fee for teaching, let him have what he seeks from the gods.

H46 *CIL* IV 8565

Atilius 1 *as*
Atilius 1 *as*
Atilius 1 *as*
Albanus 1 *as*
Albanus 1 *as*
Albanus 1 *as*
Albanus 2 *asses*
Agathemerus 2 *asses*
Acathemerus 1 *as*
Acanthus

Prominent individuals (H47–50)

In a few cases, we can trace some of the sources of wealth of prominent members of the elite, whose names loom large on the town's monumental inscriptions. It is unlikely that any of them relied solely upon a single source of income, but they all probably owned significant tracts of land beyond the town walls, which could raise revenue both through exploiting natural resources and through agricultural cultivation and processing.

Eumachia (H47–48)

Some of Eumachia's wealth, in virtue of which she was able to act as such a generous benefactor of the town (E41–47), was derived from the business activities of her father, Lucius Eumachius. His name has been found stamped upon several bricks and roof-tiles found in the town and surrounding area (*CIL* X 8042.47): H47 was found on roof-tiles (dating from *c.*50–25 BC) used in a villa at modern Scafati just to the south-east of Pompeii. In addition, some roof-tiles bear a name that may belong to a freedman of the family (H48). The former's business interests apparently extended well beyond Pompeii: his name also appears on wine *amphorae* (Dressel 2–4) found in the Fos Gulf (south of France), Carthage (north Africa), Ampurias (Spain) and Alésia (France). These inscriptions probably relate to the manufacturing of the *amphorae* themselves rather than to wine production. The theory that Eumachia's family was heavily engaged in sheep-farming and wool production relies chiefly upon the fact that she was patron of the fullers (E43, which does not actually state that she is their patron) and upon the conjecture that her building on the Forum was a wool market (E41–45).

H47 *AE* (1995) 302a (roof-tile)

Of Lucius Eumachius

H48 *CIL* X 8042.48 (roof-tile)

Of Lucius Eumachius Eros.

Holconii (H49)

It seems likely that the Holconii (D51, D53–55, F89, F96) were connected with viticulture, and that the Horconian vine was named after them (H5). In addition, the name of a Holconia appears stamped upon a roof-tile (H49).

H49 *CIL* X 8042.57 (roof-tile)

Of Holconia, daughter of Marcus.

Alleius Nigidius Maius (H50)

This painted notice shows clearly that one of the most prominent individuals in Pompeii was involved in making money out of property rental, shortly before the eruption. His use of his slave as an agent is typical (see also H69, H71–72, H75). Compare the role of freedmen and freedwomen in commerce on behalf of their patrons (D109, H21, H29, H48).

H50 *CIL* IV 138 = *ILS* 6035 (VI.vi.1)

To let from the 1st July next in the *Insula Arriana Polliana*, now owned by Gnaeus Alleius Nigidius Maius: shops with upper rooms, quality apartments and houses. Lessees contact Primus, slave of Gnaeus Alleius Nigidius Maius.

Trades and occupations (H51–63)

The table (H51) shows trades mentioned in written sources found at Pompeii. Over half the examples occur on electoral notices: sometimes an individual has added his trade (e.g., Euhode, the bath attendant begs you to make L. Ceius Secundus duumvir); in other cases the recommendation apparently comes from a group of tradesmen (e.g., Barbers support Trebius for aedile); in a few cases (marked in the table by 'U') the recommendation from a group of tradesmen is described as *universi* (e.g., All the carpenters ask for Cuspius Pansa). This term, found in connection with carpenters, goldsmiths, fruiterers, fullers and mule-drivers, has led to the suggestion that this indicated the official backing of a particular trade association.

In some cases, the indication of a trade seems to serve to help identify an individual, perhaps as a sort of nickname (*cognomen*), rather like the origin of many British surnames. For example one graffito refers to 'Marcus Faustus who is called the herdsman', while D90 insults 'Successus the Weaver' presumably to make the target clear.

Relatively few trades are known from written shop signs, though an outfitter and tanner both seem to have advertised their workshops with written signs (H55 and H61).

H51 does not take into account trades or occupations known from archaeological evidence alone. Good examples include the House of the Surgeon (VI.i.10) where 40 surgical instruments in metal cases were found. A sample of Region I, *insulae* 6–12 suggests good evidence for a fuller's, ironmonger's, potter's, dyer's shop with kiln and plant for making pigments, textile workshop, workshop for *garum* production, as well as several bars and unidentifiable shops, but also one workshop variously stated to be a surveyor's or bronzesmith on meagre evidence.

In the table (H51), gladiators and actors are not included (see notes on D45–50, D63–70) nor those involved in writing electoral notices (see F74–81).

H51 Trades mentioned in written sources

Occupation	Source	Ref. (CIL IV unless stated)	Elect -oral	Comment
Architect	D52	X 841	✗	Freedman
	D81	4755		Slave?
Baker		677	✓	
Banker	H52	See H52	✗	Freedman
	H69	3340.1		Freedman?
	H70–82	3340.2–151		Wax tablets of Caecilius Iucundus
Barber		743	✓	See introductory note above
Bath-attendant		840	✓	See introductory note above
Builder	H53	X 868	✗	
Carpenter		960	✓ U	See introductory note above
Carriage driver	F86	X 1064	✗	
Chicken-keeper	F62	241	✓	
Clapper-beater	G24	AE (1994) 398	✗	
Cloak-seller		753	✓	
Cobbler		1995	?	Rest of graffito makes no sense
Cushion-seller	G24	AE (1994) 398	✗	
Doorman		1894	✗	Love poem appealing to the doorman
Dyer		864	✓	
Engraver	H54	8505	✗	
Farmer		490	✓	
Felt-worker		7809	✓	
Fisherman		826	✓	
Fruiterer		202	✓ U	
Fuller	D71	9131		
	E43b	X 813		
	F20	7164	✓ U	
Furnace-stoker		1150	✓	
Gem-cutter	H54	8505	✗	
Goldsmith		710	✓ U	
Grape-picker		6672	✓	
Guard		3081	✗	Soldier records patrol duty in Basilica
Herdsman		4379	✗	See introductory note above
Innkeeper		1048	✓	
	H10	AE (1967) 86d		
Lupin-seller		3423/3483	✓	
Miller	F60	7273	✓	
Money-lender	H39–41	4528	✗	
Mule-driver		97	✓ U	
Ointment seller		2184	✓	
Outfitter	H55	3130	✗	
Painter	H57	7535	✗	
Pastry-cook		1768–9	✗	
Pig-breeder		D'Ambrosio and De Caro (1983) 5OS	✗	Freedwoman; 'public' pig-breeder

Porter		274 and 497	✓	
Priest's attendant		2612	✗	
Prostitute	D98–99	1751 8356	✗	Most frequent by far; many different terms used
Rag-and-bone man		7643	✓	
Scorer		1147	✓	
Scribe		3376	✗	4 named scribes 'were here' (in inn)
Soothsayer		5182	✗	Word alone
Surveyor	H60	See H60 5405	✗	'Agilis surveyor' on tomb
Tanner	H61	4014	✗	
Theatre official	F111	768	✓	
Waggoner		485	✓	
Weaver	D90	8259	✗	
Wine-seller		1819	✗	Female
Wool-worker?		1190	✓ ?	Wool-worker, wake up

Banker (H52)

This tomb may date from the late Republic.

H52 D'Ambrosio and De Caro (1983), Tomb 3OS

Lucius Ceius Serapio, freedman of Lucius, a banker and his wife, Helvia, daughter of Marcus, dedicated (this).

Builder (H53)

This name appears on a plaque located on an external wall near the corner of *insula* VII.xv, depicting a mason's tools.

H53 *CIL* X 868

Diogenes, builder.

Engraver and gem-cutter (H54)

H54 *CIL* IV 8505 (II.vii.6)

Priscus the engraver wishes good fortune to Campanus the gem-cutter.

Outfitter (H55–56)

The graffito recording the outfitter (**H55**) appears on the wall of a house (VII.ii.16). His work-shop is thought to be in a nearby *insula*. The workshop is decorated with pictures of the process of making cloth through rubbing and pressing animal skins or wool. It also has a furnace thought to be used for making a coagulant. **H56** appears to the right of the entrance of a felt workshop (IX.vii.5–7). Linen was a luxury product. One of the wax tablets of Caecilius Iucundus (**H80**) records the import of linen from Alexandria (Egypt).

H55 *CIL* IV 3130

Marcus Vecilius Verecundus, outfitter

H56 *CIL* IV 9083–5

Golden linen tunic

Painter (H57)

This painter's signature (the only one known from Pompeii, although the name of Dioscourides of Samos appears on two mosaics in the so-called Villa of Cicero) appears next to wall paint-ings of Narcissus, and Pyramus and Thisbe. These are at the end of a water channel between masonry dining couches, which forms a feature for an outdoor summer dining-room.

H57 *CIL* IV 7535 (II.v.2)

Lucius painted (this).

Sailor (retired) (H58)

The following two military men (**H58–59**) are not included in the table (**H51**), since they were probably not permanent inhabitants of Pompeii.

A retired sailor (H58)

From the mid-first century AD, auxiliaries in the Roman army could be granted full Roman citizenship on their retirement after years of loyal service. This award was inscribed on a bronze tablet displayed on the Capitoline Hill in Rome, and each individual beneficiary was given an official copy of the document for his personal use, on a small portable bronze tablet. One of these (dating to AD 71) was found in a bedroom in a small shop, in VIII.v. It belonged to a veteran of the fleet stationed at nearby Misenum, on the Bay of Naples, who came from a town in Syria. The same text is repeated on the outside of the tablet too.

H58 *CIL* X 867 = *CIL* XVI 15 = *ILS* 1990

Inside

Imperator Caesar Vespasian Augustus, chief priest, in his second year of tribunician power, hailed victorious general six times, father of his country, consul three times, designated consul for a fourth time,

to the veterans, who served in the fleet at Misenum under Sextus Lucilius Bassus, who had served for twenty-six years or more and have been settled at Paestum, whose names are written below; to themselves, their children, and their descendants, gave citizenship and the right of marriage with the wives whom they had already at that time, when citizenship was given to them, or, if any were unmarried, with those women whom they later married, provided that each man marry only a single wife.

On 5 April, in the consulship of Caesar Domitian, son of Augustus and Gnaeus Pedius Cascus; to the rank-and-file soldier Marcus Surus Garasenus, son of Dama.

Transcribed and authenticated from the bronze tablet which is affixed at Rome on the Capitol, on the podium of the altar of the Julian family, on its exterior part.

> Appius Didius Praxiles, from Laodicea, Roman equestrian
> Gaius Julius Agathocles from Laodicea
> Gnaeus Cessius son of Gnaeus, of the Collatina tribe, Cestius from Antioch
> Lucius Cornelius Simon from Caesarea Straton
> Tiberius Claudius Epaphroditus from Antioch
> Gaius Julius Theopompus from Antioch
> Tiberius Claudius Demosthenes from Laodicea

Soldier from the Praetorian Guard (H59)

In addition to burials of some members of the guard (the emperor's personal bodyguard) (G66–69), some graffiti have also been found mentioning members of different units. (See also *CIL* IV 1711, 1994, 2145, 4311.)

H59 *CIL* IV 8405 (I.x.11, to the right of door to bedroom)

Gaius Annaeus Capito, cavalryman of the 10th praetorian cohort, Gratus' unit.

Surveyor (H60)

This tombstone was found reused in a later tomb. The epitaph itself makes no allusion to the deceased's profession, but on either side of it are sculpted in relief the tools of a surveyor: *groma* (instrument for taking bearings), stakes, measuring rod and rope.

Plate 8.3 H60a Tomb of the surveyor Popidius Nicostratus

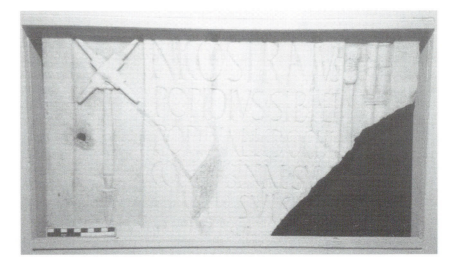

H60b D'Ambrosio and De Caro (1983), Tomb 17a/b OS

Nicostratus Popidius (erected this monument) for himself and his concubine Popidia Ecdoche and his family.

Tanner (H61)

This is an inscription in carbon on the wall of shop I.v.2, leading to a tannery.

H61 *CIL* IV 4014

Tannery of Xulmus

Textile worker (H62–3)

In shop (IX. xii. 1–2) two graffiti were found relating to textile production and trade.

H62 *CIL* IV 9109

I have written down that the weaving was begun on 26 December.

H63 *CIL* IV 9108

6 July. Tunic 15 sesterces.

COMMERCIAL LIFE

The organization of trade (H64–68)

Measuring table in the Forum (H64)

The official set of standard measures (*mensa ponderaria*) was displayed in a niche on the west side of the Forum. This public measuring table was radically modified *c*.20 BC. New measuring holes were cut into it: in addition to the already existing five central basins, which were enlarged, four smaller ones were also added at the corners, and the Oscan inscriptions (Vetter no. 22; Poccetti 1979: no. 109; Antonini 1978: 871) labelling the basins in use up to that time were erased. The local magistrates in charge of the operation to standardize the measures in accordance with those at Rome recorded their action in a Latin inscription across the front of the table. Compare the standardized weights found at Herculaneum (*CIL* X 8067.1–2), which the local aediles had approved.

Plate 8.4 H64a Measuring table in the Forum

H64b *CIL* X 793 = *ILS* 5602

Aulus Clodius Flaccus, son of Aulus, and Numerius Arcaeus Arellianus Caledus, son of Numerius, duumvirs with judicial power, saw to the standardization of the measures in accordance with a decree of the town councillors.

Market stalls by Amphitheatre (H65)

The aediles were in charge of regulating trading matters. Painted inscriptions from the outside of the Amphitheatre appear to have marked off trading booths within the arched openings (**H65**). For fragments of similar notices, see *CIL* IV 1096a–97b, 2485. See the riot painting (**D37**) for evidence of temporary stalls in the piazza around the Amphitheatre.

H65 *CIL* IV 1096

By permission of the aediles. Gnaeus Aninius Fortunatus occupies (this space).

Trade in the Forum (H66–68)

Sixteen fragments of wall painting from a single room in the estate of Julia Felix (II.iv.2) portray different aspects of life in the Forum. The best preserved scenes are the following.

Plate 8.5 H66a Market stalls in the Forum

H66b NM inv. 9069 (painting)

In the far background, a garlanded portico. In the foreground, two market-stalls – a cobbler and an ironmonger – with their customers.

H67 NM inv. 9068 (painting)

In the background, a double-storeyed portico hung with garlands, with three equestrian statues in front. In the foreground, four figures (three adult men, one child) are reading public notices displayed on a long whiteboard.

H68 NM inv. 9063 (painting)

In the background, columns. In the foreground, traders and their customers, including two men selling cloth and a man selling kitchen pots and pans.

The wax tablets of the banker Caecilius Iucundus
(H69–82)

A total of 153 partially legible documents relating to the business affairs of the banker (*coactor argentarius*) Lucius Caecilius Iucundus have been deciphered from writing-tablets found in V.i.26 in 1875. Generally, the wax has perished from the tablets, but traces of their writing remain visible where the metal pen has penetrated into the wooden surface below. They had been stored in a wooden chest on the first floor, above the north side of the peristyle. This also contained some unused tablets and a large placard. The earliest tablet (H69) dates from AD 15, and relates to the business of the banker Caecilius Felix. He is generally supposed to be Iucundus' father and precursor in the same job. His identification as a freedman depends upon his *cognomen*, common among freedmen, or upon the assumption that he is identical with the freedman Lucius Caecilius Felix mentioned in another inscription (*CIL* X 891, AD 1). A freedman called Felix also dedicated a portrait bust of 'our Lucius' in the house (E55). It is also possible, however, that both ex-slave and master bore the same names, and that the banker was not a freedman. The latest tablet (H82) dates from January AD 62, only a month before the town was severely damaged by an earthquake, commemorated on the *lararium* relief in Iucundus' house (C3). We can only speculate whether this collection of tablets is an accident of chance or whether it represents an archive of important documents. It certainly does not preserve a complete record of Iucundus' business transactions.

A collection of 137 documents relate to auction sales. Iucundus acted as a go-between for seller and buyer, paying a sum to the seller for the goods sold at auction a few days later, and extending short-term credit to the buyer. Almost all (tablet 100 may be an exception) probably relate to occasional activity on the part of the seller (such as following on from an inheritance, H71) rather than to regular commercial transactions. Most of these documents are 'receipts' from the seller, acknowledging that Iucundus has paid the amount raised by auction and promised by contract. These documents are not 'receipts' in a modern sense but are formally witnessed verbal statements that payment promised by contract (*stipulatio*) has been received. They thus formally release the banker from his obligation to pay.

The amounts paid out by the banker range from 342 to 38,079 sesterces. The median, calculated from the 44 exact and approximate sums known, comes to *c.*4,500. Only three sales are worth more than 30,000 sesterces. See Appendix 3 for relative monetary values. Their contents include the names of the seller and of Iucundus or a slave acting as his representative, the date, a list of witnesses (all male, with a single exception – Umbricia Antiochis affixes her seal as witness on H76) and the sum paid out. Some receipts are written by the banker or his representative, stating that the seller has received his money before witnesses. Others are written directly by the recipient (the seller at auction) or his/her representative; in these cases, fewer witnesses are needed. It seems that the order in which the names of witnesses were listed reflected their relative status in society. Tablets 81 and 89 show that the ordering of names was a matter for concern, since the same names are erased and then rewritten in a different order. Sometimes they record the amount of commission charged by the banker. Only a few specify what has been sold – it may be that this was included for clarification only when a seller sold more than one item at auction.

In most cases, three tablets are bound together: pages 1 and 6 are often blank, but sometimes contain a summary of the document in ink; pages 2–3 contain the document in full, on wax, which is sealed; page 4 contains witnesses' names and seals; page 5 reproduces the text in full or in summary. The typical pattern of such documents can be seen in **H72** and **H74**. Each document consists of three parts: a statement of the payment made by Caecilius Iucundus in person, a list of witnesses with their seals, and finally a statement, written on behalf of the seller confirming that the banker has settled his account with him or her.

The tablets present us with a picture of variable literacy among the inhabitants of Pompeii. In Tablet 32, a Latin text is written in Greek letters. In other tablets, their writers do not always display complete competence in Latin. **H79** in particular betrays some confusion as to how to designate Roman numerals and adopts idiosyncratic spelling. The fact that women never write for themselves is not, however, a sign of their illiteracy, but reflects their legal status (specifically the requirement that a legal guardian, or *tutor*, authorize a woman's participation in a business deal of this kind: compare **H38**). Consequently, there would be no point in a woman writing in the first person that she is releasing the banker from his promised contract with her for payment of the proceeds of an auction, since she did not herself possess the legal right to do so. By contrast, one of the so-called Murecine Tablets (*TP* 46 + 44) or Archive of the Sulpicii (found just outside Pompeii but relating to business affairs in Puteoli) documents a slave writing on his master's orders 'because he says he is illiterate'.

Sixteen tablets record business between Iucundus and the town (e.g. **H81–82**). These contain receipts written by a public slave acknowledging that Iucundus has paid sums due to the town. Since they are signed by the public slave in receipt of the money, they are witnessed by only three or four individuals, including at least one duumvir. Payments relate to tax on a fullery for five years, AD 56–61 (**H81**: tablets 141–4), to the leasing from the town of a farm, the *fundus Audianus* (tablets 138–40), and to the collection of tax on pasturage, AD 56–61 (tablets 145–7) and on the market (**H82**), perhaps paid for setting up a stall. Iucundus may have been leasing the fullery and farm from the town for his own benefit or may have been collecting rental payments from a third party.

Receipt for sale of a mule, auctioned by Caecilius Felix, May AD 15 (H69)

This is the earliest document preserved, recording a business transaction by Caecilius Felix. It consists of two tablets: pages 1 and 4 are smoothed over, but blank; pages 2–3 are hollowed out for wax, but this has perished. The text is faintly legible on the wood beneath, where the metal pen (*stilus*) has scratched through the wax.

H69 *CIL* IV 3340.1

{Pages 2–3}

520 sesterces for a mule sold to [Marcus] Pomponius Nico, freedman of Marcus, the sum of money which Marcus Cerrinius Eup†h†rates is said to have received in accordance with the contract made with [Lucius] Caecilius Felix. Marcus Cerrinius Euphrates, freedman of Marcus, declared that he had received payment in full of the aforementioned sum of money, in cash from Philadelphus, slave of Caecilius Felix. {Seal}.

Transacted at Pompeii, 28 May, in the consulship of Drusus Caesar and Gaius Norbanus Flaccus.

Receipt for sale of boxwood at auction, May AD 54 (H70)

H70 *CIL* IV 3340.5

{Page 4, left column, written in ink on wood, vertically across the page}

Gaius Iulius Onesimus declared that he has received from Marcus Fabius Agathinus, acting for Lucius Caecilius Iucundus, 1,985 sesterces, less commission, the sum of money which is due for payment, as contracted with Lucius Caecilius Iucundus, by 15 July next, for the boxwood sale of Gaius Iulius Onesimus.

Transacted at Pompeii, 10 May, in the consulship of Acilius Aviola, Asinius Marcellus.

{Page 4, right column, contains a partially legible list of witnesses. Iucundus is here making a payment in advance of the agreed date (15 July).}

Receipt for auction of goods from the estate of Nasennius Nigidius Vaccula, May AD 54 (H71)

It seems that this is the last in a series of payments, and that Salvius has been receiving the money in instalments, whenever it has been required.

H71 *CIL* IV 3340.6

{Page 2, on the edge, in ink}

Handwritten document – of Salvius(?)

{Pages 2–3}

In the consulship of Manius Acilius Aviola and Marcus Asinius, on 29 May. I, Salvius, slave of the heirs of Numerius Nasennius Nigidius Vaccula, have written that I have received from Lucius Caecilius Iucundus on account of my auction the sum, raised in accordance with his contract, of 3,059 sesterces, which I have received in instalments on request up to today.

Transacted at Pompeii.

{Page 4, right column, in ink}
   {Seal of}   Salvius (slave) of the heirs of Vaccula
                 Lucius Aelius Turbo
                 Publius Vedius Primus
                 Salvius (slave) of the heirs of Vaccula

An almost completely preserved receipt for sale of slave at auction, May–June AD 54 (H72)

H72 *CIL* IV 3340.7

{In ink, on the margin of the second tablet}

Acknowledgement of Nymphius – slave of [Lucius] Iunius Aquila.

{Pages 2–3}

1,567(?) sesterces – the sum of money which is due for payment, as contracted with Lucius Caecilius Iucundus, by 13 August next, for the auction of Ni(m)[ph]ius, slave of Lucius Iunius Aquila, less commission – Lucius Iunius Aquila [declared that he has] (received this sum), in cash, from Lucius Caecilius Iucundus.

Transacted at Pompeii on 29 May {or 28 June}, in the consulship of Manlius Acilius and Marcus Asinius.

{Page 4, right column (in ink), next to seals, now missing}
   Of Sextus Numisius Iucundus
   Of Lucius Nerius Hy[ginus?]
   Of [Quintus] Caecilius Attalus
   Of Marcus Badius Hermes
   Of [Publius] Paccius Cerinthus
   Of Aulus Vettius Donatus
   Of Publius Aefulanus Crysant[us]
   Of Gaius Nunnidius Sy[n.]
   Of Lucius Iunius

{Page 5}

I, Nymphius, wrote by instruction [and request] of Lucius Iunius Aquila that he received from Lucius Caecilius Iucundus 1,567(?) sesterces for the auction of Nymphius, slave of Iunius Aquila.

Receipt for highest sum known from auction sale, January AD 55 (H73)

H73 *CIL* IV 3340.10

{Pages 2–3}
38,079 sesterces – the sum which is due for payment, as contracted with Lucius Caecilius Iucundus, for the auction of Marcus Lucretius Lerus, less 2 per cent commission – Marcus Lucretius Lerus declared that he has (received this sum), in cash, from Lucius Caecilius Iucundus.

Transacted at Pompeii on 22 January in the consulship of Nero Caesar and Lucius Antistius.

{Page 4}
{List of (probably) nine witnesses.}

Receipt for proceeds from auction for Histria Ichimas, November AD 56 (H74)

H74 *CIL* IV 3340.22

{In ink, on the margin of the second tablet}
Acknowledgement for Histria Ich†i†mas.

{Pages 2–3}
6,456½ sesterces – the sum of money which is due for payment, as contracted with Lucius Caecilius Iucundus, for the auction of Histria Ichimas – Histria Ichimas declared that she has (received this sum), less commission, from Lucius Caecilius Iucundus.

Transacted at Pompeii, 5 November, in the consulship of Lucius Duvius and Publius Clodius.

{Page 4, right column, written in ink, next to seals, now missing}
    Of Gaius Numitorius Bassus
    Of Lucius Numisius Rarus
    Of Aulus Veius Atticus
    Of Decimus Caprasius Gobio
    Of Lucius Valerius Peregrinus
    Of . . . Cestilius Philod[espotus]
    Of [Gaius] Novellius Fortunatus
    Of [Aulus] Alfius Abasca[ntus]
    Of [Lucius] Ceius Felicio

{Page 5}
In the consulship of Lucius Duvius and Publius Clodius, on 5 November.
I, [name lost], wrote at the request of [Histria Ichimas] that [part of the sum lost, but what remains, fits that mentioned above, 6,456½ sesterces] has been paid [by Lucius Caecilius] Iucundus, for the auction which her [slave] made.

Transacted at Pompeii.

Receipt for sale of fixtures and fittings at auction by
Umbricia Antiochis, November AD *56 (H75)*

Unusually, this tablet gives us a glimpse of the fees and expenses charged for the auction. The items sold fetched 645 sesterces at auction, of which the seller eventually received 560 (i.e. 87 per cent of their total value) after various deductions. In this case, the banker's commission came to around 8 per cent, whereas in Tablet 10 it is 2 per cent, suggesting that there may have been a sliding scale of commission.

H75 *CIL* IV 3340.23

{Pages 2–3}

[During the consulship of Q. Volusius S]aturninus and [P. Cornelius Scipi]o, on the 11 November.

I, [name missing], slave of Umbricia Antiochis, [have written] that she has received 645 sesterces from L. Caecilius [Iucundus], for the auction [which was performed on her behalf], for the objects removed from a property sold earlier. Out of this sum [she has received] 200 sesterces [in cash], with valuation costs adding up to 20 sesterces, incidental expenses adding up to 13 sesterces, and the banker's fee of 51 sesterces having been deducted from the price; finally I received today the sum of 360 sesterces.

Transacted at Pompeii.

Receipt for sale of a slave by Umbricia Antiochis,
December AD *56 (H76)*

H76 *CIL* IV 3340.24

{In ink, on the margin of the second tablet}

Acknowledgement – for Trophimus.

{Pages 2–3}

In the consulship of Lucius Duvius Avitus and Publius Clodius, on 10 December.

I, Marcus Helvius Catullus, wrote at the request of Umbricia Antiochis that she had received from Lucius Caecilius Iucundus 6,252 sesterces for the auction of her slave Trophimus, less commission.

Transacted at Pompeii.

{Page 4, next to seals, now missing}

> Of Marcus Helvius Catullus
> Of Melissaeus Fuscus
> Of Fabius Proculus
> Of Umbricia Antiochis
> Of Catullus

{Page 5}

In the consulship of Lucius Duvius [Avitus and Publius] Clodius, on 10 December.

I, Marcus Helvius Catullus, wrote at the request of Umbricia that she had received from Iucundus 6,252 [sesterces] for the auction of her slave Trophimus, less commission.

Transacted at Pompeii.

Receipt for goods auctioned for Umbricia Ianuaria, December AD 56 (H77)

H77 *CIL* IV 3340.25

{In ink, on the margin of the second tablet}

[Acknowledgement] for Umbricia [Ianuaria]

{Pages 2–3}

11,039 sesterces – the sum of money which is due for payment, as contracted with Lucius Caecilius Iucundus, for the auction of Umbricia Ianuaria – Umbricia Ianuaria declared that she has (received this sum), less commission from Lucius Caecilius Iucundus.

Transacted at Pompeii, 12 December, in the consulship of Lucius Duvius and Publius Clodius.

{Page 4, next to seals, now missing}

    Of Quintus Appuleius Severus
    Of Marcus Lucretius Lerus
    Of Tiberius Iulius Abascantus
    Of Marcus Iulius Crescens
    Of Publius Terentius Primus
    Of Marcus Epidius Hymenaeus
    Of Quintus Granius Lesbus
    Of Titus Vesonius Le[. . .]
    Of Decimus Volcius Thallus

{Page 5}

12 December, in the consulship of Lucius Duvius and Publius Clodius Thrasea.

I, Decimus Volcius Thallus, wrote at the request of Umbricia Ianuaria, that she had received from Lucius Caecilius Iucundus 11,039 sesterces, less commission from her auction, as confirmed on examination of sealed tablets. {Traces of two seals remain.}

Receipt for auction of goods by Tullia Lampyris,
December AD *57 (H78)*

H78 *CIL* IV 3340.40

{Pages 2–3}

8,562 sesterces – the sum of money which is due for payment, as contracted with Lucius Caecilius Iucundus, for the auction of Tullia Lampyris – Tullia Lampyris declared that she has been paid this sum, less commission, by Lucius Caecilius Iucundus.

Transacted at Pompeii, 23 December in the consulship of Nero Caesar for the second time and Lucius Caesius Martialis.

{Page 4, next to seals, now missing}
Of Lucius Vedius Ceratus
Of Aulus Caecilius Philologus
Of Gnaeus Helvius Apollonius
Of Marcus Stabius Chryseros
Of Decimus Volcius Thallus
Of Sextus Pompeius Axsioc(hus)
Of Publius Sextius Primus
Of Gaius Vibius Alcimus

{Page 5}

In the consulship of Nero Caesar for the second time and Lucius Caesius Martialis, transacted at Pompeii on 23 December. I, Sextus Pompeius Axiochus, have written at the request of Tullia Lampyris, that she has received from Lucius Caecilius Iucundus 8,560 sesterces and 2 *asses* for her auction, as confirmed on examination of sealed tablets.

Receipt for proceeds from auction sale by military personnel
at Nuceria (H79)

This is the only tablet written outside Pompeii, at a military camp, probably to the north of Pompeii, near Nuceria, where members of the praetorian guard appear to have been stationed. By the first century AD, it was quite usual for detachments of praetorians (the emperor's body-guard) to leave Rome during imperial travels (see also **G66–69**, **H59**). The document contains several other unusual features. It records that the proceeds of an auction sale by Alfenus Pollio (a *decurio*, or commander of a cavalry unit) and Eprius Nicia are being handed over to Alfenus Varus, who is a *trecenarius Augusti* (i.e. a high-ranking officer in the praetorians). The most likely scenario is that Eprius and Pollio owe some money to Varus. They then auction off some goods belonging to another party who, in turn, is indebted to them. Part of the proceeds of the auction is passed over directly to Varus, thus clearing their debt to him, and they prob-ably then received any surplus from the auction themselves. The text itself is poorly written (e.g., with Iuqundus for Iucundus).

H79 *CIL* IV 3340.45 (with *AE* 1993,454)

{Pages 2–3}

In the consulship of [. . .] and Lucius Iunius, on 27 August; I, Publius Alfenus Varus, the emperor's *trecenarius*, have written that I have received from Lucius Caecilius Iuqundus 25,439 sesterces, from the auction of Publius Alfenus Pollio, cavalry officer, and of Numerius Eprius, for that part contractually due to me as substitute debtor. Transacted at the Julian camp at the Nucerian garrison.

{Page 4, right column, in ink, next to seals, now missing}
   Of Publius Alfenus Va[rus], emperor's *trecenarius*
   Of Publius Alfenus Pollio
   Of . . . Trausus A . . .
   Of [Publius] Alfenus Varus, emperor's *trecenarius*
   Of Publius Alfenus Pollio

Ptolemy of Alexandria, seller of linen at the market (H80)

The rest of the text is mostly lost, but enough survives of the ink summary to attest the activity of an Alexandrian trader at Pompeii, nicely complementing other evidence in the town for the impact of Egyptian culture and influence there (see also E3–9).

H80 *CIL* IV 3340.100

{On edge of tablet, in ink}
   Acknowledgement of auction of linen of Ptolemy, son of Masyllus, of Alexandria.

Payment of rental for fullery, August AD 58 (H81)

This document relates to the payment of rental for a fullery for the year AD 57/58. This is the second year of rental in an agreement covering a five-year period.

H81 *CIL* IV 3340.142

{Pages 2–3}

In the duumvirate of Lucius Albucius Iustus and Lucius Veranius Hypsaeus, I, Privatus, slave of the colony, have written that I have received from Lucius Caecilius Iucundus 1,652 sesterces, from the outstanding amount for the fullery before this day, 14 July.

   Transacted at Pompeii, 14 August, in the consulship of A. Paconius Sabinus and A. Petronius.

The latest tablet: receipt of market tax/rental,
January AD 62 (H82)

H82 *CIL* IV 3340.151

{Edge of 2nd tablet in ink}
Payment. . . .

{Pages 2–3}
In the duumvirate of . . . and Tiberius Claudius Verus. . . . January. I, [Privatus], slave of the colony of Pompeii have written that I have received from [Lucius] Caecilius Iucundus 2,520 sesterces, on behalf of Marcus Fabius Agathinus, stall-holder in the market.

Transacted at Pompeii.

In the consulship of Publius Marius son of Publius and Lucius Afinius.

Town amenities (H83)

H83 Distribution map of public water fountains, bakeries and *popinae* (snack bars)

See **Figure 8.1**.

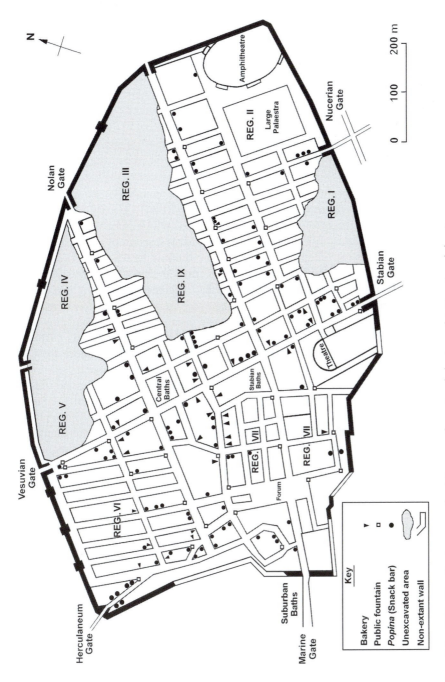

Figure 8.1 H83 Distribution map of public water fountains, bakeries and *popinae* (snack bars)

9

EXCAVATION REPORTS

This chapter contains translated excerpts from contemporary excavation day-books. *Pompeianarum Antiquitatum Historia* (*PAH*: *History of Pompeian Antiquities*) is a three-volume work (1860–1864) which published transcriptions of the manuscript notes kept by the excavators from 1748 onwards (J1–58). It was compiled by Giuseppe Fiorelli while he was a political prisoner in 1849. He is better known for his introduction of a more scientific approach to digging at Pompeii after he had become inspector of the excavations in 1860. His system of numbering every building with three numbers – region, *insula* and doorway – remains the foundation of how buildings at Pompeii are still identified today. This supplemented the previous custom of giving names to houses, some of which would accumulate more than a dozen names over the years, and which could result in confusion (see note on J55–58). One of the most memorable features of visits to the site today is seeing plaster casts of Vesuvius' victims, a technique which Fiorelli adopted extensively.

Fiorelli's publication of the day-books, however, was equally revolutionary. At the time, all publications about sites in the Kingdom of Naples required the official approval of the Royal Herculaneum Academy. When Fiorelli published the first volume in a projected series of eight (entitled *Journal of the Excavations of Pompeii: Original Documents Published with Notes and Appendixes*) in 1850, the authorities seized and burned his manuscripts, and he was unable to proceed with publication at that time. After this incident, and his brief imprisonment, he was excluded from any job in Naples Museum or at Pompeii, and was employed by Count Leopold of Syracuse as a private secretary (1853–1860), carrying out and publishing excavations at Cumae.

After the eventual fall of the Bourbon dynasty in 1860, Fiorelli was reinstated, first as inspector of excavations at Pompeii in 1860, and then, from 1863, as both superintendent of Pompeii and as director of Naples Museum. He was also then able to publish *PAH* in three volumes from 1860 to 1864. In 1875, Fiorelli was appointed director-general of antiquities. By virtue of this post, he was able to implement on an Italy-wide stage some of the innovations that he had introduced to Naples and Pompeii. Well aware of the importance of regular reporting of the latest archaeological discoveries in Italy, he established in 1876 the journal *Notizie degli scavi di antichità* (*NSc: Notes on Excavations of Antiquity*), which is still published today, to provide monthly reports of current excavations. Extracts from this journal are translated here, covering the excavation of the House of the Vettii (J59–70).

The start of official excavations at Pompeii (J1–5)

(*PAH* I, Part 1, pp. 1–2)

In the earliest days of excavation, the Spanish engineers working for Charles VII believed that they were uncovering the ancient town of Stabiae. Nearby Gragnano is the site of a villa. We learn that one of the main reasons for starting the new dig was that progress at Herculaneum was slow and difficult. This site had first been struck at the bottom of a well in 1711, and Charles VII had restarted digging there in 1738. The excavators there had to dig through many metres of solidified pyroclastic deposits, via a system of airless tunnels underground. Pompeii, by contrast, was less deeply covered by layers of generally lighter volcanic material (chiefly pumice stones). These reports set the tone for the excavations, with their search for artistic finds and lack of interest in the ruins themselves.

J1 23 March 1748

Having begun in the last days to make an on-the-spot inspection of the channel which carries water to the Munitions Factory of Torre Annunziata, and on the basis of information which I had previously received – in particular from the Officer Don Juan Bernardo Boschi – according to whom there is in these parts a place called Civita, approximately 2 miles from the aforementioned Torre, where there have been found some statues and other remains of the ancient town of Stabiae, I believed it timely to visit the place and to gather some information. I have arrived at the firm belief that some monuments and ancient treasures could be found there, with less work than we are engaged in here. And seeing that nothing special has been found in these excavations for some time now, despite the fact that digging continues in the middle of the ruins, I wanted very greatly to suspend these works for a while and to go and carry out a trial with the same men in the above-named locality of Civita, and also at Gragnano, which is another place not very far away.

J2 6 April 1748

In the excavation which we have begun at Torre Annunziata, the first thing which we have discovered is a painting 11 ft long and 4½ ft tall, which contains two large festoons of fruit and flowers; a very large and well-executed head of a man; a helmet; an owl; various birds and other things. I think that it is one of the better pieces of painting found up until now. And after the sculptor had come here this morning to see it, I gave instructions for it to be cut out on Tuesday. His Majesty was informed of this in the afternoon and he ordered a stretcher to be brought to take it, as the Officer has arranged, since this is the most convenient way of avoiding damaging it.

J3 10 April 1748

Yesterday the large painting, which had been found, was removed but because of its weight we could not transport it with the stretcher which had arrived for this purpose. This morning I arranged for it to be transported by cart, and this afternoon it arrived successfully at the royal palace, where it was handed over to the sculptor.

J4 19 April 1748

Found a skeleton and 18 coins.

J5 27 April 1748

Nothing was found, and only ruined structures were uncovered.

Temple of Isis (J6–10)

(Extracts from *PAH* I, Part 1, pp. 171–2, 177, 182–3, 188.)

For a plan of the Temple of Isis, see **E3**.

J6 and J8 illustrate some of the problems encountered by the earliest excavators. At the time, it was believed that pockets of noxious gases (such as carbon dioxide, carbon monoxide and hydrogen sulphide) were trapped underground beneath the volcanic layers deposited by the eruption. At the slightest suspicion that the excavators were coming across such a pocket, work would be immediately abandoned in that area; work was suspended at Pompeii for three months from July 1748, when a hot sirocco wind was thought to be exacerbating the problems of mofette. Nevertheless, no traces of such gases have been found in more modern excavations, and it may be that some of these fears were groundless. Another difficulty hampering the digging was leakage from the Sarno channel.

J6 8 June 1765

What is believed to be a small temple on the estate of Montemurro at Civita has been completely uncovered. This has already been mentioned in the report of 4 May this year. It is part of a larger building, which is included in the hall, already mentioned elsewhere. This second small structure is still entirely decorated with stuccowork on all sides {a description follows . . .}. This building remained uncovered, and inside nothing was found except for a small staircase, which led underground, whose function still could not be discovered because of the mofette.

To the sides of the entrance to this building, outside, there are two small altars of soft stone, and in front of these is another larger one, on which there are still ash and small pieces of burnt bones of sacrificial victims. Near to this temple, in the soil of the courtyard, is seen a square hole full of a large quantity of black ash, or of the remains of burnt fruit. At the bottom of this pit was found an iron nail, an Egyptian idol lacking its legs and broken into various pieces, and from its belt downwards decorated with many hieroglyphs . . . Among the remains of burnt fruit which were seen in the afore-mentioned pit, the following were extracted from them: various pieces of figs, many pine seeds with their shells and pieces of pine-bark, some pieces of walnut, some hazelnut-shells, and two dates. All of the things described above, as well as the remains of the little idol, and the pictures that have been found so far, reveal that this temple was dedicated to some Egyptian deity.

J7 20 September 1765

A small room was discovered adjoining the above-mentioned temple, which has been recognized as having been a kitchen, and the following kitchen utensils were discovered there. An iron tripod, and an axe of the same metal. Two earthenware frying pans, a bowl, two plates, and a lamp also of earthenware: this lamp provides a single flame, and in its upper part there is a youth in low relief, who is carrying on his shoulders a stick, from which two baskets are hanging.

J8 14 December 1765

Soil was removed in the Temple of Isis, in the place which has been uncovered already for some time, which it would have been possible to believe was the rim of a well, if it had not been found covered with the roof. Having seen to removing the volcanic debris, a large quantity of burnt fruits was discovered at the bottom; but it was not possible to reach the ancient floor, which is perhaps not very far below, because, as the channel which takes water to the Munitions' Factory passes near to this place and so much water has leaked out, it was not possible to excavate any more. The various burnt fruits which were removed from here and sent to the Museum are: pine-seeds with pine-bark, dates, hazelnuts, and what seemed to be some chestnuts and figs.

J9 4 January 1766

Soil was removed in the room in the Temple of Isis, where the painting was discovered in the presence of His Majesty, and in this place was found a bronze *sistrum* {rattle used in worship of Isis}, 11 inches tall with its handle, with four attachments, at the top of which is an animal which resembles a cat, and two flowers on the two sides: this is well preserved and perfectly intact.

J10 10 May 1766

In the same room {so-called *ecclesiasterion*} was found a table supported by a pillar and foot, the whole thing 2 feet and 11 inches tall, 3 feet and 8 inches long, and 1 foot and 8 inches wide; and a vase of terracotta, lacking almost completely its lip, 1 foot and 10 inches tall and 1 foot and 4 inches in diameter. Next to the table there was a man's skeleton, and beneath the table various chicken bones. Some time ago, during the clearance of soil in the afore-mentioned Temple of Isis, about 37 pieces of inscriptions were found. But since we were unable to put them together in such a way as to form a single word, they were sent to Paderni in the Royal Museum.

The discovery of the Gladiatorial Barracks (J11–20)

(Extracts from *PAH* I, Part 1 pp. 196–212)

J12–14 illustrate how the building was identified as a soldiers' barracks on the basis of finds. In time, these amounted to fifteen helmets, fourteen greaves (i.e. shin-guards), four belts, a sword-hilt and a shield, all in bronze and decorated with mythological scenes. The discovery of the shackles (J12) inspired one of G.B. Piranesi's imaginative sketches of Pompeii.

The excavators' general rules in documenting their finds can be seen here. Objects found were listed in categories according to the material out of which they were made (such as metal or bone) (J14). It also demonstrates the attitude to paintings found at Pompeii: if regarded as of any merit, they were copied and then cut out of the wall and transferred to the royal collection (J15–16). The main painting described here depicts Mars and Venus with trophies made out of gladiatorial weapons.

The excavation of a particular building could take many years of fitful activity, depending on the amount of excitement generated by its discovery. In the case of the Barracks, its fourth side was still being uncovered on 16 February 1792, even though this part of the building had first been located on 21 January 1769.

For a plan of the Barracks, see **D44**.

J11 6 December 1766

Continuing to clear the earth in the building which lies adjacent to the town walls, which reveals a large courtyard or piazza surrounded by a portico, with 'peperino' {tufa} columns painted red and rooms on two floors . . .

J12 20 December 1766

Continuing to dig in the building adjacent to the town walls. From the finds which have been made, this is believed to be a Soldiers' Barracks. The following was found: a room . . . in which were found shackles for ten people, made up of a bar 7 feet 10 inches long and 2½ inches wide, with three cross-bars for locking above a large plank opposite it, of which some remains were found. Above this bar there were 22 irons with eyelets protruding vertically, each one 4½ inches high, leaving spaces for ankles between them. From one of the ends of this bar there remained welded the socket of a lock 10 inches high, 13 inches wide and 3½ inches thick, and this came encased in a wooden outer-casing. Near to this, partly rusted together, was found a rod of the same length as the shackles, with a ring on one end. This rod must have worked by being inserted from the lock's exterior hole through the eyelets, thus fastening the prisoners' legs securely. At the end of this rod, towards the ring, can be seen the hole through which the lock's bolt must have passed. The whole room is painted, though plainly, and 4 skeletons were found there, perhaps of prisoners. In another room of the same building . . . four helmets were found, believed to be of copper; judging from the place in which they were found, and from some nails which fitted them on the wall, these must have been attached to that wall. {Description of the four helmets follows.}

J13 30 December 1766

Having cleared some of the earth, which remained beneath the helmets mentioned in the previous report, 4 copper greaves were found . . . {description follows}.

J14 10 January 1767

In the current week, another room adjacent to the last one found was uncovered in the Barracks building. It has a flooring of crushed tiles, and is entirely painted inside, though plainly. The following was found there. Four helmets . . . {description of the helmets}. Two large copper greaves, similar to those described in the report for 20 December . . . A piece of weaponry, of unknown purpose, more or less semicircular in shape . . . Also found in metal: a nail-head, two rings, a needle 5 inches long, and a small piece. In lead: 4 ring-like pieces, 2½ inches in diameter. In glass: a small bottle and a button. A bone pin. A shell and a heap of grass, even though it apparently came from the sea, on top of which lay some of the helmets. Also found were fragments of pots, pieces of a broken water-jar, and many pieces of broken water-jugs.

J15 14 February 1767

In the current week the room, whose initial discovery was described in the previous report, was entirely uncovered. This room, which is the centre of this side of the building {i.e. in the centre of the south-east portico}, is open towards the courtyard, and is painted as follows. All around, it has a black base with some minor decoration. In the middle of the main façade there is a picture 2 feet, 10 inches high and 2 feet, 6 inches wide with two figures, a man and a woman. But this section has deteriorated greatly and it is difficult to see anything else. Beside this picture are two architectural grotesques, and the rest of the façade has various sections. The façade to the left of the bit described has in its centre a trophy, which rises up from the paving to a height of 10 feet. It is made up of helmets, cuirasses, greaves, shields, belts, and a trident, a cloak and spear. As background to this trophy, which is all painted in naturalistic colours, is a section of architecture. On the left is a picture 2 feet, 6 inches high and 2 feet, 3 inches wide, in which appears a man who is clothed and holding a spear in his left hand, and a woman who is entirely draped.

J16 7 March 1767

Once the draughtsman Morghen had finished copying the whole of the room painted as described above, Canart, as advised, immediately gave instructions for the cutting out of the four pieces which were worth it:

1   Picture with two figures: 2 feet, 10 inches high and 2 feet, 6 inches wide.
2   Picture with a trophy: 9 feet, 9 inches high and 4 feet, 3 inches wide.
3   Picture with two figures – a man with a spear in his left hand and a woman: 2 feet, 7 inches high and 2 feet, 4 inches wide.
4   Picture with part of a trophy: 3 feet, 6 inches high and 5 feet wide.

{Further discoveries of helmets, armour . . .}

J17 23 May 1767

{Ends report with discovery of} some tiny part of a woollen cap, which sat beneath a helmet.

J18 20 June 1767

{They found} a man's skeleton all intact, which remains crouched on the ground, a curious sight.

J19 29 August 1767

Continuing to dig in the usual place, some skeletons were found, one of which had two gold rings on its fingers. One of these is a small circle weighing two 'trappesi' {i.e. 1.78 grammes}, the other is a small bar, which ends in two snakes' heads, which, drawing together, make a discontinuous circle, weighing 16½ 'trappesi' {i.e. 14.685 grammes}.

J20 5 December 1767

In digging in the Barracks in a space under the stairs, a human skeleton was found . . . In the same room was also found a skeleton, which appears to be of a horse, and nearby the following pieces, which are believed to be its tack . . . {describes bits of buckles, bell, part of a saddle}.

Unusual finds in the Theatre (J21–23)

(*PAH* I, Part 1, pp.223–4; *PAH* I, Addenda IV: *Epitome diurnorum ex cod. mss. Aloys. Ribau* (*Summary of the Daybooks from the manuscript of A. Ribau*) p. 154)

For the double honorific chair, see **G37** and **G47**.

J21 22 October 1768

Digging continued in the building next to the Theatre, and the following was found: a musical instrument consisting of a bronze trumpet without mouthpiece . . . The trumpet is 20 inches long. Another instrument consisting of a bone pipe 19 inches long was found.

J22 29 April 1769

A magistrate's {'curule'} or double honorific chair {*bisellium*}, or some other similar piece of furniture, of iron, decorated with ivory turned on the lathe, was found in the portico behind the stage building of the Large Theatre, through which one used to enter into the Odeion Theatre.

J23 3 June 1769

Other pieces of similar furniture, of magistrate's or double honorific chairs. Cushion of afore-mentioned furniture.

A royal visit (J24)

(*PAH* I, Part 1, pp. 228–9)

The year 1748 heralded the start of official excavations at Pompeii (J1–5), under the authority of the Bourbon King Charles VII of Naples. On the death of his half-brother Ferdinand VI in 1759, he handed over this realm to his son, so that he could return to Spain as King Charles III.

The following account illustrates how the young King Ferdinand IV (about 18 years old at this time) had to be prodded into showing much interest in the excavations, which his father had eagerly initiated. The Hapsburg Emperor Joseph II (his brother-in-law) was much more aware of the kudos which could be derived from canny exploitation of the excavations, and played an important role in trying to convince his younger relation of this, even by appealing to Ferdinand IV's obsession with hunting.

Access to the site by visitors was severely restricted, so it is no surprise to find the antiquity-mad English Ambassador to Naples (from 1764 to 1800), Sir William Hamilton, taking the opportunity to join in this inspection. Marquis Bernardo Tanucci, formerly a professor in law at Pisa University, was an influential figure in the Naples court: he founded the Royal Herculaneum Academy in 1755 and acted as Regent for Ferdinand IV.

Entries like this one, recording visits to the excavations by royal dignitaries, are often accorded more space in the excavation diary than actual episodes of archaeological digging!

J24 7 April 1769

Yesterday at about the 20th hour, His Majesty the King {Ferdinand IV} came to observe the excavation of Pompeii, together with the Queen {Maria Carolina} and Emperor Joseph II. Besides their entourage were Count Kaunitz, the English Ambassador {Sir William Hamilton}, and that ambassador's antiquary Mr. D'Ancrevil. When the King saw the antiquary entering the site, he told him to carry out his duties, and did me (F. La Vega) the honour of saying that I should follow the King himself; whereas the aforementioned antiquary was there for the express purpose, to explain things to the Emperor en route. Their Majesties first entered the Barracks; they wanted to give all parts of it special attention, as well as the material with which it had been overwhelmed. The Emperor asked how this excavation had had its beginnings, which I answered, and I also added, that it had not been carried out in earlier times because a forest had stood in this place, which had been cut down about 28 years ago. The Sovereign examined this building with pleasure and disapproved of the fact that the earth in the middle of the courtyard had not also been cleared. From this place, their Majesties proceeded to the west to a house, where they admired the vaults still intact, the stairs and plaster. In this site they found work proceeding in four rooms and they observed the digging with pleasure. Through the previous instruction of His Excellency Marquis Tanucci, the number of workers had been increased for some days, in anticipation of the visit. In these rooms the earth remained at a height of only 2 feet, and a good part of this had been cleared, where it was less probable that one could find something. After a short time a bronze vase began to be excavated, and so from one thing to another there was uncovered in the 2 rooms all that which is noted down here in order by material, with the exception of some small things which had already been found. {List of finds includes 12 pieces of silver plaque with relief figures; bronze objects – basin, vases, coins, door-hinges, brooches; items in iron, lead, glass, bone, and pottery.}

And the following pieces of plaster had been found in the same rooms shortly before . . . {description follows}. The Emperor was surprised, and even wondered whether all these things had been placed there artificially in order to flatter their good fortune; but he came to realize the truth as I pointed out the position of the finds, the type of earth that contained them, and when I reported what had been done. He then congratulated the King on such a good day's hunting, which was in effect to apologize; and I added that such a pleasure had been reserved for him alone of all Sovereigns. The English Ambassador, Sir William Hamilton, with his passion for antiquity, did not fail in the midst of this to make known the value of the discoveries with the most detailed observations. The King displayed the greatest pleasure in this encounter, and was so enthused that, besides not wanting to move a step from the place where excavations were being carried out, he actually said two or three times to La Vega to let him know when places were ready to be uncovered, because he wanted to be present when discoveries were being made; and he would be very happy for a day to be set aside for seeing discoveries being made. The Queen was also very joyful at these finds and impatient to see them soon. In the other two rooms nothing was found except for a skeleton, and two coins of the type already described. Afterwards their Majesties went to see some rooms, which had been exposed, where an intact skeleton was still preserved. From this place they proceeded to the Theatre . . . The Emperor asked La Vega how many workmen were employed in this task, and having been informed that there were 20, asked the King how he allowed such a task to proceed so slowly. When he said that little by little it would all be done, the Emperor added that this was a job for employing 3,000 men, and that he would have thought that nothing like this existed in Europe, Asia, Africa, and America, and that this created a special honour for the Kingdom; and he asked the King who was looking after these antiquities; he replied that it was the Marquis Tanucci. Her Majesty expressed disapproval of this, and joined in urging the King to devote some energy to such a task. From this place they continued, after having observed the signs that an Odeion had been found, to a whole private house, to see the Temple of Isis, which brought forth praise from the Emperor; and in the meanwhile he did not cease to encourage the King in the most vigorous manner to value these things most highly. In the temple, La Vega showed to their Majesties the drawings, which he had made, towards which the King graciously condescended to show favour. The Emperor particularly enjoyed seeing what remained as an impression of the wooden door, preserved as an imprint on the ground. After having examined all these buildings, which formed a unit as it were, they proceeded to the town gate, where the Emperor was displeased not to see any workmen. La Vega showed to the Sovereigns the plan, which fixes the location of all the buildings excavated in Pompeii, and what had been done at other times, to make them understand the situation and the shape. The Emperor asked what there was of those buildings which they had not seen, and was assured that they had been covered over again (as perhaps Ancrevil had told him, as he was coming together with the rest of the Emperor's retinue). And he asked the King why he had allowed this. His Majesty replied to this that it had been done in the time of his Esteemed Father {Charles VII}; and La Vega added that it had been done 20 years ago when there was no sign that the site could be a town; but being assured about 6 years ago that it was Pompeii from an inscription found near the site where they were, they had left buildings uncovered, no measures having been taken before this other than for creating the Museum. Their Majesties after this departed at around the 22nd hour and a quarter.

A royal telegram (J25)

(*PAH* I, Part 2, p. 46)

J25 2 December 1789

Telegram. In conformity with the deputation of Your Most Noble Excellency of the 20th of last month, the King approved that for now the excavation of private houses in Pompeii be suspended, and instructed all workers to dig the ancient Theatre, which is already partly uncovered. In the Royal name I am reporting it to Your Most Noble Excellency for your information and for whatever is necessary to be done. The Palace, 2 December 1789.

The varied fortunes of inscriptions (J26–29)

Bronze inscription in the Covered Theatre (J26–28)

(*PAH* I, Part 2, p. 54; *PAH* I, Addenda from manuscript of Ribau, p. 231, 277)

A large bronze inscription was found running across the *orchestra* of the Covered Theatre in 1793 (see D57). Its letters were individually set into the marble paving, and were particularly attractive and susceptible to marauding visitors. It is clearly represented in an early watercolour (H. Wilkins, *Suite de vues pittoresques des ruines de Pompeii et un précis historique de la ville* (Rome 1819), plate xxvii), but no trace of it now remains. These extracts show how it was gradually destroyed by visitors to the site.

J26 7–21 November 1793

Continuing to uncover the Covered Theatre, there was found in the *orchestra*, which is entirely decorated with slabs and strips of a variety of marbles, above a strip of cipollino marble, which takes up the whole diameter of the *orchestra*, the following inscription in bronze letters: M . OCVLATIVS. M. F. VERVS. II. VIR. PRO LVDIS. This is being kept covered in the same place, until the Director La Vega issues instructions.

J27 15 April 1809

Last week between 12 and 15 soldiers came to Pompeii, of those who are stationed at Torre Annunziata. They did not want to be escorted by anyone, and among their fooling about and drunkenness they knocked over some pilasters at the entrance to the Theatre, and they tore out and seized two bronze letters of the inscription, which remains on the paving of the Odeion, an R and an O. The veterans assigned to this part of the site did not believe in worrying themselves about them; the curators were afraid of their sabres.

J28 25 May 1815

On the 24th, at 8 o'clock Italian time, some officers from the Austrian troops, who are passing, came to the excavations of Pompeii. Having gone to look at the Theatre, they removed from it some bronze letters, which had been fixed in the paving there; but when the sergeant of veterans informed their general, who joined them there a few moments later, he summoned them and forced them to return to the curators what they had removed.

The perils of reconstruction: funerary inscription of Umbricius Scaurus (J29)

(*PAH* I, Addenda from manuscript of Ribau, pp. 258–9)

The funerary inscription of Umbricius Scaurus (**F91**), which was found in pieces on the Street of Tombs outside the Herculaneum Gate, is still displayed today on the wrong tomb (see **D31**), following a mistaken restoration.

J29 23 January 1813

The inscription of Scaurus has been placed on the tomb decorated with bas-reliefs in stucco on the above-mentioned street. A.L. Millin, in his pamphlet entitled *Déscription des tombeaux qui ont été decouverts à Pompei dans l'année 1812* (Naples 1813, p. 51ff), doubts that this inscription belonged to the monument on which it has been set, and gives the following reasons for this. {Summary of the reasons: ancient stucco covering brickwork had to be removed to allow the inscription to be attached; there was no sign of the ancient clamping to hold the inscription; the inscription does not fit properly; the lettering is out of proportion to the monument; the style of lettering on the inscription is later in date than the style of the stucco bas-relief.}

Visits to the site (J30–31)

Military troops (J30)

(*PAH* II p. 30)

J30 30 June 1821

Yesterday, Friday, a troop of German soldiers, which is stationed at the garrison in Torre Annunziata, having made their way into various parts of this royal area, committed a series of insolent acts. For example, they took the liberty of breaking into pieces a large terracotta storage jar, which stood beside an entrance to an ancient house, and which had been excavated in the presence of His Majesty the Emperor of Austria; and of also throwing to the ground some column-shafts, which form the peristyle of the public building believed to be a School, which is an extension of the Temple of Isis. But I saw to it that the columns were immediately replaced in their original location, so that this important place should not remain disfigured; and I did not fail at the same time to ask them to co-operate, as a result of which a command was given to the officer of this detachment, which forbade his soldiers from coming to the excavations in the future in so great a number; otherwise there is the risk that they could be the cause of still greater troubles.

Dowager Queen Adelaide of England (J31)

(*PAH* II, p. 361)

The vagueness of this report has misled some scholars into thinking that the visit was by the new Queen Victoria, rather than by the wife of the late William IV.

J31 7 November 1838

On this day, Her Majesty the Queen of England honoured these royal works by visiting with a large entourage, and in her presence an excavation was performed in the shop to the left of the Street of Tombs – the one where a furnace can be seen.

Excavation of the Forum (J32–46)

The Forum and its surrounding buildings were excavated in 1813–1824. The excavation reports of this period are particularly patchy, with whole periods remaining unaccounted for. This was a time of considerable political upheaval, with the Bourbons being driven into exile by Napoleon, followed by the Napoleonic rulers of Naples being ousted in their turn by the return of the Bourbon monarchy from exile in 1815. It is especially difficult to judge, therefore, whether absence of evidence can be taken to be evidence of absence (J33–39). 'Nothing to report' does not necessarily mean that nothing was being found, merely that nothing thought worthy of attention at the time was being uncovered (compare the dismissive attitude even to sizeable blocks of dismembered architecture: J38–39). On the other hand, the tiny handful of workers engaged in this demanding task must have found it difficult to make much headway in their digging. As soon as fragments of statues and significant buildings start to be found, however, the reports contain more details (J40–44). Presumably the earlier reports relate to the clearance of the open piazza.

As a result of these reporting techniques, scholars today hold diametrically opposed views about the state of the Forum in AD 79. Some argue that the town's citizens neglected to repair the Forum following earthquake damage in AD 62 (compare C1–5) and that this is indicative of changing attitudes to public space, with the Forum receiving less attention than the Amphitheatre, for example. Others, however, contend that the Pompeians were actually engaged in executing a lavish building programme, not realizing that their plans would go unfinished.

The apparent lack of material in the Forum is not just the result of reporting techniques. It is likely that much material was salvaged from it in antiquity, both in the immediate aftermath of the eruption and in the centuries following it (J32).

Possible signs of salvaging in antiquity (J32)

(*PAH* I, Part 3, p. 158)

Compare C17–19.

J32 14 August 1814

At the Basilica, we finished clearing the large room, which I mentioned in my previous report, and some broken marble slabs were found there: both their small number and their being found all in confusion indicate that already the ancients had salvaged some of them.

A lean period in the dig (J33–39)

(*PAH* I, Part 3, pp. 181–2)

J33 10 August 1816

While working in excavating the Forum with 2 carts and 7 workmen, nothing to report happened last week.

J34 17 August 1816

Last week we worked in the Forum with 2 carts and 7 workmen, without anything worth any notice happening.

J35 24 August 1816

We continued to clear the Forum with 3 carts and 7 workmen: last week nothing to report happened there.

J36 31 August 1816

Continuing to excavate in the Forum with 2 carts and 7 workmen, nothing noteworthy happened.

J37 7 September 1816

Nothing remarkable happened in excavating in the Forum last week, working with the usual 2 carts and 7 workmen.

J38 28 September 1816

In continuing to excavate the Forum, we again came across the usual size-able pieces of travertine and tufa, consisting of architraves, friezes, cornices and other shapeless pieces, of the sort which are removed by a group of 5 workmen, whom Aquila's contractor had employed, besides the usual 8 workmen and 2 carts.

J39 5 October 1816

In the excavations, last week, nothing to report. The usual 8 workmen, 2 carts and 5 men were employed for taking off the useless pieces and putting back those pieces which belong to various sites, and a craftsman for restoring the pavings. Curators were employed in cleaning the cleared areas.

Temple of Jupiter (J40)

(*PAH* I, Part 3, p. 188)

J40 11 January 1817

It seems that there are beginning to be signs of Signore Arditi's idea, that one day statues must be found in the Forum. In the inner chamber {*cella*} of the afore-mentioned temple, last Saturday, two large feet were found, and a separate arm with a right hand, corresponding in size to them. The feet are each 2¾ feet long, wearing imperial sandals, and the hand grasps a sceptre, or perhaps the handle of some weapon, so that they seem to belong to a colossal imperial statue, about 19 feet tall.

Problems in excavating the Forum (J41–44)

(Extracts from *PAH* I, Part 3, pp. 192–3, 195–6)

The Sarno aqueduct was built at the end of the sixteenth century between Sarno and Torre Annunziata. It mostly proceeded above ground, but some parts of it went underground, including a section lasting about 1,600 metres beneath the hill known as Civita (which later was found to be the site of Pompeii). For other problems encountered by the excavators, see J6 and J8.

J41 7 June 1817

Last week we worked in the usual places indicated many times, with 73 workmen and 4 carts, without anything noteworthy happening. On day 3 of the current month, contrary to Aquila's contractor and the supervisors, we set about searching the small cellar which remains beneath the upper rubble of the Forum, in accordance with instructions of Your Most Noble Lordship. After various searches we finally found a most beautiful bronze statue, broken into 3 pieces, and lacking the right foot, an arm, and a hand. It depicts a young nude male, 5½ feet tall, with a small piece of drapery, which he holds hanging down over his arms, and which covers his loins; this is being kept safe by supervisor Imparato.

J42 19 June 1817

The clearing undertaken in the ancient water tank, where we had the good luck to find the fine bronze statue, has been completely suspended by order of Signore Arditi: with regard to this, Signore Bonucci refers to what he wrote to him last week, without having anything else to add. But we ought to mention that removal of the material extracted from the afore-mentioned tank does not interfere in the slightest with the air vent of the Sarno aqueduct, which powers the engines of the Iron-Foundry directed by Signore Colonel Salinieri . . . {Instead, the workmen concentrate on clearing the Forum's east side.} We proceeded to uncover notable pieces of marble architecture, which can be matched to the buildings so far discovered around about: in addition, some fine fragments of statues, among which a right foot attached to part of its base, of excellent and elegant craftsmanship; with the result that we still hope to find one statue intact of the many which must have stood on the large number of pedestals set up in this large area.

J43 12 July 1817

In this week work was carried out in the Forum, and the only noteworthy occurrence there was the discovery on the 5th of a spear-point of gilded bronze, which is being kept. Aquila's contractor kept employed in the work 62 workmen, 4 carts, a master-plasterer and a band.

J44 15 July 1817

The materials that have been extracted and are still being extracted from the Forum district, and that are being dumped from part of the king's public highway, have by now reached such an extent that the continuation of such tipping could, with the rain of the coming season, block and impede the free flow of traffic on this road . . .

During continuing clearance in the Forum's open space, in order to level it off, among the countless pieces of plain and decorated marble architecture, there were found fragments of various inscriptions, which may perhaps belong to others previously found nearby, and which are kept locked up in the storeroom, of which Signore Arditi holds the key. It would therefore be necessary to carry out a detailed study of them, to try to put together in this way some whole inscriptions, which are so interesting for the study of venerable antiquity.

The fate of Lord Bulwer-Lytton's villain (J45)

(*PAH* I, Part 3, p. 203)

The Last Days of Pompeii by Edward Bulwer-Lytton was a popular historical novel (1834), which drew its inspiration from recent discoveries at Pompeii. The villainous Egyptian priest Arbaces meets his end when a column falls on top of him in the Forum, next to the Temple of Jupiter, during the earth tremors accompanying the eruption.

J45 5 May 1818

This morning in clearing beside the hexastyle temple in the Forum, two skeletons were found, and having looked again at them with every care, nothing else was found near one of them, except only a large bronze coin, and nothing next to the other (who had fallen victim under a marble column).

Eumachia's Building (J46)

(*PAH* II, p. 14)

J46 15 January 1820

Continuing during the last days of last week to clear the secret passage, which leads from the entrance to the left of the public building near to the Forum {i.e. Eumachia's Building} to a temple adjacent to it. A store was found of 16 large white marble slabs, each one 7 ft long, 4 ft high . . . This marble store must perhaps have served for the restoration of the building, as is apparent from various pieces of cornices and marble decoration, which were found in an unfinished state, scattered everywhere in the area.

Excavation of the Amphitheatre (J47–52)

(*PAH* I, Part 3, pp. 169–71)

Although the Amphitheatre was one of the earliest buildings excavated on the site, in 1748, it was the policy at that time to cover over again any buildings uncovered, once finds (such as paintings) had been removed from them. The Estate of Julia Felix also received such treatment (compare J24). Consequently, the Amphitheatre was actually excavated twice, the second time in 1813–1816. Although in general we now deplore the eighteenth-century practice of removing paintings from the site for display in the royal collection, such paintings were at least preserved in this way. By contrast, the scenes painted around the balustrade, or parapet, between the Amphitheatre's arena and seating, depicting wild beast fights, were destroyed by frost (J47–51). They are now known only through watercolour scenes painted by F. Morelli some time before 1816, and through the brief descriptions in these excavation notebooks. Aquila, a character of dubious reputation who owned a private house within the confines of the site, was later critically dubbed by Fiorelli 'the real boss of the excavations'.

J47 2–9 February 1815

Nothing to report. In the road to the east at the rear of the Amphitheatre, another door was found, which is entirely in ruins. In the Amphitheatre, we proceeded to discover the paintings with which the final parapet was decorated. 45 workmen, 12 carts.

J48 12 February 1815

Work was carried out with 12 carts and 51 workmen, whom Aquila's contractor had employed. The section of the wall towards the east was passed over as far as the walls towards the north, in order to search for the other door which enters the town. In the Amphitheatre, the corridor has been entirely buttressed on the right as one descends from the door, on the instructions of Commissioner Signor Minervini, who came on 7 February. The pictures around the last parapet continued to be discovered: among them has emerged a picture with a green background, depicting a tiger chasing a boar.

J49 23 February 1815

In the Amphitheatre, in the last parapet, which separates off the arena on the right as one descends from the door, a small space was discovered, an entrance into another corridor, with two gladiators painted on either side of this space. Workmen 52, carts 12.

J50 8 March 1815

Work was continued; nothing to report. In the defensive wall towards the north we continued to search for another part of that wall, which still has not been found. In the Amphitheatre we proceeded to uncover the final parapet which separates off the arena, on which towards the west has emerged another picture, which depicts a panther chasing a deer.

J51 6 April 1815

On these two days of the current week (there was a holiday on Monday because of the festival of the Annunciation), work was carried out with 70 workers and 14 carts, whom Aquila's contractor had employed. All of the above workmen were solely employed in clearing the interior of the Amphitheatre, and particularly in finding the arena, which is almost totally covered, with only a small portion of it remaining, and which we hope in the course of the current week to see entirely cleared. Following the emergence of the other pictures on the last parapet, which separates off the arena, we saw another one, which depicts a mastiff fighting a bull.

J52 7 April 1815

At 22 hours today the arena of the Amphitheatre was entirely uncovered.

Eruption of Vesuvius in 1822 (J53–54)

(*PAH* II, p. 63–4)

Following a large explosive eruption in 1631, Vesuvius was at its most active in (relatively) recent times during the reign of the Bourbons. Other eruptions occurred in 1737, 1751, 1754, 1760, 1767, 1779, 1786 and 1794. These extracts illustrate the hazards of an eruption for the excavations.

J53 27 October 1822

The terrible explosion of Vesuvius, of which you know, occurred at the beginning of just last week, and I was obliged to flee from Torre Annunziata on Wednesday morning in the direction of Naples on foot, after having spent Tuesday night amidst terrifying thunderous roaring and frightful showers of stones, ash and pumice; consequently I cannot give you information on the excavations of Pompeii. Only I must inform you that I have made all possible provision that great care be taken by those employees who succeeded in remaining there, in spite of the afore-mentioned explosion, in removing the material which has fallen especially onto the roofs, under which are preserved the paintings and statues recently found in these excavations; and in taking other necessary precautions, as a result of which that notable place may be guarded as much as possible. However, up to this point I have received no other news of it, perhaps because the roads are made entirely impassable by the material which has accumulated on them. As soon, therefore, as I receive news and a detailed report of what I have arranged in this respect, I will not fail to give you an accurate report of this.

J54 28 October 1822

According to what I promised you with yesterday's report, I can relate that I have now received news from the supervisor of the Excavations of Pompeii: that the volcanic explosion of stones, ash and pumice, of which you know, although it reached that far in a considerable quantity, nevertheless did not cause any actual damage, except that under the weight of its material, two rafters of roof-covering gave way. These had been recently built above paintings found in a building uncovered a short while ago, to the right of the road north of the civil Forum. But this damage was immediately repaired by the afore-mentioned supervisor, who did not neglect to make his way there during such dangerous circumstances, in accordance with the arrangements I had made and the tasks entrusted to him; and now he is not omitting to continue to get the workmen to remove the afore-mentioned material, in order to see all those ancient buildings clear as much as possible of this material, in the hope that the awe-inspiring volcano does not continue to cause damage of a similar character, inasmuch as it seems now to have abated its fury against this region to some degree.

House of the Faun (VI.xii.2) (J55–58)

(*PAH* II, pp. 232, 240–2)

Until the advent of Fiorelli, there was no accurate system for identifying a house, with the result that the location of a particular building was often described by a long paraphrase. Houses might be named after some distinctive feature, but that name could change over time. What is now commonly known as the House of the Faun (VI.xii.2), for example, has been called 'House of Pan', 'House of Goethe', 'House of the Large Mosaic', 'House of the family of Purius Magius', 'House of Arbaces the Egyptian', 'House of the Battle of Alexander', 'House of M. Cassius' and 'House of the Lucretii Satrii'. The following extracts report the excavation of what is one of the grandest houses in the town, famous for its multicoloured mosaics, especially the so-called Alexander Mosaic (A19). For a plan of the house, see A18.

J55 October–December 1829

Along the road from the Temple of {Augustan} Fortune towards the Gate of Isis {now 'Nolan Gate'}, crossing the heart of the town, on the right was discovered the façade of a magnificent house, decorated with pilasters and Corinthian cornices. Its entrance was covered with a ceiling with elegantly worked coffering and of a design so far unparalleled in Pompeii.

J56 October 1830

Once the Street of Mercury had been completely cleared, we were left free to direct our efforts once more to the street which leads from the Temple of Fortune to the Gate of Isis, passing through the heart of this ancient town.

At once we came across the entrance to a private building, which must be considered among the most surprising things to have been discovered. This entrance was equipped with a high and wide wooden door, made up of three pieces, which were held together by every kind of iron fitting and large rings of bronze. The walls inside displayed an order of coffering as decoration, resting above brackets in the shape of dogs in stucco, represented in energetic and swift movement. Above, rise up 4 small Corinthian columns, which imitate the entrance to a luxurious building, whose doors appear in the background, and which support a second order of coffering, representing the roofing of the afore-mentioned entrance. The interior of these last cofferings was gilded, and contained the miniature busts in stucco of some protecting deities. A lead palette with various colours and with gold leaf, which were perhaps being used to finish the work in this part of the house, was found nearby. The mosaic threshold of the second door, which leads directly into the *atrium*, is a unique monument in terms of its preservation and art. It is 11 feet long by 2¼; and it depicts a large festoon of flowers and fruit, which supports two tragic masks and two circular frames, all of it of incomparable craftsmanship, design and colouring. The *atrium* is decorated with rusticated walls, which appear as if of coloured marbles {i.e. 1st style painting}; in the middle is the *impluvium* with a small fountain. On one of its sides was found a statue of Pan {'the Faun'}, about 3 feet high, of bronze. {Description follows.}

J57 November 1830

The *tablinum* is opposite. To its sides are two splendid rooms, and in front of these the usual covered rooms, or *alae*. In the room to the right of the *tablinum* one admires a mosaic on the floor, 4¼ by 4¼ feet, which depicts a sea shore covered with a large number of fish, lifesized and coloured in a lively way and with surprising accuracy. {Description follows.}

J58 December 1830

In the room to the left of the *tablinum* another mosaic was uncovered this month, 4¼ by 4¼ feet, depicting the Divine Spirit of Bacchus on a panther . . . Festoons of flowers and fruit surround this picture, and from them hang many stage-masks, of a new and varied design. The execution, colouring, style, sensitivity and freshness of this peerless monument cannot be described. {Continues with the right *ala*, where there is a more ordinary mosaic of birds, and the left *ala*, where there is a mosaic of a cat with a dead bird, judged to be possibly the best mosaic discovered.} It is to be noted that apart from the decorations and the rusticated walls imitating coloured marbles, no painting adorns this dwelling. One might say that its owner, scorning a glory which he would have shared in common with more lowly houses, has reserved for himself a type of decoration and of luxury, which it would not be easy to emulate. Thus, this house's *atrium* alone offers enough to create a gallery in the Royal Museum of unparalleled richness.

House of the Vettii (VI.xv.1) (J59–70)

(*NSc* (1894) p. 406; (1895) pp. 31–4, 234)

The following extracts belong to the publication in the *Notizie degli Scavi* of the 'Journal of the excavations compiled by the assistants'. It is worth noting how the report describes only mythological paintings, and does not mention other types of scenes. For the lead weight in J69, see *CIL* X 8067.5.

J59 1–5 November 1894

The excavations to the east of the House of the Labyrinth were restarted, in Region VI, insula 12 [9]. The workmen are directing their attention towards the clearance of the rooms to the right as one looks towards the doorway and in the first of these, which is opposite the peristyle, three paintings came to light, with depictions of the punishment of Dirce in the first, the punishment of Pentheus in the second, and of Hercules with the snakes in the third. In the last room were found another two paintings, one depicting Bacchus and other figures present at the struggle between Cupid and Pan; and the other depicting Cyparissus. The two panels which used to decorate the walls on the east and west sides are missing.

J60 1–2 December 1894

Attention was paid to clearing the large peristyle in *insula* 12 of Region VI, and no discoveries of objects occurred.

J61 4 December 1894

Excavations continued in the same place; and in the upper layer of the soil was found: *Glass.* A small carafe, 0.092 m high, found near the *andron* {men's room}. *Bone.* Twenty-three cylindrical pieces, belonging to hinges.

J62 5–9 December 1894

No finds occurred.

J63a 10 December 1894

The excavations continued in the same place. In the *atrium*, to the left of the *impluvium* the strongbox was found, leaning against a pilaster. It was covered with bronze and iron, and now its restoration is awaited, since it was in fragments.

Plate 9.1 J63b Strongbox in the *atrium* of the House of the Vettii

J64 11 December 1894

The excavations continued in the peristyle of the house in *insula* 12 of Region VI. Near the strongbox previously recorded was picked up: *Bronze*. A casing for a lock with the four corresponding small nails. Seal on which was read in raised letters:

{in *NSc*, the text is shown as it would appear on the seal, in reverse}

A. VETTI
RETVSTT

It is surmounted by a ring, in whose setting is cut an *amphora*. Another seal with the legend also in raised letters:

{again in *NSc*, the text is shown as it would appear on the seal, in reverse}

A. VETTI
CONVIVAES

It is also surmounted by a ring, in whose setting is a *caduceus* {wand}. Ring with the legend:

{again in *NSc*, the text is shown as it would appear on the seal, in reverse}

A V CO

in which is clearly repeated the name of the previous seal, i.e. *A(uli) V(etti) Co(nvivae)*.

J65 12 December 1894

Work continued in the same place; and in the upper layer of soil the following finds were made: *Gold.* Finger-ring, with cornelian on which a Victory is engraved. It was found in the alley to the east of the excavation, near the *andron* {men's room}. Small necklace-chain, with very fine links, in the centre of which is suspended a tiny ring and a small pearl. *Silver.* Circular mirror with engraved work around it; diameter 0.093 m. There is a ring for holding it suspended. Bangle in fragments. *Bronze.* A brooch, 0.072 m high. Another one 0.070 m high. Fluted ring 0.043 m in diameter. *Lead.* A rectangular weight, with handle consisting of an iron ring; 0.055 m high. *Bronze.* A broken dish, also badly preserved, 0.240 m in diameter. It was found in the space under the stairs, which exists in the corridor which leads from the shop on the south side into the *atrium*. Decoration formed of a disk from which hangs a leaf; 0.080 m high. Another one, also formed of a disk, from which hangs another piece of rhomboid shape; 0.085 m high. 10 small pieces, of various shapes, belonging to ornaments. Small brooch, 0.025 m long. {More small finds of bronze, glass and terracotta follow.}

J66a 31 December 1894

Work on excavation in the same places was restarted (except for the part on the north side), and almost the whole peristyle is now completely cleared. This peristyle consists of 7 columns on the short side.

On the south side, are 4 pilasters next to 4 columns, carrying marble statuettes of a Bacchus and 2 Satyrs. The statuette from the column at the south-east corner is missing. In front of the statuette next to the column at the south-west corner is a circular marble basin; and in front of the 2 statuettes of the central columns is also a marble basin, and another circular basin is in front of the south-east column where the statuette is missing.

On the east side, starting from the south side, the fourth and fifth columns were also equipped with statuettes, although these have not been found, and in front there was the usual marble basin, which was found in several pieces; in the next intercolumniation a circular table came to light, also in several pieces, which is supported by 3 table legs with lion's head and feet. On the north side, which is not completely cleared, as was said, has come to light at a distance of 3.50 m from the columns, and in the centre, a rectangular basin of Greek marble, shell-shaped, in the middle of which is a sea creature in low relief and further in front on the same axis a column for jetting out water. Two herms with small columns decorated in relief with leaves stand further in front, topped by two-faced heads, of a bearded figure on one side and a woman on the other; and finally another small column rises up nearby, without its table. On the west side, between the north-west column and the other one to the west, between the third and fourth columns, next to which are two statuettes depicting two cherubs, is another marble basin.

Plate 9.2 J66b **Peristyle garden in the House of the Vettii**

J67 14 May 1895

In the kitchen of the house currently being excavated the following came to light: *Bronze*. A cauldron 326 mm in diameter, in a poor state of preservation. Another, its belly and lip damaged, also poorly preserved; 336 mm in diameter. Another, 337 mm in diameter. A fourth, its edge broken, 286 mm in diameter. Cauldron with moveable handle, 223 mm in diameter. *Iron*. A gridiron in fragments. A fragmentary tripod. A second tripod, also broken. *Terracotta*. Pot-bellied vessel, with a handle, with neck ending in the shape of an oil jar; 254 mm high. Ordinary vessel with narrow and short neck, with a thin handle, 268 mm high. Six other similar vessels, 193–257 mm high. A narrow-necked flask with thin handles, 344 mm high. A wide-mouthed vessel, and two thin handles, 328 mm high. A shallow basin 300 mm internal diameter. *Marble*. Statuette of male figure, headless, and lacking left arm, right forearm and toes; 830 mm high. Another statuette, restored by the ancients themselves, with head of Satyr and club in left hand. Lacks right leg, left foot, and right hand; 840 mm high.

J68 15–17 May 1895

No finds.

J69 18 May 1895

In the second room, to the right of the peristyle of the house currently excavated, was found: *Lead*. A weight, on one side of which is inscribed: EME and on the other: HABEBIS. In the room to the left of the large reception room were found three bronze hinges.

J70 20 May 1895

In the room mentioned were found another two bronze hinges {and another two also found on 23 May}.

KNOWN DATES OF GAMES AT POMPEII AND OUTSIDE

Data for bar chart (D10)

Table 1 Games at Pompeii

CIL IV number	Source number	Venue	Date of games	Gladiators	Hunt	Other	Duration (days)
1179	D19	Pompeii	24, 25, 26 November	30 pairs plus replacements	✓	V	3
1180	D23	Pompeii	4 July	troupe	✓	V	1
1183		Pompeii	16 May	troupe	✓	V	1
1185	D13	Pompeii	28 March	? troupe	✓	V	1
1186		Pompeii	from 20 April	troupe	✓	V	2?
1189	D16	Pompeii	31 May	troupe	✓	V	1
1199		Pompeii	27, 28, 29, 30 November	?	✓	V	4
1204		Pompeii	from 1 June	30 pairs	?	?	3?
1989		*Pompeii*	*28 August*		✓	*bears*	*1*
1989a		*Pompeii*	*5 January*			*bull*	*1*
2508	*D32*	*Pompeii*	*1?, 2 May*	*results name*			*2*
			11, 12, 13, 14, 15 May	*30 or more gladiators*			*5*
3884	D11	Pompeii	8, 9, 10, 11, 12 April	30 pairs	✓	V	5
7988		Pompeii	4, 5 June	?	?	?	2
7989a		Pompeii	25, 26 February	none	✓	Ath & Sp	2
7992	D12	Pompeii	from 4 April	30 pairs	✓	V	3?
7993	D21	Pompeii	13 June	none	✓	Ath & P	1
7995	D14	Pompeii	from 28 March	30 pairs	✓	V	3?
9974		Pompeii	12, 13, 14 May	?	?	?	3
9980		Pompeii	4, 5, 6, 7 November	20 pairs	✓	✗	4
9986		Pompeii	23 and? January	more than 40 pairs	?	?	1+

Pompeii notices of games with dates only partly legible: *CIL* IV 1184 – ?May; 1187 – 2 A[pril] or 2 A[ugust]; 1193 – 5 A[pril] or 5 A[ugust]; 9962 (**D18**) – 30 January or 11 February

Pompeii notices of games with dates not legible or not given: *CIL* IV 1177 (**D22** = 7993?); 1178; 1192; 1192a; 1194; 1196; 1200; 1201; (3883 = 1177/ 7993?); 7986a; 7991 (**D20** no date given = 1179?); 9963; 9965; 9967; 9968; 9975; 9982; 9985

Table 2 Games outside Pompeii

CIL IV number	Source Number	Venue	Date of games	Gladiators	Hunt	Other	Duration (days)
3881		Nola	1, 2, 3 May	20 pairs	✓	✗	3
3882		Nuceria	5, 6, 7, 8 May	20 pairs	✓	✗	4
4299	*D49*	*Nuceria*	*28 July*	*(record of victories by one gladiator)*			*1*
		Herculaneum	*16 August*				*1*
7994	D30	Puteoli	12, 14, 16, 18 May	49 pairs	✗	V	4
9969		Puteoli	9 ?December	?	?	V	1
9970		Puteoli	17, 18, 19, 20 March	20 pairs	✓	Ath	4
9972		Nuceria	31 October, 1, 8, 9 November	36 pairs	✗	✗	4
9973	D29	?Nuceria	30 ?October	20 pairs	?	?	1
9976		?Cumae	18, 19, 20 May	?	?	?	3
9977		?Cales	5, 7 June	20 pairs	✗	V	2
9983a		Cumae	1, 5, 6 October	20 pairs	✓	V & Cruc	3
10161		Nuceria	21 April	?	?	O	1
AE 1990, 177b		Capua	23, 24 January	40 pairs	✗	V	2
AE 1990, 177c		Forum Popilii	20, 21, 22, 23 May	24 pairs	✓	✗	4

Notices of games held outside Pompeii with dates not legible: *CIL* IV 9978 – Nola; 9984 – Puteoli Most of the inscriptions tabulated here are painted notices of games to be given. Entries in italics indicate other written evidence, e.g. results and scratched messages relating to individuals: these may give the date, but could not be expected to give information about what else may have happened at the games. Several sets of games are advertised as being from a given date: here the number of gladiators usually suggests that the games would have lasted several days (perhaps depending on the weather and/or how quickly the fights ended). We have given an estimate for the duration. A question mark indicates that part of the notice cannot be read. Where crosses appear, the whole notice is preserved, without mention of a particular feature.

For other types of entertainment/facilities advertised:

Ath	athletes
Cruc	crucifixions
P	procession
Sp	sprinklings of water
U	uncovered (i.e. no *vela*)
V	*vela* (awning)

Appendix 2

TABLE SHOWING QUOTATIONS OF LITERATURE FOUND WRITTEN ON THE WALLS OF POMPEII

Author	Work		Freq	Reference (CIL IV)
Ennius	*Annals* (Ed. Skutsch fr.110)		4	3135, 7353, 8568 (adapted), 8995
Homer	*Iliad*	various	1	4078
Lucretius	*On the Nature*	1.1	5	3072, 3118, 3139, 3913, 4373 (?)
	of Things	1.86	1	5020
		2.1	1	*CErc* (1973) 102 n.28
Ovid	*Art of Love*	1.9.1	1	3149
		1.475–6	1	1895* (var.)
	Amores	1.8.77–8	1	1893*
		3.2.1	1	1595* (adapted)
		3.11.35	2	1520* (adapted), 9847* (adapted)
	Heroides	4.17	1	4133
		20.205	1	1595* (adapted)
Propertius	*Elegies*	1.1.5	6	1520, 1523, 1526, 1528, 3040, 9847* (all adapted)
		2.5.9–10	1	4491*
		4.5.47–8	1	1894*
		4.16.13–14	1	1950* (var.)
Seneca	*Agamemnon*	730	1	6698
Tibullus	*Elegies*	2.6.30	1	1837* (?badly preserved)
Virgil	*Aeneid*	1.1	12	1282, 2361, 3198, 4757, 4832*, 5002, 5337, 7131, 8416, 8831, 10059(?), 10086
		1.135	1	4409(?)
		1.192–3	1	8630b (adapted)
		1.234	1	5012*
		2.1	14	1672, 2213, 3151(?), 3889, 4036, 4191, 4212, 4665, 4675, 4877(?), 6707, 8222, 8247(?), 10096b
		2.148	1	1841*
		5.110/9.269	1	1237* (adapted)
		7.1	3	3796, 4127, 4373(?)
		8.1	1	10190 (with *AE* (1989) 185) (adapted)
		9.404	1	2310k*

Eclogues	2.21	2	8625, *AE* (1992) 279
	2.56	3	1527 (var.), 1524, 4660 (?var.)
	3.1	1	5007 (adapted)
	5.72	1	5195
	8.70	3	1982, 4401 (?), 5304 (?)
Georgics	1.163	2	8560, 8610

Notes:

* – denotes quotation beyond a couple of words

var. – variation: some difference from our known versions in manuscript

adapted – deliberate reworking

CIL IV 2400a is a one-line palindrome from the Greek Anthology (Planudes 6.13) written in Greek and underneath in Roman letters.

CIL IV 733 reproduces in Greek a quotation by the philosopher Diogenes the Cynic, as reported by the Greek writer Diogenes Laertes at 6.50.

Appendix 3

A GUIDE TO MONETARY VALUES

	sesterces
A member of Rome's equestrian class had to possess property worth	400,000
Local councillors might have had to possess (figure for Pompeii unknown)	100,000
A legionary received on discharge after 25 years' service	12,000
Sale of the slave Trophimus	6,252
The large marble basin in the Forum Baths cost	5,250
Funeral costs for M. Obellius Firmus	5,000
Two slaves, Simplex and Petrinus, sold for	2,000
On occasion, the town council paid towards public funerals	2,000
12 pints of *garum* fetched	1,000
Basic legionary annual pay was	900
Sale of a mule raised	520
A tunic (of unknown quality) cost	15
The prostitute Attice charged	4
A cup of Falernian wine at a bar	1
A cup of poor quality wine at a bar	¼

These figures can be assumed to apply to the last decades of Pompeii's history. Inflation was not an important factor at this time.

1 sesterce = 4 *asses*; 4 sesterces = 1 *denarius*

Appendix 4

BRIEF LIST OF DATES OF
RELEVANCE TO POMPEII

510 BC	Establishment of Republican government in Rome
323 BC	Death of Alexander the Great; start of period of Hellenistic culture
89 BC	Pompeii captured by Sulla during Social War
c.81 BC	Roman colony established at Pompeii
73 BC	Slave revolt of Spartacus
63 BC	Cicero consul; Catiline declared public enemy
49 BC	Julius Caesar begins civil war with Pompey the Great. End of Roman Republic?
44 BC	Julius Caesar assassinated
31 BC	Octavian defeats Mark Antony to become undisputed sole ruler of the Roman empire
27 BC	Octavian adopts the name Augustus and reigns until AD 14
AD 14–37	Tiberius emperor
AD 37–41	Gaius Caligula emperor
AD 41–54	Claudius emperor
AD 54–68	Nero emperor
AD 59	Riot in Pompeii's Amphitheatre
AD 62	February: major earthquake affecting Pompeii
AD 68–69	Civil war; 'Year of the four emperors'
AD 69–79	Vespasian emperor
AD 79–81	Titus emperor (from 24 June AD 79)
AD 79	24 August: eruption of Vesuvius

GLOSSARY

aedile   local magistrate, elected annually, in charge of streets, sacred and public buildings

amphora/-ae   large pottery container, often used for olive oil and wine

as (**pl.** *asses*)   the base unit of Roman currency, a small value coin

atrium   main reception room of a house, with *impluvium* in the middle, leading to other rooms

Augustalis   a priest involved in emperor-worship

Augustus   name adopted by the emperor Octavian, and used as part of the title of subsequent emperors

Basilica   public building where legal business was usually conducted

bisellium   an honorific double-width seat

Caesar   the *cognomen* of Julius Caesar (the general and *dictator*); used as a family name by his heir, Augustus, and his family; occasionally used to refer to the current emperor

client   a citizen who voluntarily paid his respects to a richer, more powerful patron, in return for his protection; an ex-slave with obligations to his or her former master

cognomen   the last of a Roman's names, sometimes a type of nickname, but often distinguishing not just an individual, but a branch of a large family

Colonia Veneria Cornelia   the official title for Pompeii as a Roman colony, taken from the names of Venus (its guardian deity) and Cornelius Sulla, the founder of the colony

colonist   citizen of a colony; at Pompeii in the period after it became a colony, a Roman settler rather than original inhabitant

colony   a settlement of Roman citizens (often army veterans) with its own local constitution

consul   the highest political office in the Republic, and still in existence under the emperors, though without real political power. Two were elected each year to serve for one year

decurion   local town councillor

denarius   Roman coin, worth 4 sesterces

dictator   official appointed in time of emergency in Rome

dipinti   inscriptions painted on walls

duumvirs   the two senior annually elected magistrates at Pompeii

epitaph   inscription on a tomb, honouring the deceased

equestrian (1) a member of this class in Rome, almost equal in status to the senatorial class; (2) equestrian statue: statue of a man on horseback (compare *pedestrian statue*)

Etruscan   the language and culture of an indigenous Italian people, from the area of modern Tuscany. Around 500 BC, their empire was the most important in Italy

exedra   a large funerary monument also providing a seat

Forum   open piazza in a town, surrounded by public buildings; the focus of religious, commercial, administrative and judicial affairs

freedman, freedwoman   an ex-slave, set free by his or her master, automatically becoming a Roman citizen (and the client of his or her former master)

fullery   laundry where clothes were cleaned and finished

garum   fish sauce

genius   the guardian spirit of a person (or place)

graffiti   writing scratched upon a hard surface with a metal implement

Hellenistic   describes Greek culture originating after the death of Alexander the Great (323 BC) in the areas of his conquest

herm   a small stone pillar with the representation of a human head

Ides   the thirteenth or fifteenth day of the Roman month

imperator   originally a title given by Roman troops to their general after a major victory, adopted by Augustus and by later emperors as part of the emperor's official title

impluvium   square pool in the middle of the *atrium*'s floor, leading to a cistern, for collecting rainwater from roof

insula   block of buildings defined by streets on all sides

Kalends   the first day of the Roman month

lararium   shrine for the household gods (*lares*)

lares   guardian spirits, of households and of crossroads

libation   liquid (usually wine) poured as an offering to gods or spirits of the dead

Macellum   meat and fish market in the Forum

magistrate   a politician elected for a year – at Pompeii, aediles and duumvirs

military tribune   properly an officer in the Roman army, but sometimes a purely honorary title given by popular demand

necropolis   area for burial of bodies or ashes of the dead and their monuments

Nones   the fifth or seventh day of a Roman month

orchestra   semicircular area of a theatre in front of the stage

Oscan   one of the local languages of Italy, used in Campania, which was gradually replaced by Latin

palaestra   large open area, surrounded by a colonnade, originally for exercise

patron   a more wealthy and important citizen who looked after the interests of poorer clients in return for their support and public deference; a town's patron protected its interests at Rome

pedestrian statue   statue of a man standing up (compare *equestrian*)

peristyle   a garden area in a Roman house, surrounded by a colonnade

portico   a colonnade around a central (open-air) area

prefect   at Pompeii, a magistrate appointed only in special circumstances

pumice   a light volcanic rock

quaestor   at Pompeii, before *c*.80 BC, a magistrate responsible for financial matters; also an officer responsible for a cult's finances

quinquennial   the highest political office in Pompeii, elected every five years

Republican   modern usage to refer to the period when Rome was governed by elected magistrates (rather than emperors)

Samnite   the name of a people from the region to the north of Campania

senate   the ruling council of Rome

sesterces   Roman unit of currency

Sibyl   a woman, often a priestess, thought to act as the mouthpiece of a god

stucco   decorative plasterwork

tablinum   room in a house between *atrium* and garden area, thought to be where the householder conducted his business

travertine   white limestone

tribe   all citizens of the Roman empire were formally members of one of thirty-five tribes

tribunician power   a legal power adopted by Augustus and by subsequent emperors and their chosen successors. Its use as part of an emperor's title enables inscriptions to be dated.

triclinium   room in a house for dining, with couches

tufa   stone formed from compacted volcanic ash

urceus   small pottery storage container

vela   canvas awning providing shelter for spectators at the theatre or amphitheatre

FURTHER READING

General books

Possibly the best introduction to the overall history of the site is Zanker (1998). This is available in English translation, contains a large number of illustrations, and presents some interesting analyses of the development of the town over time. For up-to-date guidebooks, two Italian archaeological guides are the most comprehensive: de Vos and de Vos (1982) and La Rocca *et al.* (1994). There is no equivalent in English, although the relevant section in the *Blue Guide* to Southern Italy (Blanchard 1990) is a guide of manageable proportions (albeit outdated in parts) for accompanying a visit to the site. Cooley (2003) explores the political and cultural context of the site's excavation, and presents recent vulcanological research for a non-specialist readership. For thoughtful studies of housing and town planning, see Wallace-Hadrill (1994) and Laurence (1994).

We have limited our discussion and illustration of artefacts relevant to the study of Pompeii. Some of the outstanding artefacts found at Pompeii, as well as more mundane ones, are often made available to viewers outside the site and museum storerooms via exhibition catalogues, such as Ward-Perkins and Claridge (1976). There is also much useful material in a catalogue of Naples Museum: De Caro (1996).

An excellent series of pamphlets, available in English translation, was produced by the Soprintendenza to commemorate the 250th anniversary of the beginning of the excavations. D'Ambrosio (1998b) provides a succinct introduction to the site's early excavation; for visitors to the site who wish to escape from the crowds in the town, a peaceful walk has been designed around the town's perimeter, illustrated by Ciarallo and De Carolis (1998b); Berry (1998) presents the latest research on Pompeii's early history. A series of short thematic picture books has also begun to be published (Pompei – Guide tematiche), including De Carolis (2000) and d'Ambrosio (2001).

'Coffee-table' books exist seemingly by their hundreds, often with fantastic photography, but with rather poor quality captions and text. One of the best and most up-to-date of these is Nappo (1998).

If hunting for information about a particular topic, turn to the *Nova biblio-theca pompeiana* (García y García 1998), which provides an exhaustive list of everything ever published about Pompeii, with 14,596 entries in all. It contains useful indexes by topography and theme.

Chapter 1 Pre-Roman Pompeii

Etruscan graffiti from Pompeii are published by Cristofani *et al.* (1996) 59–64, nos. 8747–75. Many of them were found in the Temple of Apollo, on which see De Caro (1986).

The standard publication of Oscan inscriptions is Vetter (1953) nos. 8–22, updated by Antonini (1977) and Poccetti (1979) nos. 107–10. For the possibility that the inscription **A9** was deliberately preserved in Roman times, see Cooley (2002).

The impact of Hellenistic culture on the town is considered by Zanker (1998) pp. 32–60 and De Caro (1991). Brief archaeological reports have been published on the Sanctuary of Dionysus – Maiuri (1947), Van Buren (1948), Elia and Pugliese Carratelli (1979) – but no full-scale publication exists.

Chapter 2 Roman colonization of Pompeii

For a completely different interpretation of the military notices (Vetter (1953) nos. 23–8, **B5**), as somehow related to electioneering, see Campanile (1996).

On the impact of Sulla's colonization of the town, especially upon its urban development, see Andreau (1980), Castrén (1976), Kockel (1987), Zanker (1998) pp. 61–77 and Zevi (1995). Gabba (1972) remains the classic article on the wider Italian context of this transformation. For Gaius Quinctius Valgus (**B9–10**) see Dessau (1883) and Harvey (1973).

Berry (1996) is now the standard edition of Cicero's speech, *pro Sulla*, while the particular problem of Pompeii is succinctly analysed by Wiseman (1977).

Chapter 3 Destruction of Pompeii

Some books on Pompeii persist in incorrectly dating the major earthquake to AD 63, despite the generally accepted arguments of Onorato (1949) in favour of AD 62. Hine (1984) gives a plausible explanation of the discrepancy between Tacitus and Seneca. Extensive discussion and photographic evidence for earthquake damage and repairs can be found in Adam (1986) and in *Archäologie und Seismologie* (1995). Gradel (1992) makes some new suggestions about the Forum earthquake relief (**C3**).

For modern assessments of the accuracy of Pliny's account of the eruption, in the light of recent scientific discoveries, see Sigurdsson *et al.* (1982) and Varone and Marturano (1997). For a critical discussion of the minority view that the eruption took place in November, not August, see Ciarallo and De Carolis (1998a).

For discussion of **C28–29**, see Brenk (1999). For a general analysis of both earthquake and eruption, and contemporary responses to the eruption, see Cooley (2003) chs 2–3.

Chapter 4 Leisure

The architecture and history of Pompeii's amphitheatre are clearly outlined by Bomgardner (2000) pp. 39–58, with helpful plans. The archaeological evidence for awnings over the Amphitheatre and Theatre is presented by Graefe (1979). The standard work on the painted notices advertising shows is Sabbatini Tumolesi (1980). For detailed discussion of the 'tomb of Scaurus' and its reliefs (**D31**), see Kockel (1983) pp. 75–85. Moeller (1970) examines the historical significance of the riot. The career of Alleius Nigidius Maius is analysed by Franklin (1997) and Van Buren (1947).

On the significance of the building work of the Holconii in the Large Theatre and its relationship to Augustan Rome see D'Arms (1988) and Small (1987). Contrasting views on the function of the Odeion can be found in Zanker (1998) pp. 65–8 and Zevi (1995). On actors in general and Norbanus Sorex in particular, see the new material from Nemi discussed by Granino Cecere (1988–1989); Franklin (1987) discusses the troupe of Actius Anicetus.

Literary graffiti are catalogued and discussed by Gigante (1979). Graffiti accompanying pictures (not just from Pompeii) are superbly published by Langner (2001), complete with a CD-Rom containing extensive documentation and a searchable database. On **D82**, see further Maulucci Vivolo (1993) p. 189.

For basic data on the baths at Pompeii, see Nielsen (1993), catalogue nos. C40–47.

Chapter 5 Religion

Individual aspects of religion at Pompeii, rather than the overall picture, have attracted discussion. The cult of Isis is particularly well documented, with one catalogue of finds from the Temple of Isis (De Caro 1992) and another of finds relating to the cult of Isis in general (Tran Tam Tinh 1964).

The identity of the temple dedicated by Mamia is discussed further by Gradel (1992) and Fishwick (1995), with Wallat (1995b) arguing that the door-frame currently displayed on Eumachia's Building actually belonged to this neighbouring temple.

An article by Van Andringa (2000) usefully collates evidence for all crossroad shrines. Household shrines are catalogued by Boyce (1937) and Fröhlich (1991), with discussion of their significance in Foss (1997).

Chapter 6 Politics and public life

On political life at Pompeii in general, see the contrasting approaches of Castrén (1975), Franklin (2001) and Mouritsen (1988). On electoral notices, see further Franklin (1978, 1980). For other urban features producing a distribution pattern similar to the one in **F29** (**Figure 6.1**), see Laurence (1994) Map 5.3 (bars), Maps 6.1–4 (doorways), Maps 6.5–8 (messages).

Chapter 7 Tombs

The standard publications of the so-called 'Street of Tombs' outside the Herculaneum Gate and of the necropolis outside the Nucerian Gate are Kockel (1983) and d'Ambrosio and De Caro (1983). The most recent discussion of tombs at Pompeii, including new material and analysis of other little known material, is an exhibition catalogue, *Pompei oltre la vita* (1998).

The tomb of Vestorius Priscus has been published in detail by Mols and Moormann (1993–1994); the tomb of Obellius Firmus by De Franciscis (1976), with further important discussion by Jongman (1978–1979) and De Caro (1979); tomb of the Lucretii Valentes by De' Spagnolis Conticello (1993–1994). For the burials of praetorians outside the Nolan Gate, see De Caro (1979).

Chapter 8 Commercial life

The fascinating work of Jashemski (1979, 1993) in uncovering gardens and vineyards is superbly and lavishly illustrated. In aiming to cover every known garden area in Pompeii, she provides information on a large number of houses and on far more than horticulture. Her work is discussed by Cooley (2003), ch. 6. For the Inn of Euxinus, see Jashemski (1967, 1979, pp. 172–6, 1993, pp. 51–2). Jashemski and Meyer (2002) provide an exhaustive analysis of data pertaining to the natural environment of the town.

The House of Amarantus was re-excavated in the mid-1990s by a team from the University of Reading and British School at Rome; their results are published by Berry (1997, 1998) and Fulford and Wallace-Hadrill (1999).

For discussion of Umbricius Scaurus' fish sauce, see Curtis (1984, 1988); Curtis (1979) reports the excavation of a fish sauce shop in I.xii.8. The *amphorae* of Eumachius are discussed briefly by Tchernia and Zevi (1972).

Pirson (1997) compares the information given about property in the rental notices (**H44** and **H50**) with the buildings on which the notices are displayed, trying to discern which parts of the *insula* were for rent. For a related discussion of the mixed commercial interests of the elite, see Parkins (1997). The sample of trades in I.vi–xii is taken from that recorded by Wallace-Hadrill (1994) pp. 187–97.

The paintings of the Forum from the Estate of Julia Felix are republished, with pictures, by Nappo (1989).

The tablets of Caecilius Iucundus were published by Zangemeister (1898); their historical significance and the wider context of banking have been discussed by Andreau (1973, 1974, 1999).

Chapter 9 Excavation reports

For Fiorelli's outstanding contribution to the excavation of Pompeii, see Cooley (2003) ch. 5 and Castiglione Morelli (1999).

The exhibition of paintings and statues from the Temple of Isis in Naples Museum is accompanied by a catalogue commenting on the temple's excavation and listing the finds (De Caro 1992).

For further background on the Bourbons' attitudes to the site, see Cooley (2003) ch. 4.

For discussion of the state of the Forum in AD 79, see Andreau (1984), Cooley (2003) ch. 1, Dobbins (1994), Wallat (1995a) and Zanker (1998) pp. 129–33.

BIBLIOGRAPHY

Adam, J-P. (1986) 'Observations techniques sur les suites du séisme de 62 à Pompéi', in C. Albore Livadie (ed.) *Tremblements de terre, éruptions volcaniques et vie des hommes dans la Campanie antique*, Naples: Bibliothèque de l'Institut français de Naples, Centre Jean Bérard, 67–87.

d'Ambrosio, A. (1998a) 'Scavi e scoperte nel suburbio di Pompei', *Rivista di studi pompeiani* 9: 197–9.

—— (ed.) (1998b) *Discovering Pompeii: Itineraries for Visitors on the Occasion of the 250th Anniversary of the Beginning of the Excavations*, Milan: Electa.

—— (2001) *La bellezza femminile a Pompei*, Rome: «L'Erma» di Bretschneider.

d'Ambrosio, A. and De Caro, S. (1983) *Un impegno per Pompeii: fotopiano e documentazione della necropoli di Porta Nocera*, Milan: TOTAL, Touring club italiano.

Andreau, J. (1973) 'Remarques sur la société pompéienne (à propos des tablettes de L. Caecilius Jucundus)', *Dialoghi di Archeologia* 7(2–3): 213–54.

—— (1974) *Les Affaires de Monsieur Jucundus*, Rome: Ecole française de Rome.

—— (1980) 'Pompéi: mais où sont les vétérans de Sylla?', *Revue des Etudes Anciennes* 82: 183–99.

—— (1984) 'Il terremoto del 62', in F. Zevi (ed.) *Pompei 79*, Naples: G. Macchiaroli, 40–4.

—— (1999) *Banking and Business in the Roman World*, trans. J. Lloyd, Cambridge: Cambridge University Press.

Antonini, R. (1977) 'Iscrizioni osche pompeiane', *Studi etruschi* 45: 317–40.

—— (1978) 'Pompei', in A.L. Prosdocimi (ed.) *Popoli e civiltà dell'Italia antica* VI. *Lingue e dialetti*, Rome: Biblioteca di storia patria, 865–73.

Archäologie und Seismologie (1995) *La regione vesuviana dal 62 al 79 d.C. Problemi archeologici e sismologici*, Munich: Biering and Brinkmann.

Berry, D.H. (1996) *Cicero Pro P. Sulla Oratio*, Cambridge: Cambridge University Press.

Berry, J. (1997) 'The conditions of domestic life in Pompeii in AD 79: a case-study of Houses 11 and 12, Insula 9, Region 1', *Papers of the British School at Rome* 52: 103–25.

—— (ed.) (1998) *Unpeeling Pompeii: Studies in Region I of Pompeii*, Milan: Electa.

Blanchard, P. (1990) *Southern Italy: From Rome to Calabria*, 7th edn, London: A. & C. Black.

Bomgardner, D.L. (2000) *The Story of the Roman Amphitheatre*, London: Routledge.

Boyce, G.K. (1937) *Corpus of the Lararia of Pompeii*, Rome: American Academy in Rome.

Brenk, F.E. (1999) *Clothed in Purple Light: Studies in Vergil and in Latin Literature, including Aspects of Philiosophy, Religion, Magic, Judaism, and the New Testament Background*, Stuttgart: Steiner.

Campanile, E. (1996) 'Le iscrizioni osche di Pompei attribuite al periodo della Guerra Sociale', in L. Breglia Pulci Doria (ed.) *L'incidenza dell'antico: Studi in memoria di Ettore Lepore* II, Naples: Luciano editore, 361–75.

Castiglione Morelli, V. (ed.) (1999) *A Giuseppe Fiorelli nel primo centenario della morte*, Naples: Arte tipografica.

Castrén, P. (1975) *Ordo Populusque Pompeianus: Polity and Society in Roman Pompeii*, Rome: Bardi.

—— (1976) 'Hellenismus und Romanisierung in Pompeji', in P. Zanker (ed.) *Hellenismus in Mittelitalien*, Göttingen: Vandenhoeck and Ruprecht, 356–65.

Ciarallo, A. and De Carolis, E. (1998a) 'La data dell'eruzione', *Rivista di studi pompeiani* 9: 63–73.

—— (eds) (1998b) *Around the Walls of Pompeii: The Ancient City in its Natural Environment*, Milan: Electa.

Cooley, A.E. (2002) 'The survival of Oscan in Roman Pompeii', in A.E. Cooley (ed.) *Becoming Roman, Writing Latin? Literacy and Epigraphy in the Roman West*, Portsmouth, RI: *Journal of Roman Archaeology* supplement 48, 77–86.

—— (2003) *Pompeii*, London: Duckworth.

Cristofani, M. *et al.* (eds) (1996) *Corpus Inscriptionum Etruscarum* II.2, Rome.

Curtis, R.I. (1979) 'The garum shop of Pompeii', *Cronache pompeiane* 5: 5–23.

—— (1984) 'A personalized floor mosaic from Pompeii', *American Journal of Archaeology* 88: 557–66.

—— (1988) 'A. Umbricius Scaurus of Pompeii', in R.I. Curtis (ed.) *Studia Pompeiana et Classica in Honor of Wilhelmina F. Jashemski*. I *Pompeiana*, New York: Aristide D. Caratzas, 19–50.

D'Arms, J.H. (1988) 'Pompeii and Rome in the Augustan age and beyond: the eminence of the *Gens Holconia*', in R.I. Curtis (ed.) *Studia Pompeiana et Classica in Honor of Wilhelmina F. Jashemski*. I *Pompeiana*, New York: Aristide D. Caratzas, 51–74.

De Caro, S. (1979) 'Scavi nell'area fuori Porta Nola a Pompei', *Cronache pompeiane* 5: 61–101.

—— (1986) *Saggi nell'area del tempio di Apollo a Pompei: Scavi stratigrafici di A. Maiuri nel 1931–32 e 1942–43*, Naples: Istituto universitario orientale, Dipartimento di studi del mondo classico e del Mediterraneo antico.

—— (1991) 'La città sannitica urbanistica e architettura', in F. Zevi (ed.) *Pompei I*, Naples: Banco di Napoli, 23–46.

—— (ed.) (1992) *Alla ricerca di Iside: Analisi, studi e restauri dell' Iseo pompeiano nel Museo di Napoli*, Rome: Arti.

—— (1996) *The National Archaeological Museum of Naples*, Naples: Guide Artistiche Electa Napoli.

De Carolis, E. (2000) *Dei ed eroi nella pittura pompeiana*, Rome: «L'Erma» di Bretschneider.

De Franciscis, A. (1976) 'Sepolcro di M. Obellius Firmus', *Cronache pompeiane* 2: 246–8.

De' Spagnolis Conticello, M. (1993–1994) 'Sul rinvenimento della villa e del monumento funerario dei Lucretii Valentes', *Rivista di studi pompeiani* 6: 147–66.

Dessau, H. (1883) 'C. Quinctius Valgus, der Erbauer des Amphitheaters zu Pompeii', *Hermes* 18: 620–2.

de Vos, A. and de Vos, M. (1982) *Pompei, Ercolano, Stabia*, Rome: G. Laterza.

Dobbins, J.J. (1992) 'The altar in the sanctuary of the Genius of Augustus in the Forum at Pompeii', *Mittheilungen des deutschen archaeologischen Instituts Rom* 99: 251–63.

—— (1994) 'Problems of chronology, decoration, and urban design in the Forum at Pompeii', *American Journal of Archaeology* 98(4): 629–94.

Elia, O. and Pugliese Carratelli, G. (1979) 'Il santuario dionisiaco di Pompei', *Parola del Passato* 34: 442–81.

Fishwick, D. (1995) 'The inscription of Mamia again: the cult of the *Genius Augusti* and the temple of the imperial cult on the *Forum* of Pompeii', *Epigraphica* 57: 17–38.

Foss, P. (1997) 'Watchful *Lares*: Roman household organization and the rituals of cooking and eating', in R. Laurence and A. Wallace-Hadrill (eds) *Domestic Space in the Roman World: Pompeii and Beyond*, Portsmouth, RI: *Journal of Roman Archaeology* supplement 22, 196–218.

Franklin, J.L., Jr (1978) 'Notes on Pompeian prosopography: *programmatum scriptores*', *Cronache pompeiane* 4: 54–74.

—— (1980) *Pompeii: The Electoral Programmata, Campaigns and Politics, AD 71–79*, Rome: American Academy in Rome.

—— (1987) 'Pantomimists at Pompeii: Actius Anicetus and his troupe', *American Journal of Philology* 108: 95–107.

—— (1997) 'Cn. Alleius Nigidius Maius and the amphitheatre: *munera* and a distinguished career at ancient Pompeii', *Historia* 96: 434–47.

—— (2001) *Pompeis difficile est: Studies in the Political Life of Imperial Pompeii*, Ann Arbor, MI: University of Michigan Press.

Fröhlich, T. (1991) *Lararien und Fassadenbilder in den Vesuvstädten: Untersuchungen zur 'volkstümlichen' pompejanischen Malerei*, Mainz: Zabern.

Fulford, M. and Wallace-Hadrill, A. (1999) 'Towards a history of pre-Roman Pompeii: excavations beneath the House of Amarantus (I.9.11–12), 1995–98', *Papers of the British School at Rome* 67: 37–144.

Gabba, E. (1972) 'Urbanizzazione e rinnovamenti urbanistici nell' Italia centro-meridionale del 1 sec. a.C.', *Studi classici e orientali* 21: 73–112.

García y García, L. (1998) *Nova bibliotheca pompeiana: 250 anni di bibliografia archeologica*, Rome: Bardi.

Gigante, M. (1979) *Civiltà delle forme letterarie nell'antica Pompei*, Naples: Bibliopolis.

Giordano, C. and Casale, A. (1991) 'Iscrizioni pompeiane inedite scoperte tra gli anni 1954–1978', *Atti della Accademia Pontaniana* n.s. 39: 273–378.

Gradel, I. (1992) 'Mamia's dedication: emperor and Genius. The imperial cult in Italy and the Genius Coloniae in Pompeii', *Analecta Romana Instituti Danici* 20: 43–58.

Graefe, R. (1979) *Vela erunt: die Zeltdächer der römischen Theater und ähnlicher Anlagen*, Mainz am Rhein: P.v. Zabern.

Granino Cecere, M.G. (1988–1989) 'Nemi: l'erma di C. Norbanus Sorex', *Atti della Pontificia Accademia Romana di Archeologia. Rendiconti* 61: 131–51.

Harvey, P.B. (1973) 'Socer Valgus, Valgii, and C. Quinctius Valgus', in E.N. Borza and R.W. Carrubba (eds) *Classics and the Classical Tradition: Essays Presented to Robert E. Dengler*, University Park, PA: Pennsylvania State University, 79–94.

Hine, H. (1984) 'The date of the Campanian earthquake: AD 62 or AD 63, or both?', *L'Antiquité Classique* 53: 266–9.

Jashemski, W.F. (1967) 'The caupona of Euxinus at Pompeii', *Archaeology* 20: 36–44.

—— (1979, 1993) *The Gardens of Pompeii, Herculaneum and the Villas Destroyed by Vesuvius*, 2 vols, New York: Caratzas Brothers.

Jashemski, W.F. and Meyer, F.G. (eds) (2002) *The Natural History of Pompeii*, Cambridge: Cambridge University Press.

Jongman, W.M. (1978–1979) 'M. Obellius M. f. Firmus, Pompeian duovir', *Talanta* 10–11: 62–5.

Kockel, V. (1983) *Die Grabbauten vor den Herkulaner Tor in Pompeji*, Mainz am Rhein: P. v. Zabern

—— (1987) 'Im Tode gleich? Die Sullanischen Kolonisten und ihr kulturelles Gewicht in Pompeji am Beispiel der Nekropolen', in H. von Hesberg and P. Zanker (eds) *Römische Gräberstrassen: Selbstdarstellung, Status, Standard*, Munich: Bayerischen Akademie der Wissenschaften, 183–96.

La Rocca, E., de Vos, M. and de Vos, A. (1994) *Pompei*, 2nd edn, Milan: A. Mondadori.

Langner, M. (2001) *Antike Graffitizeichnungen: Motive, Gestaltung und Bedeutung*, Wiesbaden: L. Reichert.

Laurence, R. (1994) *Roman Pompeii: Space and Society*, London: Routledge.

Maiuri, A. (1947) 'Pompeii: Santuario Dionisiaco in località S. Abbondio', *Fasti archaeologici* 2: 197 no. 1656.

Maulucci Vivolo, F.P. (1993) *Pompei: i graffiti figurati*, Foggia: Bastogi.

Moeller, W.O. (1970) 'The riot of AD 59 at Pompeii', *Historia* 19: 84–95.

Mols, S.T.A.M. and Moormann, E.M. (1993–1994) '*Ex parvo crevit*. Proposta per una lettura iconografia della Tomba di Vestorius Priscus fuori Porta Vesuvio a Pompei', *Rivista di studi pompeiani* 6: 15–52.

Mouritsen, H. (1988) *Elections, Magistrates and Municipal Elite: Studies in Pompeian Epigraphy*, Rome: «L'Erma» di Bretschneider.

Nappo, S. (1998) *Pompeii: Guide to the Lost City*, London: Weidenfeld and Nicolson.

Nappo, S.C. (1989) 'Fregio dipinto dal "praedium" di Giulia Felice con rappresentazione dal foro di Pompei', *Rivista di studi pompeiani* 3: 79–96.

Nielsen, I. (1993) *Thermae et Balnea: The Architecture and Cultural History of Roman Public Baths* II. *Catalogue and Plates*, 2nd edn, Aarhus: Aarhus University Press.

Onorato, G.O. (1949) 'La data del terremoto di Pompei, 5 febbraio 62 d.Cr.', *Rendiconti dell'Accademia Nazionale dei Lincei. Classe di scienze morali, storiche e filologiche*, ser. 8, vol. 4, fasc. 11–12: 644–61.

Parkins, H.M. (1997) 'The "consumer city"' domesticated? The Roman city in elite economic strategies', in H.M. Parkins (ed.) *Roman Urbanism beyond the Consumer City*, London: Routledge, 83–111.

Pirson, F. (1997) 'Rented accommodation at Pompeii: the evidence of the *Insula Arriana Polliana* VI 6', in R. Laurence and A. Wallace-Hadrill (eds) *Domestic Space in the Roman World: Pompeii and Beyond*, Portsmouth, RI: *Journal of Roman Archaeology* supplement 22, 165–81.

Poccetti, P. (1979) *Nuovi documenti italici: a complemento del Manuale di E. Vetter*, Pisa: Giardini.

Pompei oltre la vita (1998) *Nuove testimonianze dalle necropoli*, Naples: Soprintendenza Archeologica di Pompei.

Sabbatini Tumolesi, P. (1980) *Gladiatorum Paria: annunci di spettacoli gladiatorii a Pompei*, Rome: Edizioni di storia e letteratura.

Sigurdsson, H. *et al.* (1982) 'The eruption of Vesuvius in AD 79: reconstruction from historical and volcanological evidence', *American Journal of Archaeology* 86: 39–51.

Small, D.B. (1987) 'Social correlations to the Greek cavea in the Roman period', in S. Macready and F.H. Thompson (eds) *Roman Architecture in the Greek World*, London: Society of Antiquaries, 85–93.

Solin, H. (1968) 'Pompeiana', *Epigraphica* 30: 105–25.

Tchernia, A. and Zevi, F. (1972) 'Amphores vinaires de Campanie et de Tarraconaise à Ostie', in P. Baldacci *et al.* (eds) *Recherches sur les amphores romaines*, Rome: Ecole française de Rome, 35–67.

Tran Tam Tinh, V. (1964) *Essai sur le culte d'Isis à Pompéi*, Paris: E. de Boccard.

Van Andringa, W. (2000) 'Autels de carrefour, organisation vicinale et rapports de voisinage à Pompéi', *Rivista di studi pompeiani* 11: 47–86.

Van Buren, A.W. (1947) 'Gnaeus Alleius Nigidius Maius of Pompeii', *American Journal of Philology* 68: 382–93.

—— (1948) 'Archaeological news: Italy: Pompeii', *American Journal of Archaeology* 52: 508–9.

Varone, A. and Marturano, A. (1997) 'L'eruzione vesuviana del 24 agosto del 79 d.C. attraverso le lettere di Plinio il Giovane e le nuove evidenze archeologiche', *Rivista di studi pompeiani* 8: 57–72.

Vetter, E. (1953) *Handbuch der italischen Dialekte*, Heidelberg: C. Winter.

Wallace-Hadrill, A. (1994) *Houses and Society in Pompeii and Herculaneum*, Princeton, NJ: Princeton University Press.

Wallat, K. (1995a) 'Der Zustand des Forums von Pompeji am Vorabend des Vesuvausbruchs 79 n. Chr.', in *Archäologie und Seismologie: La regione vesuviana dal 62 al 79 d.C. Problemi archeologici e sismologici*, Munich: Biering and Brinkmann, 75–89.

—— (1995b) 'Der Marmorfries am Eingangsportal des Gebäudes der Eumachia (VII, 9, 1) in Pompeji und sein ursprünglicher Anbringungsort', *Archäologischer Anzeiger*, 345–73.

Ward-Perkins, J. and Claridge, A. (1976) *Pompeii AD 79*, Bristol: Imperial Tobacco Ltd.

Wiseman, T.P. (1977) 'Cicero, *pro Sulla* 60–1', *Liverpool Classical Monthly* 2: 21–2.

Zangemeister, C. (1898) *Corpus Inscriptionum Latinarum* IV. *Inscriptionum Parietarum Pompeianarum Supplementum* – I. *Tabulae Ceratae Pompeis Repertae Annis MDCCCLXXV et MDCCCLXXXVII*, Berlin: G. Reimerum.

Zanker, P. (1998) *Pompeii: Public and Private Life*, trans. D. Lucas Schneider, Cambridge, MA: Harvard University Press (originally published as *Pompeji: Stadtbild und Wohngeschmack*, 1995).

Zevi, F. (1995) 'Personaggi della Pompei sillana', *Papers of the British School at Rome* 63: 1–24.

INDEX OF SOURCES

Literary Sources

Appian, *Civil Wars* 1.39: **B1**; 1.50: **B3**

Cato the Elder, *On Agriculture* 22.3: **H35**
Cicero, *Letters to Atticus* 2.1.11: **B17**;
 10.15.4: **B20**; 10.16.4: **B21**; 13.8:
 B19; 16.11.6: **B22**; *Pro Sulla* 60–62:
 B15

Dio Cassius 66.21–23: **C14**; 66.24.1,
 3–4: **C18**
Diodorus of Sicily 4.21.5: **C6**

Eusebius, *Chronicle* AD 79: **C15**

Florus, *Epitome* 1.16: **H1**
Frontinus, *Strategems* 1.5.21: **B13**

Isidore, *Etymologies* 15.1.51: **A2**

Josephus, *Jewish Antiquities* 20.7.2: **C16**

Livy 9.38.2: **A7**

Macrobius, *Saturnalia* 2.3.11: **F1**
Martial, *Epigrams* 4.44: **C24**

Orosius, *Histories against the Pagans*
 5.18.22: **B4**

Pliny the Elder, *Natural History* 2.137:
 B16; 3.60–2: **A6**; 14.35: **H5**;
 31.93–4: **H18**; 35.110: **A21**

Pliny the Younger, *Letters* 6.16: **C9**;
 6.20: **C12**
Plutarch, *Life of Cicero* 8: **B18**;
 Moralia 398E, The Oracles at Delphi:
 C29

Quintus Curtius Rufus, *History of
 Alexander* 3.11.7–12: **A20**

Seneca the Younger, *Natural Questions*
 6.1.1–3, 6.1.10, 6.27.1, 6.31: **C1**
Servius, *Commentary on Virgil's* Aeneid
 VII, 662: **A3**
Sibylline Oracle 4.130–6: **C28**
Silius Italicus, *Punic Wars* 8.653–5:
 C27
Statius, *Silvae* 3.5.72–5: **C20**; 4.4.78–85:
 C21; 4.8.3–5: **C22**; 5.3.205–8:
 C23
Strabo, *Geography* 5.4.8: **A5**, **C8**,
 H2
Suetonius, *On Distinguished Men*: **C11**;
 Titus 8.3: **C17**

Tacitus, *Annals* 4.67: **C25**; 14.17: **D34**;
 15.22: **C2**; *Histories* 1.2: **C13**
Tertullian, *Apology* 40.8: **C30**

Valerius Flaccus, *The Argonauts* 4.507–9:
 C26
Velleius Paterculus 2.16.2: **B2**
Vitruvius, *On Architecture* 2.6.2: **C7**

237

Inscriptions

NSc (1893) 333: **G32**; (1897) 275: **G69**;
(1910) 405: **G9**; (1916) 303: **G1**, **G3**

Poccetti (1979) 107: **A16**; 108: **A17**

Pompei oltre la vita no.19: **G2**

Tran Tam Tinh (1964) 176 no.148: **E6**

Vetter (1953) 8: **A8**; 11: **A9**; 12: **A10**;
13: **A22**; 14: **A24**; 15: **A11**; 18: **A12**;
21: **A13**; 23: **B5**; 35: **B14**; 70: **A14**;
71: **A25**

INDEX OF PERSONS

The earliest recorded inhabitants of Pompeii had two names – a first name and a family name. By the first century AD, however, most Roman citizens had three names. Only a few first names (the *praenomen*) were in common use. The second name (the *nomen*) was the family name. The third name (*cognomen*) could be used to differentiate between members of the same family, or branches of a large family.

Slaves would have only one name, usually easily distinguishable from a Roman name. On being freed, a slave would take his former master's first and second name, with his own former name as a third name.

INDEX OF PLACES

Page references in **bold** indicate an illustration.

INDEX OF SUBJECTS

Page references in **bold** indicate an illustration